THE HARRAP ANTHOLOGY OF SPANISH POETRY

THE HARRAP ANTHOLOGY OF SPANISH POETRY

With an Introductory Essay on the Development of Metrical Forms

edited by

JANET H. PERRY, M.A.

FORMERLY LECTURER IN SPANISH IN THE UNIVERSITY OF LONDON

HARRAP LONDON

TO

MISS BEL CHESTNUT

OF THE HIGH SCHOOL GALWAY

WHO GUIDED MY FIRST STEPS IN SPANISH

IN AFFECTIONATE REMEMBRANCE

First published in Great Britain 1953
by GEORGE G. HARRAP & CO. LTD
182-184 High Holborn, London WC1V 7AX
Reprinted: 1954; 1960; 1962; 1964; 1967; 1970; 1977

ISBN 0 245 55137 9

Printed in Great Britain by
Biddles Ltd, Guildford, Surrey

ACKNOWLEDGEMENTS

My thanks are due in the first place to the critics and literary historians who have taught me to enjoy and appreciate all that is most worth while in Spanish poetry. To D. Marcelino Menéndez Pelayo, that sturdy and indefatigable pioneer who broke so much ground for others to cultivate, our debt is great and unforgettable. Among the living we owe much to D. Ramón Menéndez Pidal, the master guide to the Medieval Epic, and to D. Dámaso Alonso, who has rendered such service to the student of Spanish poetry by restoring the early Spanish lyric to its rightful place in the literature of Spain—not to mention the light he has thrown on the technique of the poets of the Renaissance and Baroque periods, especially that of Góngora. In examining the intricacies of versification D. Pedro Henríquez Ureña has added to our knowledge of verse forms and their development, though dealing mainly with the aspect of irregularity so typical of the Spaniard. For others who have given and continue to give valuable information and guidance I refer the reader to the list of reference books.

My warm thanks also to Professor E. M. Wilson and Mrs Rita Hamilton of King's College, London, Mrs Helen Grant of Girton College, Cambridge, and Dr A. K. Jameson for their help and encouragement. I am deeply grateful also to D. Eduardo Torner, who devoted some of his valuable time and specialist knowledge to explaining to me the various forms of the *seguidilla*.

I wish also to express my gratitude to the following poets and poets' relatives and representatives who have so kindly permitted me to reproduce my selection from their poems: D. Rafael Alberti; D. Vicente Aleixandre; D. Dámaso Alonso; D. Manuel Álvarez de Lama (Antonio Machado); Doña Josefina Blanco V. de Valle-Inclán (Ramón del Valle-Inclán); D. Luis Cernuda; H.E. Dr Rubén Darío (Rubén Darío); D. Gerardo Diego; D. Jorge Guillén; D. Jesús Gabriel y Galán (José María Gabriel y Galán); D. Juan Ramón Jiménez; D. Rafael Nadal and the other trustees of Federico García Lorca; Sra Salinas and

Doña Soledad Salinas de Marichal (Pedro Salinas); and D. Pablo Unamuno Lizarraga (Miguel de Unamuno).

J. H. P.

NOTE

CONTENTS

INTRODUCTION

METRE IN SPANISH POETRY

Introductory Remarks

SOME general observations on Spanish as a medium for verse may be helpful before embarking on a study of metre in Spanish poetry.

Spanish is similar to Italian in having a very marked stress or accent of intensity on one syllable in each word, and this gives a pleasant undulating rhythm to a sentence, even in prose. This rhythmic intonation makes it easy to pass almost insensibly from prose to poetry. For example:

El mar estaba en calma, la luna estaba crecida.

is an ordinary prose statement. We have only to change *el* to *la* and alter the order of the words a little and the sentence becomes an actual line of an old ballad:

Estaba la mar en calma,   la luna estaba crecida.

The importance of this stress on one syllable has given rise to special names for different types of word-endings according as the stress falls on the final, penultimate, or antepenultimate syllable, and these endings are called *aguda, grave* (or *llana*), and *esdrújula* respectively.

Terminación aguda: can*tar*, vo*ló*, continua*ción*.
Terminación grave or *llana*: *li*bre, *qui*so, es*pe*ran.
Terminación esdrújula: *pá*jaro, an*gé*lico, oro*pén*dola.

A Spanish prosodic convention makes the final stressed syllable, the *terminación aguda*, count as two syllables, the equivalent of a *terminación grave*, at the end of a line of verse or a definite half-line marked by a cæsura or pause. In like circumstances a *terminación esdrujula*, though actually of three syllables, counts as two.

Another tendency in Spanish phonetic usage which affects ordinary speech as well as verse is that of combining in one syllable two or more vowels which follow one another either in the same word or at the end of one and the beginning of the next. The simplest combinations of vowels within the same word are the diphthongs and triphthongs produced when *i* and *u* come into contact with any other vowel. In these cases the *i* or *u* is converted into a semi-consonant or semi-vowel according as the other vowel follows or precedes, as in the diphthongs in the words: *pie*, *peine*, *anual*, *causa*, *viuda*, *cuida*. Triphthongs occur in the verbal endings *-iáis* and *-uáis*. When the contiguous vowels are *a*, *e*, *o*, the tendency is to separate by what is known as hiatus, but they are sometimes combined and this combination is called synæresis. Hiatus may also occasionally separate the elements of a diphthong and make it two syllables. Here are some examples:

Hiatus	Synæresis
cre-ar	*crear*
nive-o	*niveo*
cru-el	*cruel*
vi-aje	*viaje*

In a line of verse diæresis is sometimes used to indicate the hiatus, as in *süave*. The tendency to unite successive vowels in one syllable when they occur in separate words is known as synalepha, and is of particular importance in reckoning the number of syllables in a metric line. Synalepha may combine as many as six vowels, as Tomás Navarro Tomás has shown in the section, *Los sonidos agrupados* in his *Manual de pronunciación española*, in which he quotes a number of verse lines to illustrate the use of synalepha, winding up with the following line in which six vowels are combined in one syllable:

Y el móvil ácueo a Europa se encamina

making a line of eleven syllables. Synalepha, after the hesitations of early poetry, is now an established practice, but the Spanish poet has always allowed himself a certain licence with regard to synæresis and hiatus. A stanza from a poem, *Sonatina*, by Rubén

Darío will demonstrate the use of simple synalepha as well as the convention applied to the *terminaciones aguda*, *grave*, and *esdrújula*:

> ¡ Oh, quién fuera hipsipila que dejó la crisálida !
> (La princesa está triste. La princesa está pálida)
> ¡ oh visión adorada de oro, rosa y marfil !
> ¡ Quién volara a la tierra donde un príncipe existe !
> (La princesa está pálida. La princesa está triste)
> más brillante que el alba, más hermosa que abril !

Each of these lines contains fourteen syllables and is divided by a cæsura into two half-lines of seven syllables.

Another aspect of Spanish verse we should mention here is rhyme. We find in Spanish poetry both assonance or rhyming of vowels only and consonance or perfect rhyme of vowel and consonant. Assonance, which characterizes the French *Chansons de Geste*, is also typical of early Spanish narrative poetry. A distinction is made between single and double assonance; single assonance occurs when the rhyming words end in a *terminación aguda* and double assonance when they end in a *terminación grave*. In the following examples taken from two ballads we have in one a single assonance in *á* and in the other a double assonance in *i-o*:

> (1) ¡ Quién hubiese tal ventura sobre las aguas del mar,
> como hubo el conde Arnaldos la mañana de San Juan !

> (2) Nunca fuera caballero de damas tan bien servido,
> como fuera Lanzarote cuando de Bretaña vino,
> que dueñas curaban dél doncellas del su rocino.

Perfect rhyme appears in many types of verse from the thirteenth century onwards, but assonance was maintained in the ballad and in traditional verse forms like the *seguidilla*. It was revived in lyric poetry in the nineteenth century and is much in favour nowadays with those poets who use rhyme at all.

Words of classical origin are used in Spanish as in English to denote the length in syllables of the metrical line. These are not applied as a rule to lines of more than twelve syllables and the word enneasyllable which corresponds to the Spanish *eneasílabo*, is not in common use in English.

Line	*verso*	*syllables*
dodecasyllable	*dodecasílabo*	12
hendecasyllable	*endecasílabo*	11
decasyllable	*decasílabo*	10
enneasyllable	*eneasílabo*	9
octosyllable	*octosílabo*	8
heptasyllable	*heptasílabo*	7
hexasyllable	*hexasílabo*	6
pentasyllable	*pentasílabo*	5
tetrasyllable	*tetrasílabo*	4
trisyllable	*trisílabo*	3
dissyllable	*disílabo*	2

Note on the Hendecasyllable

Various kinds of hendecasyllable occur in Spanish verse:

(1) The Petrarchan hendecasyllable with stresses on the sixth and tenth syllables and usually on the second, called in Spanish *común* or *propio*.

(2) An alternative line also much used by Renaissance poets, but considered less correct and called *impropio*, has stresses on the second, fourth, eighth, and tenth syllables.

(3) The Sapphic hendecasyllable with stresses on the fourth, eighth, and tenth syllables and with a cæsura after the fifth syllable.

The first stress in any of these lines may fall on the first syllable instead of the second and usually does so in the Sapphic hendecasyllable.

(4) The hendecasyllable with the rhythm of the *verso de gaita gallega* (described below) with stresses on the first, fourth, seventh, and tenth syllables was used by D. Juan Manuel in the fourteenth century and revived by Rubén Darío in the nineteenth.

Types of Stanza

Each type of stanza (Spanish *estrofa*) is given below, with length in lines (*versos*) and the appropriate length of these in syllables with the most usual rhyme schemes.

Estrofa	*versos*	*sílabas*	*rima*
estancia / *silva*	varied	11 and 7	varied
soneto	14	11	*abbaabbacdecde*
décima	10	8	*ababacddcd* or *abaabcdccd*
espinela	10	8	*abbaaccddc*
octava real	8	11	*abababcc*
octavilla	8	8	*abbaacca*
octava de arte mayor	8	12	*ababacca* or *abbaacca*
septina	7	8	*abbaacc* or *abbacdc*
sextina	6	11 or 11 and 7	*ababcc* or *abbacc*
sextilla	6	8	*ababcc* (varied)
quinteto	5	11	*abbab*
lira	5	7 and 11	*ababb*
quintilla	5	8	*abaab*
estrofa sáfica	4	11 and 5	no rhyme
cuarteto	4	11	*abba*
serventesio	4	11	*abab*
cuarteto	4	8	*abab*
redondilla	4	8	*abba*
terceto	3	11	*ababcbcdc*, etc.
tercetillo or *tercerilla*	3	8 or 6	*aba* or *abb* or as in *terceto*
pareado	2	11 or 8 or 11 and 7 combined	*aa*, *bb*, etc.

The *estrofa sáfica* imitated from the Latin of Horace has three hendecasyllables followed by a so-called Adonic pentasyllable stressed on the first and fourth syllables.

In the short poems of the *cancioneros* of the fifteenth century there are stanzas of nine, eleven, twelve, and thirteen lines which have no special names.

Types of Line with Special Names

Verso alejandrino: the Alexandrine. This metrical line appeared in France towards the end of the twelfth century and took its name from the *Roman d'Alexandre*. It was used in both France and Spain in the thirteenth century for semi-historical, religious, and didactive narratives, frequently in monorhymed quatrains known in Spanish as the *cuaderna vía*. According to the French convention the line had twelve syllables and was divided into two hemistiches of six syllables by a definite cæsura, the mute *e* not counting as a syllable at the end of the half-line. In Spanish the line may seem to have twelve to sixteen syllables according as the final word of the hemistich has a *terminación aguda, grave,* or *esdrújula*. The conventional length, however, is fourteen syllables. Here are two lines, (1) in French and (2) in Spanish, for comparison:

(1) A seignor et a maestre qui toz maus fet venir.
RUTEBEUF. *Miracle de Théophile*

(2) Del pleito de Teófilo vos querría fablar . . .
G. DE BERCEO. *El milagro de Teófilo*

Both types agree in having an emphatic stress on the sixth syllable of each hemistich, though the French count six syllables and the Spanish seven in each half-line. Modern versions of the Alexandrine take liberties with both stress and cæsura.

Verso de romance. This name is applied either to the old ballad line of sixteen syllables with a marked cæsura and with continuous assonance or to the modified version used from the fifteenth century on, with lines of eight syllables and alternate assonance.

Verso de gaita gallega. This line has a so-called anapæstic rhythm and may have ten, eleven, or twelve syllables with two stresses in each half-line. The name comes from the *gaita* or bagpipe and suggests a rhythm similar to that of the dance it accompanies, the Galician *muñeira*.

Verso de arte mayor. This name, though strictly speaking applicable to any long metrical line, is specially applied to a line much in vogue in the fifteenth century. This is basically a twelve-syllabled line with a strong cæsura after the sixth syllable, but as it is really rhythmic rather than syllabic, the actual number of syllables varies greatly. The main requirement is that there should be two stresses in each half-line, though even in this, practice is not invariable. There is much variety in the grouping of the stressed and unstressed syllables, but the rhythm is anapæstic rather than iambic. This line is considered by some authorities to be a variant of the *verso de gaita gallega.*

Verso de arte menor. This name is used for lines of nine or fewer syllables.

Verso de pie quebrado. A short line of four or five syllables used in combination with longer lines, usually octosyllables.

Other Terms in Frequent Use

Copla: (1) A short poem, usually a quatrain in traditional style and often serving as an *estribillo* for a longer poem. (2) An equivalent of *estrofa,* as in: *Copla de pie quebrado:* a stanza in which *versos de pie quebrado* occur.

Estrambote: a few lines occasionally added at the end of a complete stanza or even a sonnet as a summary or comment on what precedes.

Estribillo: a short verse of two or three lines setting the theme for a poem in one or more stanzas and providing the refrain or merely the rhyme for the last lines.

Letra or *letrilla:* words of a song set to music. *Letrilla* is used for a poem in lighter vein, often satirical or amusing.

Estrofas paralelísticas: these are characteristic of a type of Galician poem in which each stanza is duplicated, changing some of the words slightly and their order in the lines. There may also be *encadenamiento* when the third stanza begins with the second line of the first and is followed by a new line and so on. The term *leixa-pren* is also used in this connexion. The Castilian *cossante* of Diego Furtado de Mendoza is a variant of this type.

Endecha: a composition in several stanzas in the sad tone of a lament. The stanza consists of lines of five, six, or seven syllables with assonance or perfect rhyme in the even lines. The rhyming words frequently end in a stressed syllable.

Seguidilla: a short poem of four lines of popular Castilian origin. The lines vary in length from eight to four syllables in the early *seguidillas*. There is assonance or rhyme in the even lines. The standard literary form has heptasyllables in the uneven and pentasyllables in the even lines. An *estrambote* of three lines may be added with five, seven, and five syllables respectively and with assonance or rhyme in the first and third.

Villancico: a typical Castilian folk-song. It has an initial *estribillo* of two, three, or four lines stating the theme which is developed in the following stanzas. Each stanza ends with all or part of the *estribillo* or sometimes merely echoes the rhyme. The name *villancico* is usually applied in modern usage to Christmas songs.

Zéjel: the colloquial name given to a type of Arabic poem or song of Andalusian origin. The *zéjel* was similar in form to the *villancico*, and had many varieties. The most usual arrangement of the *zéjel* in Castilian poetry was that in which the *estribillo*, a rhymed couplet, is followed by a varying number of stanzas each composed of a rhymed triplet called a *mudanza* and ending in a fourth line rhyming with the *estribillo* and known as the *vuelta*. The name *zéjel* is now often replaced by the Castilian word *estribote*.

Early Narrative Metres

Mester de juglaría: craft of minstrelsy

The earliest type of poetry in Castilian of which we have any written record is the epic or narrative poem known as the *Cantar de Gesta* and comparable to the French *Chanson de Geste* as relating the deeds of local or national heroes. As the name *cantar* suggests, these poems were composed to be sung or recited by a minstrel, called in Spanish a *juglar*, from which we get the name of his craft, the *mester de juglaría*. His business was to entertain, and reciting poems was only one of his many accomplishments. The *juglar* had entry into the castles of the great lords and the houses of the wealthy clergy, but he also entertained a more popular audience in street and market-place. These early poems told of persons and events ranging from the defeat of Rodrigo, the last Gothic king, by the invading forces of the Moors in the eighth century to the exploits of another Rodrigo, "el Cid," the national hero who fought successful battles against a fresh horde of invaders in the eleventh century and won from the Moors the city of Valencia.

The only text of this kind of early epic to be preserved at all complete is the *Poema del Cid* or as it is now called *Cantar de mio Cid*, in a version which probably dates from about the middle of the twelfth century. The other *cantares* are not extant in their original form but have been fragmentarily incorporated in the prose chronicles of the thirteenth and fourteenth centuries. This *cantar* will therefore have to serve as a basis for the study of the versification of the *mester de juglaría*. The whole poem, containing some 3730 lines, is divided into three parts, also called *cantares*: (1) *Cantar del destierro*, (2) *Cantar de las bodas*, (3) *Cantar de Corpes*. For purposes of recitation the *juglar* divided each *cantar* into sections corresponding roughly to a special incident and varying greatly in length, from three to one hundred and nine lines. The same assonance is maintained throughout each of these sections as in the *laisses* of the *Chansons de Geste*. Each line is interrupted by a cæsura, as in the *Chansons*, but instead of the regular French line of ten syllables, the Spanish poet uses a highly irregular metre in which the line may contain anything from ten to twenty syllables. If it were not for the assonance which marks the end of the line, the effect would be that of rhythmic prose. Here are two examples of two short sections in the first of which we find single assonance in *o* and in the second double assonance in *a-o*.

	Number of syllables
(1) Aun era de día, non era puesto el sol,	14
mandó veer sus yentes mio Cid el Campeador:	16
sin las peonadas e omnes valientes que son,	15
notó trezientas lancas que todas tienen pendones.	15

Cantar del destierro, Sect. 21

(2) Vino Per Vermúdoz que la seña tiene en mano,	15
metióla en somo en todo lo más alto.	13
Fabló mio Cid Roy Diaz el que en buen ora fué nado:	16
" grado a Dios del cielo e a todos sos santos,	14
ya mejoraremos posadas a dueñas e a cavallos."	17

Cantar del destierro, Sect. 30

It will be noticed that in (1) a double assonance *o-e* is used in conjunction with a single assonance in *o*. This occurs fairly often when the unstressed vowel is *e*. Occasionally a paragogic or additional *e* is added to the stressed ending to complete a double assonance, as in the following example:

	Number of syllables
En todo sodes pro, en esto assí fagades;	15
saludadnos a mio Cid el de *Bivare*,	12
somos en so pro quanto lo podemos *fare* . . .	13

The longer extracts given in the anthology show even greater variety in the length of line and irregularity in placing the cæsura. It is extremely difficult to assess the number of syllables in a line of this early poetry, as it is uncertain to what extent synalepha prevailed. Ramón Menéndez Pidal has analysed the metre in great detail in his three-volume edition of the *Cantar de mio Cid*, and calculated the number of lines of different lengths. He states that the line of fourteen syllables is the most frequent, and running it fairly close is the line of sixteen syllables. Both these foreshadow more regular metrical lines with which we shall deal later. There are a number of lines of eleven syllables similar to the French epic line of ten syllables, but they are much rarer. It is interesting to note in this connexion that the metre of a fragment of a *cantar* dating from the first half of the thirteenth century, the *Cantar de Roncesvalles* (published by Menéndez Pidal in the *Revista de Filología Española*, Vol. IV), evidently derived from French sources, is, like that of the *Cantar de mio Cid*, equally irregular and with the same predominance of the fourteen-syllabled line. An extract from this poem is given in the Anthology, where it may be compared with extracts from the *Cantar de mio Cid* and a fragment from a *Cantar de los infantes de Lara* reconstituted from a prose version in a chronicle of the fourteenth century by Dámaso Alonso. It is taken from his excellent anthology *Poesía de la edad media*.

The irregular rhythmic quality of the metre of these old poems is considered by some modern critics to be typical of indigenous Spanish verse. The student interested in this aspect of versification should consult *Versificación irregular en la poesía castellana* by

Pedro Henríquez Ureña. In our next section we shall consider a tendency to greater regularity in metre due perhaps to the influence of French models.

Mester de clerecía: clerkly craft

A new type of narrative poem appears in the thirteenth century composed by men of letters, usually clerics, or clerks as they were called in England in those days. These poems were written in a style known as *Mester de clerecía*, which may be translated 'clerkly craft.' Some students of the period have thought that these poets wrote for those who would read their compositions in study or cell, but there are signs of a direct approach to an audience by word of mouth, as Menéndez Pidal points out in his interesting book *Poesía juglaresca y juglares.* Some of these poems are anonymous or of doubtful attribution, but one poet, an outstanding and well-characterized figure, Gonzalo de Berceo, may serve as a model for all the others. He was a priest who lived in the first half of the thirteenth century, and his works consist mainly of lives of saints such as San Millán, Santo Domingo de Silos, and Santa Oria, but his masterpiece is the *Milagros de Nuestra Señora.* The French clerics were writing similar poems in a similar metre and he may have imitated them. The line used is the Alexandrine, described elsewhere, arranged in monorhymed quatrains known in Spain as the *cuaderna vía,* which has been translated the 'fourfold way.' The Alexandrine in Spanish poetry has usually fourteen syllables, seven in each half-line with a definite stress on the sixth syllable. The poets who used this new clerkly craft prided themselves on the counting of syllables, and made a point of the superiority of their regular lines and perfect rhymes over the rude craft of the minstrels, the *mester de juglaría.*

Other poems written in this metre are the *Libro de Alexandre,* a life of Alexander the Great such as had already given its name to the metric line used by the French in the *Roman d'Alexandre*; the *Libro de Apolonio,* a romantic Byzantine tale of the adventures of Tarsiana, daughter of Apolonio, King of Tyre; and the *Poema de Fernán González,* which relates the exploits of the great Count of Castile and which belongs in subject-matter rather to the domain of the *mester de juglaría.*

Though Gonzalo de Berceo was the most careful writer in this new craft, he disclaims any title to learning and says he wishes to use the homely romance speech of the common people.

> Quiero fer una prosa en román paladino
> en que suele el pueblo hablar con su vecino,
> ca non so tan letrado por fer otro latino:
> bien valdrá como creo un vaso de bon vino.[1]
>
> *Vida de Santo Domingo de Silos*, st. 2

In a later stanza of the same poem he addresses the saint and says he wishes to be *tu juglar*. He does not despise the title of minstrel rejected by others much less exact in their handling of the *mester de clerecía*. Berceo consistently avoids synalepha even in the case of identical vowels as may be seen from the *suele el* of the above example. We can rely on Berceo to provide the correct seven syllables for each hemistich, but other authors using the *cuaderna vía* are less particular and hemistiches of eight, six, and even five syllables can be found. Henríquez Ureña has detected many octosyllables in the *Libro de Alexandre*—yet we find the author declaring:

> Mester traigo fermoso no es de juglaría,
> mester es sin pecado, ca es de clerecía,
> hablar curso rimado por la cuaderna vía,
> a sílabas cuntadas, ca es gran maestría.[2]
>
> *Libro de Alexandre*

The metre in this passage is quite regular, allowing for diæresis in *maestría* and giving it four syllables. The reader may be interested to spot irregularities in the passages in the Anthology.

A very interesting composition, the *Historia Troyana*, a free adaptation in prose and verse of Benoît de Sainte Maure's *Roman de Troie*, is assigned by Menéndez Pidal to the end of the thirteenth century (1270). The fragments preserved have been edited

[1] I wish to write a story in homely romance such as the people use in talking to their neighbours, for I am not so learned as to make one in Latin: I think it will deserve a glass of good wine.

[2] I use a fair craft, but not of minstrelsy; it is faultless, as becomes a clerkly craft, composed with perfect rhyme and called the fourfold way, with counted syllables, a work of mastery.

and published by Menéndez Pidal in *Tres poetas primitivos* with a detailed analysis of the metres used in the verse portions. The author employed six different verse forms to match the various themes: the regular *cuaderna vía* for the narrative of a battle, octosyllabic and heptasyllabic *cuartetas* for love poems, an octosyllabic *sextina* for Achilles' lament for Patroclus, and a most unusual form of *décima* for Cassandra's prophetic warning of coming doom. This *décima* is composed of two tetrasyllabic *cuartetas* with alternate rhymes followed by two rhyming octosyllables as in this example:

¡ Gent perdida,
mal fadada,
confondida,
desesperada,
gente sin entendimiento,
   gente dura,
gente fuerte
sin ventura,
dada a muerte,
gente de confondimiento !

On the other hand, Hector rejects the advice of his friends in regular octosyllabic couplets, a regularity uncommon at the time as will be seen in the succeeding paragraph.

Poems in Irregular Metre in the Thirteenth Century

In this century we find four poems in irregular metre which form a striking contrast with the regular lines and stanzas of the *mester de clerecía*. They are composed mainly in lines of eight and nine syllables varied by the introduction, as occasion arises, of lines of five or six, ten, eleven, twelve, or even thirteen syllables. There is no division into stanzas, but the lines rhyme in couplets, usually with perfect rhyme, though assonance occurs at times. To the first half of the century belong (1) *Razón d'Amor*, a lyrico-narrative account of the meeting of a scholar with his beloved, and ending rather unaccountably with a discussion as to the respective merits of water and wine; (2) *Libre dels tres reys d'Orient* is a mere fragment relating the flight into Egypt of Joseph and

Mary and the child Jesus; (3) *Vida de Santa María Egipciaca*, telling of that lady's adventurous life and pious end; (4) *La disputa de Elena y María* is a dispute in which two young women vie with one another in praising their lovers, one a knight and the other a cleric.

'*Mester de clerecía*' *in the Fourteenth Century*

In the fourteenth century the *mester de clerecía* was employed and considerably modified at times by two notable poets, Juan Ruiz, Archpriest of Hita, and Pero López de Ayala, Chancellor of Castile. The former made use of this metre in the narrative parts of his delightful miscellany, the *Libro de Buen Amor*. He deliberately varied the monotony of the Alexandrine by introducing lines of sixteen syllables, and definitely connected his style of writing with that of the *juglares* when he says:

> Señores, hevos servido   con poca sabiduría,
> por vos dar solaz a todos,   fablévos en juglaría;
> yo un gualardón vos pido;   que por Dios en romería
> digades un paternoster   por mí e ave María.

Every hemistich of this quatrain has eight syllables, if we maintain the hiatus between the contiguous vowels in the last line. The introduction of this line of sixteen syllables is interesting, as we find it replacing the Alexandrine in the *cuaderna vía* and predominating to a great extent in the still irregular metre of the latest extant example of the *mester de juglaría*.

The Chancellor, Pero López de Ayala, in his *Rimado de Palacio*, a satirical poem dealing with contemporary life, followed Juan Ruiz in interpolating lines of sixteen syllables among the Alexandrines of the *cuaderna vía*, but he also combines an octosyllabic quatrain later known as a *redondilla* with a quatrain of sixteen-syllabled lines of which the first two rhyme as a couplet and the last two pick up the rhymes of the preceding quatrain:

> Sennor, si tú has dada
> tu sentencia contra mí,
> por merced te pido aquí
> que me sea revocada.

Tú, señor, tienes judgado por tu alta providencia
que emendando el pecador se mude la tu sentencia.
Por ende con penitencia e con voluntad quebrada,
he mi vida ordenada, por complir lo que fallí:

The *Poema de Yusuf*, the story of Joseph's life according to the Koran, from a *texto aljamiado*, a Spanish composition written in Arabic characters, shows the *cuaderna vía* in the last stages of decay in which the lines vary in length from twelve to sixteen syllables. With this and a didactic poem entitled *Libro de miseria de omne* in which the sixteen-syllabled line definitely predominates the *mester de clerecía* takes its farewell. For a revival of the Alexandrine we must wait until the nineteenth century when, mainly through French influence, it is reintroduced but this time as a vehicle for lyrical poetry.

Short Metre Poems in the Fourteenth Century

Apart from the two *mesteres* we must take note of two poems, one an historical narrative, the *Poema de Alfonso XI* (*c.* 1350). The author, Rodrigo Yáñez, probably a Galician, told his story in *cuartetas octosilábicas*, octosyllabic quatrains, rhyming *abab* with perfect rhyme as will be seen from the following stanza:

Por onra e prez ganar
ayuntó la su compaña,
su espada fué tomar
en Santiago de España.

The other is a didactic work, the *Proverbios morales* of the Jewish rabbi, Sem Tob, who dedicated his poem to Peter the Cruel. The stanza and the rhyme scheme are the same as the above, but the lines vary in length, the heptasyllable predominating. These two quatrains are interesting not merely from the point of view of the metre:

Por nascer en espino
la rosa, yo no siento
que pierde, nin el buen vino
por salir del sarmiento.

Nin vale el açor menos
porque en vil nido siga,
nin los enxemplos buenos
porque judío los diga.

These verses are given in slightly different wording and arrangement in the anthology as presented by González Llubera in his edition of the *Proverbios morales*.

The Last Example of the 'mester de juglaría'

At the very end of the fourteenth century there appeared the last example of the *poema juglaresco* on an heroic theme. This is the *Crónica rimada del Cid*, otherwise known as the *Mocedades de Rodrigo*. It is a refashioning of an older poem of which a prose version is incorporated in the *Crónica de 1344*. The subject is the youthful exploits of the Cid and it is important as a source of the ballads which deal with his early life and through them of Guillén de Castro's play in two parts: *Las mocedades del Cid*, from which Corneille took the substance of his famous drama *Le Cid*. The poem is composed in sections of varying length with continuous assonance in each, thus carrying on the tradition of the *mester de juglaría*. The lines are irregular in length but the sixteen-syllabled line is by far the most frequent, thus suggesting the influence of the *verso de romance*, the typical metre of the ballads which took up the historical and legendary themes and gave them a more popular form.

'Los romances': the Ballads

Though no *romances* appear in print until the fifteenth century and were not collected in any quantity until the middle of the sixteenth, they were most probably recited earlier to a popular audience by a *juglar* or minstrel such as formerly recited the epic *cantares de gesta*. We have seen that the *Mocedades de Rodrigo* was composed mainly in sixteen-syllabled lines, though with many irregularities. This line made more regular and with a marked cæsura after the eighth syllable is considered to be the typical *verso de romance*. In this form the assonance is uniform throughout, corresponding to one section of the old *cantar*. As a matter of fact, however, the sixteen-syllabled line is mainly conjectural, for when the ballads were printed they were arranged in octosyllabic lines with assonance in the alternate even lines, and all subsequent ballads follow the same model.

Romance in Spanish has not the same connotation as the word romance in English, as it originally means any composition in the vulgar tongue—compare Berceo's *román paladino*. These *romances* probably to begin with took scenes and incidents from the *cantares de gesta* chosen as specially interesting and recited them apart from their context. The arguments in favour of the epic origin of the ballads can be found in the introduction to *Flor nueva de romances viejos*, an annotated selection of some of the most interesting ballads, edited by Menéndez Pidal, the greatest authority on this matter. As the ballads passed from one reciter to another they were altered and in many cases shortened, and often in the process made more dramatic and vivid. New ballads were composed about contemporary events in the fourteenth and fifteenth centuries, and as they dealt chiefly with incidents in the frontier fighting with the Moors they are generally known as *romances fronterizos*. The older historical ballads can be divided into groups, or cycles as they are sometimes called, according to the epic theme from which they derive their matter. It is very difficult for anyone, even an expert, to distinguish between the genuine old ballads, *romances viejos*, and those written in imitation of them in the sixteenth century or later, and known as *romances juglarescos*. These very often draw their material from the prose chronicles of the thirteenth and fourteenth centuries, or, as in the case of the cycle of *Rodrigo el godo*, from a pseudo chronicle like the *Crónica Sarracina*, a kind of early historical novel by Pedro de Corral. Incidents connected with Charlemagne and his peers may be taken directly or indirectly from French sources, though subject to many changes due to national pride or to the poet's inventive imagination. Bernardo del Carpio, for example, is a hero of whom the French had never heard, while the Spanish ballad makers ascribe to him the defeat and death of Roland at Roncesvalles. The Arthurian tales, and episodes from Greek and Roman history, are also reflected in the Spanish *romancero*. Other ballads treat common international ballad matter or deal with imaginary themes. These are classed as *romances novelescos*, and they are predominantly lyrical in tone, all trace of epic origin completely lost.

To show the kind of variations produced by traditional transmission here are two versions of a well-known *romance novelesco*, the *Romance del prisionero*:

(1) Por el mes era de mayo cuando hace la calor,
cuando canta la calandria y responde el ruiseñor,
cuando los enamorados van a servir al amor,
sino yo triste cuitado, que vivo en esta prisión,
que no sé cuando es de día, ni cuando las noches son,
sino por una avecilla que me cantaba al albor:
matómela un ballestero; déle Dios mal galardón!

(2) Que por mayo era, por mayo, cuando los grandes calores,
cuando los enamorados van servir a sus amores,
sino yo triste, mezquino, que yago en estas prisiones,
que no sé cuando es de día, ni menos cuando es de noche,
sino por una avecilla que me cantaba al albor:
matómela un ballestero; déle Dios mal galardón!

The last two lines evidently imprinted themselves on the memory of the reciter and his hearers, and indeed they could hardly be improved on. The effect is even heightened in (2) by the change from the softer *terminación grave* in *o-e* to the abrupt vigour of the *terminación aguda* in *albor* and *galardón*. There is a longer version which tells how the prisoner grew old, how his wife sent him a file in a pasty and how in the end the King pardoned him, but most people will agree with Menéndez Pidal that the shorter versions stopping on the note of anger and despair are the best.

The earliest versions of the older ballads are those printed on loose sheets (*pliegos sueltos*) in the first half of the sixteenth century, and these started a great vogue for collecting them. These ballad collections were called variously *cancioneros*, *silvas*, or *rosas de romances*. The first *Cancionero de romances* published in Antwerp is undated but the second is dated 1550. The word *romancero* appears for the first time with that of Sepúlveda in 1551. It has been applied to a collection of ballads from various sources, to ballads grouped round one figure like the *Romancero del Cid*, or to the whole body of *romances* which is so vast that Menéndez Pidal has called Spain *el país del romancero*.

The first *Romancero general* appeared in 1600 and was followed by another edition in 1604. Here, however, the older type of ballad is not represented. The historical ballad disappears from the scene of literary production in the seventeenth century, with notable exceptions such as the anonymous ballads on the deaths of Don Alvaro de Luna and Pedro el Cruel. The poets represented in the *Romancero general* often use the ballad form to dilate on their own experiences and feelings in lyrico-narrative poems, known as *romances artísticos*. Those who imitated the older ballads more closely made a continuous narrative in octosyllables with alternate assonance, but as time went on there was a tendency to divide the poem into quatrains, though maintaining the same assonance throughout. In many ballads from now onwards the narrative element disappears and they are made the vehicle for lyrical expression, description of scenery, or even for semi-philosophical reflections on life.

The Rise of Lyric Poetry in the Peninsula

In reviewing the narrative poetry of the thirteenth century, we saw that French influence had given to the Spanish poets a model of regular versification in the Alexandrine quatrain, which in Spain was called the *cuaderna vía*. In the rise of formal lyric poetry in the Peninsula the impulse again came from beyond the Pyrenees. In this case it was the poetic school of the Provençal troubadours which provided varied forms for the expression of lyrical emotion hitherto only found in the folk-songs of the less literate people. This Provençal school stimulated a similar movement in Catalonia where the Catalan speech was a dialect akin to those of Southern France. Another part of the Peninsula which came more completely and fruitfully under the spell of Provençal lyricism was Galicia, the north-western region of Spain to which the tomb of St James attracted crowds of pilgrims, and with them the troubadours. From there its influence spread not only to Portugal, where the Galician dialect was in process of becoming the Portuguese language, but also to León and Castile.

The language used in these lyrics was Galician, though Menéndez y Pelayo says in the prologue to Vol. II of his *Antología de poetas líricos castellanos*, that it is a conventionalized language which should rather be called the *lengua de los trovadores españoles*. Poets of all classes were eager to claim the title of *trovador* as that of an original composer, while the old name of *juglar* was despised as indicating a mere reciter or entertainer. In the twelfth century Provençal troubadours attended the brilliant court of Alfonso VII, who held the title of emperor and claimed sway over territories in the South of France, while in the thirteenth century Galician poets thronged the courts of the Castilian monarchs Fernando III and Alfonso X, who earned the surname of *el sabio* for his patronage of letters. The most notable royal poets of this period were King Dinis of Portugal and King Alfonso of Castile. The latter composed a volume of poems in Galician dialect, the *Cantigas de Santa María*, dedicated to the Virgin Mary and relating miracles attributed to her.

Galician-Portuguese ' cancioneiros '

The bulk of this poetry was collected in the so-called Galician-Portuguese *cancioneiros—Cancioneiro da Vaticana*, *Cancioneiro de Colocci-Brancuti*, and *Cancioneiro da Ajuda*—the latter, published in a critical edition by Carolina Michaelis de Vasconcelos, gives an elaborate analysis of the metres used.

The *Cancioneiro da Ajuda* contains only the more artificial types of court poetry, but the others contain poems evidently derived from or greatly influenced by Galician folk-song. One of the most noticeable effects of the Provençal influence was to establish greater syllabic regularity in the line and to set the fashion for stanzas of a certain number of lines and a rhyme scheme repeated in each fresh stanza. The lines vary in length as a rule from four to twelve syllables, but longer lines of fifteen, sixteen, and even eighteen syllables are found. The poems showing the influence of folk-song and dance reflect the rhythm of the music.

A few examples will illustrate this variety of line and stanza, and give an idea of the rhythm. In the first example the stanza has six lines, four of twelve syllables and two of six syllables more or less. It displays also the parallelistic repetition of the same ideas in slightly varying words characteristic of Galician folk-song. In this poem the fair maidens, *as belidas*, are summoned to dance under the flowering nut-trees, *avelaneiras floridas*, and in the second stanza the word praised, *louvadas*, is substituted for *belidas* while the poetical word for fine, *granadas*, replaces *floridas*, the assonance changing from *i-a* to *a-a*.

> ¡ Bailemos agora, por Deus, ay, belidas,
> so aquestas avelaneiras floridas !
> ¡ E quen for belida como nos belidas,
> se amigo amar
> so aquestas avelaneiras floridas
> virá bailar !
>
> ¡ Bailemos agora, por Deus, ay, louvadas,
> so aquestas avelaneiras granadas !
> ¡ E quen for louvada como nos louvadas
> se amigo amar
> so aquestas avelaneiras granadas
> virá bailar !
>
> JUAN ZORRO. *Cancioneiro da Vaticana*

This is evidently a dance song for love-sick maidens, but the following is definitely a *cantar de amigo*, in which an enamoured girl tells her lover that she is alone in Vigo, unaccompanied and unguarded. It is a good example of *estrofas paralelísticas* with *encadenamiento*, the second line of the first verse providing the first line of the third verse, and that of the second verse the first line of the fourth.

> ¡ Ay Deus, sab'ora o meu amigo,
> com'eu senlleira estou en Vigo,
> e vou namorada !
>
> ¡ Ay Deus, sab'ora o meu amado
> com'eu en Vigo senlleira maño,
> e vou namorada !
>
> ¡ Com'eu senlleira estou en Vigo,
> e nullas guardas non son comigo,
> e vou namorada !

¡ Com'eu senlleira en Vigo maño,
e nullas guardas migo trayo,
e vou namorada ! .. . .
MARTÍN CODAX. *Cancioneiro da Vaticana*

The *estrofa* here is a decasyllabic couplet followed by the hexasyllable of the refrain.

The length of the stanza may vary from three to eight lines, and there may be a refrain repeated after each. Here is one which has a stanza of four lines with alternate assonance followed by a rhymed couplet as a refrain. The lines fluctuate a little but are mainly heptasyllables. The poem introduces the theme of the sea common in Galician poetry and tells how the sight of the waves dashing against the shore stirs waves of love in the poet's heart and makes him curse the sea :

Cuando eu vejo as ondas
e as muit' altas ribas,
logo me veen ondas
ao cor pola belida !
Maldito sea o mare
que me faz tanto male.

Se eu vejo as ondas
e vejo as costeiras,
logo me veen ondas
ao cor pola ben-feita !
Maldito sea o mare
que me faz tanto male.

Octosyllables and hexasyllables are common and these are the lines preferred by later Castilian poets. We also find an occasional enneasyllable as in a *Canción de amigo* by Pero Ponte which begins :

Ay madre o que me namorou
foi-se n'outro día d'aquí,
e por Deus ¿ qué faremos
ca namorada me leixou ?

We find this typical folk-song line reappearing combined with a pentasyllable in the Arcdiano de Toro's farewell to love in the *Cancionero de Baena* which begins:

A Deus amor, a Deus el Rey
que eu ben serví . . .

There is one metrical line which is of special interest in view of later developments, and that is the eleven-syllabled line or hendecasyllable. Menéndez y Pelayo has traced its history from classical Latin through the Latin hymns of the Middle Ages to the French epic line, a decasyllable according to the French method of counting. Through Provençal poetry it passes into Galician and thence into Castilian verse. To distinguish its rhythm from the later Italian version Menéndez y Pelayo calls it anapæstic while Milá y Fontanals refers to it as dactylic. It is rather confusing to introduce these classical terms referring to types of feet or prosodic groups. There are, of course, no actual feet in Romance metres, but iambic is used to indicate a tendency to stress alternate syllables and anapæstic or dactylic indicates that two stressed syllables either precede or follow a stressed one. It is evident that if a line begins with a stressed syllable it may change an anapæstic line into a dactylic one. This Galician hendecasyllable is characterized by a pause after the fifth syllable. It has two stresses in each half-line and of these one usually falls on the fourth and one on the seventh syllable with an invariable one on the tenth; a fourth stress falls variously on the first or the second syllable and may be a weak stress falling on a word or syllable not usually emphasized. There is a certain freedom allowed in distributing the stresses so long as the lilting rhythm is maintained. The metre of the following stanza from one of the *Cantigas* of Alfonso el Sabio is fairly regular as to pauses and stresses.

Bèn vennas, Máyo, con muítos ganádos;
èt nos roguémos a què os pecádos
fáz que nos séian de Déus perdõádos,
què de seu Fíllo nos fáça privádos.

The third line is a good example of dactylic rhythm, regular in every particular; note the synæresis in *seian* and *Deus*. This line, with its four beats or *altas* as they are called, is known as the *verso de gaita gallega*, the Galician bagpipe line, and has the rhythm of the Galician folk-dance, the *muñeira*.

Types of Poem in Provençal and Galician Poetry

It may be of use to summarize here the main types of poem composed by the Provençal troubadours and reflected in the Galician-Portuguese *cancioneiros*. There is the *canson*, a love-song often of a very conventional kind and running into many verses; the *serventés*, which dealt with a moral, political, or religious subject and often degenerated into a bitter personal attack; the *tenson*, a discussion in verse on any subject proposed, in which two or three persons took part, the speaker changing with each stanza but keeping to the same metre and rhyme scheme; the *descort*, a poem in irregular metre of varying lines showing the discord created in the poet's mind by the pangs of unrequited love. There is one type of particular interest to the student of Spanish poetry and that is the *pastorela*. This is of popular origin but given a conventional form and setting by the troubadours. The poet going on a journey meets a fair young shepherdess, singing and minding her flock. The poet compliments her and offers her his love, which is usually rejected on the grounds of difference of station, or because the maiden loves her own faithful shepherd. Lastly there is the *alba* or dawn-song in which the poet laments the coming of dawn which brings separation to the lovers.

Similar types appear in the *cancioneiros*. The *canson* is here the *cantiga de amor* addressed by the lover to his lady, the *cantiga de escarnio* or *maldecir* is a satirical or abusive poem like the *serventés*; the *tenson* and the *descort* have become the *recuesta* and the *discor*. Corresponding to the *pastorela* is the Galician *villanesca* which in Castilian appeared as a *serranilla*, for the maiden courted by the Castilian poet was frequently a *serrana* or mountain maid. There are two types of poem which are purely Peninsular and owe nothing to Provençal models. They are the *cantiga de amigo* addressed by a lovelorn maiden to her mother or absent sweetheart complaining of her sad fate, as we have seen in poems quoted above, and the *cantiga de romería*, a variation of this theme, for the visit to a sanctuary was often a pretext for the maiden to seek out her lover. The Galician *alba* too owes more to native tradition than to Provençal influence.

Traditional Poetry in the Peninsula

Though we do not find the court poets deliberately imitating the compositions of the Provençal and Galician type in their own language until the end of the fourteenth century, Ramón Menendez Pidal maintains in his essay *Primitiva poesía lírica española* that folk-poetry comparable to the Galician existed in earlier times in Castilian. As examples he quotes a *canción de romería, So ell encina, encina*, and a *canción de amigo, Al alba venid, buen amigo*. The latter differs from the usual type of *alba* or dawn-song, for in it the girl does not lament her lover's departure but summons him to meet her. It is composed in the parallelistic style usually considered typically Galician but which is also found in the Asturian song *Ay! un galán d'esta villa*, which accompanies the regional dance, *la danza prima*. Fresh light has lately been thrown on the early traditional poetry of the Peninsula by the discovery of certain Arabic and Hebrew poems written in Moorish Spain during the eleventh and twelfth centuries. At the end of these poems, which are often panegyrical rather than lyrical, there is a couplet in a recognizable Romance dialect, though disguised in Arabic and Hebrew characters. These Romance endings appear to be fragments of primitive *cantigas de amigo*. Colloquial Arabic poems known as *zéjels*, the most usual form of which has been described above, seem to be imitations of a song similar to the Castilian *villancico*. This would give support to the theory that such songs were common to the local Romance dialects all over the Peninsula and not confined to any one region. It cannot, however, be denied that the poets of the *cancioneiros* led the way in making the form of such traditional songs the vehicle for literary composition.

Traditional Lyric Forms in Castilian

It may be an appropriate moment to mention some types of Castilian lyric of traditional origin. The basic form is that of the *villancico*, a name suggestive of a rural theme and assuredly so applied to begin with, but also used habitually for love poems and for lyrics in praise of the Virgin. In modern usage the name is applied to songs celebrating the birth of Christ like Christmas carols. The theme is stated in a preliminary *estribillo* of two, three, or four lines giving a rhyme or rhymes to be repeated in the last one or two lines of each stanza. Sometimes the whole *estribillo* is repeated as a refrain. A charming anonymous love poem will serve as an example:

Que no cogeré yo verbena
la mañana de San Juan,
pues mis amores se van.

Que no cogeré yo claveles,
madreselva ni mirabeles,
sino penas tan crueles
cual jamás se cogerán,
pues mis amores se van.

Romancero general (1600)

The lines here are mainly octosyllabic, but the two initial ones beginning with *que* have nine syllables. The lines may have six syllables as in the following:

Vi los barcos, madre,
vilos y no me valen.

Madre, tres mozuelas,
no de aquesta villa,
en agua corriente
lavan sus camisas
sus camisas, madre,
vilas y no me valen.

Cancionero de Uppsala

The *endecha* or lament is composed in lines of five, six, or seven syllables and differs from the *villancico* in having no *estribillo* and it is characterized by assonance in the even lines which often end in a final stressed syllable as in the quatrain at the head of the famous *endecha*, *Los comendadores de Córdoba*:

¡Los comendadores,
por mi mal os vi!
Yo vi a vosotros,
vosotros a mí.

There are many songs for special occasions like the third of May (*la cruz de mayo*), St John's Day and Christmas Eve, and occupational songs for sowing, reaping, etc., and for the watchman on the look-out in his tower. These are mostly composed in octosyllables or hexasyllables with various arrangements of rhyme or assonance. The *seguidilla*, another verse form of popular origin, will be dealt with at length later on.

The Archpriest of Hita, Don Juan Manuel and Pero López de Ayala

Apart from the main stream of court poetry mostly inspired by Galician and Provençal models, the fourteenth century produced a versatile and original poet, Juan Ruiz, Archpriest of Hita, already mentioned as using a free version of the *mester de clerecía* in the fables and other narrative parts of his book, the *Libro de buen amor*. Juan Ruiz wrote in Castilian a number of *Cánticas de serrana* in popular style, and some charming lyrics. In some instances the Archpriest used the *zéjel* verse form for the first time in Castilian, probably influenced by strolling singers from Moorish Spain. The best-known example is the satirical poem addressed to his faithless messenger, and based on an octosyllabic couplet followed by a series of stanzas of the usual type—*i.e.*, a monorhymed tercet and a fourth line rhyming with the initial couplet. It begins:

Mis ojos no verán luz,
pues perdido he a Cruz.

Cruz cruzada, panadera,
tomé por entendedera,
tomé senda por carrera,
como hace el andaluz.

Four of his *serranillas* are composed in lines of six or eight syllables preceded by a *copla* or *estribillo*, while two others have no introductory lines. The *serranas* depicted by the Archpriest are not the gentle maidens of the Provençal *pastorela*, but, following the Peninsular tradition, are strong, at times aggressive young women who demand gifts as a reward for entertainment and guidance over the mountain passes.

The devotional poems in praise of the Virgin display a number of short-lined metres with or without *estribillo*. The stanzas vary in length and the main lines of the poem of six, seven, or eight syllables may be interrupted by a shorter one of four or five, an early example of the *verso de pie quebrado*. We even find a couplet of lines of fourteen to sixteen syllables followed by an octosyllabic quatrain rhymed *abba* (a *redondilla*).

The most charming of these songs is the *Cántica de loores a Santa María*, beginning:

Quiero seguir a ti ¡ flor de las flores!

which Menéndez y Pelayo took for a continuous line and noted as an early example of a Renaissance hendecasyllable. It seems more likely that the stanza is composed of seven lines of five and seven syllables rhyming *ababaab*, as Julio Cejador gives it in his edition of the *Libro de buen amor* in *Clásicos castellanos*. The version in the Anthology follows the arrangement by María Rosa Lida in her selection published by Losada. The long lines are divided so as to show the probable shorter ones.

In his more popular style Juan Ruiz composed songs for begging students of which the one example we possess is in the form of a *zéjel* and begins:

Señores, dat al escolar
que vos viene demandar.

Dat limosna e ración:
faré por vos oración,
que Dios vos dé salvación:
quered por Dios a mi dar . . .

Songs for blind minstrels ascribed to him are written in stanzas of five or six octosyllabic lines with the same sing-song rhythm.

Spaniards are notoriously difficult to group in classes and categories, so we are not surprised to find in the fourteenth century a prose writer dropping into verse. Don Juan Manuel, a pioneer in prose style, is also a pioneer in the use of certain metric lines. In his book, *El conde Lucanor*, he appended to his fables and tales rhymed couplets to emphasize and sum up the moral. In many of these he used hendecasyllables, some of a recognizable Renaissance type, as Menéndez y Pelayo points out, with a stress on the sixth syllable as three of the following lines will show, though the second line of the first couplet reverts to the rhythm of the *verso de gaita gallega*:

(*a*) En el comienço deve ome mostrar
a su mujer cómo deve passar.

(*b*) Non aventures muncho tu riqueça
por consejo del ome que ha pobreça.

In other couplets we find an approximation to the *verso de arte mayor* typical of the next century as in:

Quien por grand cobdicia de haber se aventura,
será maravilla que el bien muchol' dura.

In the latter half of the fourteenth century another distinguished writer, Pero López de Ayala, whose satirical poem the *Rimado de Palacio* has already been mentioned (as a late irregular example of the *mester de clerecía*), interspersed his narrative with lyrical poems in octosyllables, and in one section used the verse and stanza of the *arte mayor*, but he forms a definite link with the poets of the *Cancionero de Baena* and the movement of which we are about to speak in the next section.

Castilian 'cancioneros' of the Fifteenth and Sixteenth Centuries

From about the middle of the fifteenth century onward there began to appear a number of Castilian *cancioneros* in the style of the Galician-Portuguese *cancioneiros*. Though these include some works of the preceding and following centuries the bulk of their content belongs to the fifteenth century. The first of these collections was the *Cancionero de Baena*, compiled by Juan Alfonso de Baena and dedicated to the poet king, D. Juan II, in 1445. In the work of some of the earlier poets we find *cantigas* in Galician or showing traces of this poetic dialect. Among these may be mentioned Macías, the Arcidiano de Toro, and Garcí Ferrández de Jerena. The Arcidiano composed his poetic testament in

Galician and in *versos de gaita gallega*. The *Cancionero* includes not only occasional poems, whether love lyrics, personal satires, semi-serious discussions on the most varied subjects called *recuestas* similar to the Provençal *tensons*, but also didactic and religious poems of considerable length which show the influence of the great Italian writers in matter and approach, though not yet to any extent in metrical form.

Some of the best known of the *cancioneros* that followed the *Cancionero de Baena* are (1) *Cancionero de Stúñiga*, compiled in Naples in the late fifteenth century at the court of King Alfonso V of Aragon and named for its chief contributor; (2) *Cancionero general de Hernando del Castillo*, published in Valencia in 1511; (3) *Cancionero de Resende*, published in Lisbon in 1516 and containing poems both in Castilian and Portuguese. Of these the most important is the *Cancionero de Hernando del Castillo* often referred to simply as the *Cancionero general*. An interesting point in connexion with the *Cancionero de Stúñiga* is that it contains the first *romance* attributed to a known author.

A very comprehensive collection of poems from the various *cancioneros* has been edited by Foulché-Delbosc under the title of *Cancionero castellano del Siglo XV*,[1] in which the greatest poets of the century are very fully represented.

Metrical Lines and Verse Forms in the Fifteenth Century

Our chief concern is with metre, however, so we shall now consider the lines and verse forms typical of the period. These are in many respects similar to those found in the *cancioneiros* of the preceding century. Of the shorter metres, the *versos de arte menor*, the Castilian poets on the whole preferred the octosyllable for their occasional poems in the conventional courtly style, *canciones*, *decires*, *esparsas*, *preguntas*, *respuestas*, etc. The octosyllable was also sometimes used for longer poems such as the *Claros varones de España* by Fernán Pérez de Guzmán and the *Doctrinal de privados*, a bitter satire against Don Álvaro de Luna by the Marqués de Santillana, both in stanzas of eight lines known as *octavillas*.

[1] *Nueva biblioteca de autores españoles*, Vols. 19 and 22.

The shorter lyrics usually follow the model of the *villancico* and consist of a stanza or stanzas of five, six, seven, eight, nine, or ten lines with an initial *estribillo*. Here is a *canción* by a poet called Escrivá with an *estribillo* of four and a stanza of seven lines:

> Ven muerte tan escondida,
> que no te sienta conmigo,
> porqu'el gozo de contigo
> no me torne a dar la vida.
>
> Ven como rayo que hiere,
> que hasta que ha herido
> no se siente su rüido,
> por mejor herir do quiere:
> así sea tu venida,
> si no, desde aquí me obligo
> qu'el gozo que habré contigo
> me dará de nuevo vida.

Alfonso Álvarez de Villasandino wrote several poems in the form of the *zéjel*, and one which is a petition to the King for money or remuneration of some kind recalls the Archpriest's rhyme for begging students in the *Libro de buen amor*. The initial couplet runs:

> Señores, para el camino
> dat al de Villasandino.

and the quatrains follow in the usual *zéjel* style. It is interesting to trace this verse form in many poems by different authors. The *serranillas* of the Marqués de Santillana remind us of the *cánticas de serrana* of Juan Ruiz, but rather by way of contrast. They are similar in form, written in stanzas of seven or eight lines with or without a short *estribillo*. The Marqués is, however, closer to the Provençal *pastorela* in his treatment of the theme and his presentation of the fair maiden, though the setting is local, as in the *Vaquera de la Finojosa* and the *Moçuela de Bores*, both in hexasyllables. The hexasyllable was used especially in *canciones* and *cantares* that preserve a flavour of folk-poetry. A short *cantar* by Juan Álvarez Gato addressed to *Nuestro Señor* illustrates the happy marriage of folk-rhyme and literary composition in a religious poem:

Amor, no me dexes,
que me morire.

Que en ti so yo vivo,
sin ti so cativo;
si m'eres esquivo
perdido seré.

Si mal no me viene,
por ti se detiene
en ti me sostiene
tu gracia y mi fe.

Que el que en ti se ceva,
que truene, que llueva,
no espera ya nueva
que pena le dé.

Cabo

Que aquel que tu tienes
los males son bienes,
a él vas y vienes
y muy cierto lo sé.

Amor, no me dexes,
que me morire.

When it seemed that the continuous use of one line was somewhat monotonous, variety of rhythm was obtained by introducing into the stanza one or more shorter lines, *versos de pie quebrado* usually about half the length of the others. In the cases where the octosyllable is the basic line the shorter ones have four or five syllables. The broken rhythm of the *pie quebrado* gives a pathetic lilt to this *canción* by the Marqués de Santillana:

Recuerdate de mi vida,
pues que viste
mi partir e despedida
ser tan triste.

Recuérdate que padesco
e padescí
las penas que non meresco,
desque vi
la respuesta non devida
que me diste;
por lo cual mi despedida
fué tan triste. . . .

Other notable poets used varying combinations of these two lines in poems of a serious didactic tone as in this stanza from the *Coplas* addressed by Gómez Manrique to Diego Arias de Ávila on the theme of the swift passing of time and the turning of Fortune's wheel:

En esta mar alterada
por do todos navegamos,
los deportes que pasamos,
si bien lo consideramos,
no duran mas que rociada.
¡ O, pues tú, ombre mortal,
mira, mira,
la rueda cuan presto gira
mundanal!

A stanza from the *Coplas por la muerte de su padre* by Jorge Manrique on much the same theme shows a different combination:

Los estados y riqueza,
que nos dejan a deshora,
¿ quién lo duda?
No les pidamos firmeza,
pues que son de una señora
que se muda;
que bienes son de Fortuna
que revuelve con su rueda
presurosa,
la cual no puede ser una,
ni estar estable ni queda
en una cosa.

As we have said, the lines most in use in this century are the octosyllable and the hexasyllable, but heptasyllables are fairly frequent and enneasyllables occur. The stanzas of the short poems are so varied that we do not propose to deal with them in detail. Further illustrations are provided in the Anthology and those who are interested will find a wider and carefully chosen selection of fifteenth-century lyrics in Dámaso Alonso's *Antología de la poesía de la edad media*.

In the long narrative and didactic poems, stanzas of nine, eleven, twelve, and thirteen lines are found, but the most common stanzas are the *octavilla* and the *décima* composed in octosyllabic lines. The invention of the *décima* is sometimes attributed to Vicente Espinel, a writer of the latter half of the sixteenth century. He merely set a fashion in *décimas* by composing one with a special rhyme scheme which was copied by others and given the name of *espinela*. One has only to look at the first poem in Foulché-Delbosc's *Cancionero castellano del siglo XV* to find a *Vita Christi* in *décimas* by Fray Iñigo de Mendoza which occupies fifty-two pages. The rhyme scheme in this case is *abaabcdccd*, changing the rhyme after the fifth line, and for this reason some people have called this *décima* a double *quintilla*. Espinel's rhyme scheme is *abbaaccddc* and it is interesting to note that the *décimas* of Cristóbal de Castillejo at the beginning of the sixteenth century are rhymed *abaabcdccd* or *ababacddcd*, while towards the end of the century Góngora follows Espinel's model. Lope de Vega also used this *espinela* scheme of rhyme as do all the succeeding dramatists up to the nineteenth century.

The terms that have come to be used to describe the stanzas of varying lengths in Spanish verse such as *cuartetas*, *quintillas*, *sextillas*, etc., have been listed and explained elsewhere, which makes a detailed description unnecessary here. The generic term for all these short-line poems is *arte menor*, in contrast to the term *arte mayor*, the art of the long line.

Verso de arte mayor

The Castilian poets of the fifteenth century not only made use of short-lined metres we have described, but they cultivated a new long-lined metre peculiar to the period, the so-called *verso de arte mayor*. The name should, strictly speaking, connote any long metrical line, but it is generally applied to one particular type. Its rhythm is similar to that of the *verso de gaita gallega*, but it is based on the dodecasyllable, instead of the hendecasyllable. As it is essentially an accentual rather than a syllabic line it displays many irregularities, and lines of eleven, ten, and even nine or eight syllables occur. In theory, however, the line is a dodecasyllable divided into two definite hemistiches of six syllables. Each hemistich generally bears two stresses, one often weak is variously placed, but a strong stress falls regularly on the fifth syllable. The final stress of the line should fall invariably on the eleventh syllable. The stanza employed is the *octava* with three rhymes arranged in slightly different ways. The *verso de arte mayor* first appeared somewhat tentatively in Don Juan Manuel's rhymed couplets and was one of the long metre lines used by Pero López de Ayala. It definitely took its place as a literary medium for a long didactic poem in the anonymous *Danza de la muerte* at the beginning of the fifteenth century. The first stanza of this poem gives a good idea of the rhythm and displays a few characteristic irregularities. The strong stresses have been indicated by an acute and the weak ones by a grave accent (using the French terms for the sake of convenience). The rhyme scheme is *ababbccb*.

A la dánza mortál   veníd los nascídos
que en el múndo sóis   de qualquiéra estádo,
el que nòn quisiére,   a fuérça e amídos
fazérle he venír   muy tóste prïádo.
Pues que yà el fráile   vos hà predicádo
que tódos vayáis   a fazér peniténcia,
el que nòn quisiére   ponér diligéncia
por mí non puéde   ser más esperádo.

In the *Cancionero de Baena* there are poems in this metre by Pero López de Ayala, Alfonso Álvarez de Villasandino, Francisco Imperial, and Fernán Pérez de Guzmán, and in spite of its lively cadence it was generally applied to serious and didactic matter. Special mention should be made of a poem in *arte mayor* by Fernán Sánchez de Calavera on the *Vanidades del mundo*, a forerunner in its theme of the better-known poems of Gómez and Jorge Manrique.

The poet who manipulated this curious metre with the greatest ease and freedom was perhaps Juan de Mena. An extract from his famous allegory, *El laberinto de Fortuna*, will give an idea of his style. This passage describes his meeting with Macías, the poet who died for love of a fair lady:

Tanto anduvimos el cerco mirando
a que nos hallamos con nuestro Macías,
e vimos que estava llorando los días
en que de su vida tomó fin amando;
llegué más acerca turbado yo quando
vi ser un hombre de nuestra nación
e vi que decía tal triste canción,
en elegíaco verso cantando.

The rhyme scheme here is *abbaacca*, very usual in *octavas* and *octavillas*. There is a striking irregularity in the length and division of the lines. In at least two cases the hemistich is short and the stress falls on the fourth syllable. In the last line there are only five syllables in each hemistich if we change the stress on the word *elegíaco* to make the stress fall on the fifth syllable. This metre had a great vogue in the early fifteenth century, but as time went on the fashion changed; though the Marqués de Santillana used this metre in his poem in dialogue *Comedieta de Ponça*, and Gómez Manrique wrote several poems in it, Jorge Manrique regularly preferred the short-lined metres.

First Signs of the Italian Hendecasyllable

In this century some knowledge of the works of Dante and Petrarch was beginning to penetrate into the Spanish world of letters, as is seen in the long allegorical poems. The first signs of an attempt to imitate the Italian hendecasyllable are to be found in a poem included in the *Cancionero de Baena*, *Dezir de las siete virtudes* by Francisco Imperial. Little is known of Imperial except that he was born in Genoa and lived for some time in Seville. The poem is an allegory in which Dante serves as a guide to the poet to lead him into the " Garden of the Virtues." It is composed in *octavas* and the metric line is a kind of mixture of *verso de gaita gallega* and the Italian hendecasyllable and may have been influenced at first or second hand by the current *arte mayor*. To illustrate the effect here is an *octava* describing Dante's appearance:

> Era en vista benigno e süave,
> e en color era la su vestidura
> ceniza o tierra que seca se cave;
> barva e cabello alvo sin mesura:
> traía un libro de poca escriptura
> escripto todo con oro muy fino,
> e començava: "*En medio del camino*,"
> e del laurel corona e cintura.

It will be noticed that the first six lines have a different rhythm from those that follow, for they echo the lilt of the *gaita gallega* with the three main stresses on the fourth, seventh, and tenth syllables, while the last two lines recall the Italian rhythm, the words in italics echoing a phrase from Dante's *Divina Commedia*. A longer extract in the anthology will enable the reader to judge to what extent the poet has mastered the new technique. Later on a much more successful attempt was made by the Marqués de Santillana in his forty-two sonnets "*fechos al itálico modo*" in imitation of Petrarch, a remarkable achievement for his time.

Survival of the 'versos de arte menor'

The fashion for composing poems in the short-line metres known as *versos de arte menor* did not end with the appearance and adoption in Spain of the Italian renaissance metrical forms. That they survived throughout the sixteenth and seventeenth centuries was due to a great extent to music and the drama or a combination of them both. The lyrics based on folk-rhymes and imitations of these were set to music by contemporary composers and published in collections like the *Cancionero musical de los siglos XV y XVI* (based on the *Cancionero de Palacio*) available in the edition published in 1890 by F. Asenjo Barbieri. Two notable poets who were also musicians, one a Spaniard, Juan del Encina, who is represented in the *Cancionero musical* by several pieces, and the other a Portuguese, Gil Vicente, who wrote in both languages, introduced into their rather primitive dramatic pieces called *autos* and *églogas* a number of *villancicos* and *canciones*. Gil Vicente excelled in the composition or adaptation of the traditional folk-poetry. Adoption might be a more exact description of the part he played in some cases, and Dámaso Alonso, who includes some of these songs under Gil Vicente's name in his *Antología de la edad media*, admits that the attribution to him is doubtful.

The other *cancioneros* even without music maintained their popularity in the sixteenth century, and the *Cancionero general*, re-edited by Hernando del Castillo in 1514, was reprinted nine times.

La seguidilla

There is one verse form, the *seguidilla*, which had a great vogue in literary circles of the sixteenth and seventeenth centuries, and which is probably of purely Castilian origin as it is unrepresented in the Galician-Portuguese *cancioneiros*. The early *seguidillas* have four lines with assonance or rhyme in the even lines while the uneven lines may or may not rhyme. These lines fluctuate in length as is usual in folk-poetry, the uneven varying from eight to six syllables and the even lines from six to four. When regularized for literary purposes by poets like Lope de Vega three main types frequently occur; in one the alternating lines are hexasyllables and pentasyllables, in another heptasyllables and hexasyllables, and lastly one in heptasyllables and pentasyllables which came to be considered the standard form. Of this latter type is the anonymous *seguidilla* adapted by Juan Álvarez Gato to precede and set the theme for a religious poem in hexasyllables. This application of folk-rhymes to religious poetry is very common in this century. Here are the two *seguidillas* for comparison:

Anonymous

Quita allá, que no quiero,
falso enemigo;
quita allá, que no quiero
que huelgues conmigo.

Juan Álvarez Gato

Quita allá, que no quiero,
mundo enemigo;
quita allá, que no quiero
pendencias contigo.

Disenchantment with a deceitful world replaces the false lover as the subject of the poem that follows.

The *seguidilla* begins to take definite form in Cervantes though he often arranges the quatrains as couplets, easily divided into their component lines by obvious pauses. In *Don Quixote*, Part II, Chap. XXIV, a lad going to the wars sings a *seguidilla* as he tramps along:

> A la guerra me lleva   mi necesidad;
> si tuviera dineros,   no fuera en verdad.

which makes a quatrain of heptasyllables and hexasyllables. In the *entremés* of *La guarda cuidadosa*, we find the accepted form of heptasyllables followed by pentasyllables:

> Sacristán de mi vida,   tenme por tuya,
> y fiado en mi fe   canta aleluya.

Such *seguidillas* are also sung by La Escalanta in the novel *Rinconete y Cortadillo*. In other *entremeses* we find them arranged in quatrains as in this example from the *Entremés de los romances*:

> Frescos ventecillos,
> favor os pido,
> que me anego en las olas
> del mar del olvido.

In the seventeenth century there appears a *seguidilla* with an *estrambote* of three extra lines, making seven in all, as in this one from *Las paredes oyen* by Juan Ruiz de Alarcón:

> Venta de Viveros
> dichoso sitio,
> si es cristiano el ventero
> y es moro el vino.
>
> Sitio dichoso,
> si el ventero es cristiano
> y el vino es moro.

As will be noticed in this example, the extra triplet rhymes in the uneven lines.

The *seguidilla* has survived to this day in popular form as a song set to music to accompany a dance. In the north of Spain it has only the original four lines, but in Andalusia the *estrambote* is usual except in the case of the gypsy *seguidilla* or *siguiriya*, as they call it, which has four lines of six, six, eleven, and six syllables as in:

Madre de mi alma,
¡ qué buena gitana !
De un pedacito de pan que tenía
la mitad me daba.

The popularity of the *seguidilla* continued throughout the seventeenth century and Henríquez Ureña in his book on irregular metres in Spanish poetry quotes innumerable instances from the poems and plays of Lope de Vega, one of the most striking of them being the haunting verse on which Lope based his tragedy, *El caballero de Olmedo*:

Que de noche le mataron
al caballero,
la gala de Medina,
la flor de Olmedo.

He also gives examples from Tirso de Molina, Valdivielso, and Calderón. Apart from the *seguidillas* labelled as such the reader will find in the Anthology two *Canciones a la Virgen* from Lope's *Los pastores de Belén*, the well-known *Romancillo* by Góngora, *Las flores del romero*, and a poem by Valdivielso, all developing the themes of initial *seguidillas*.

From the time of Calderón onwards the standard type has become fixed and hardly varies in cultured or popular poetry up to the present day.

Renaissance Metres in the Sixteenth and Seventeenth Centuries

As we have seen, attempts were made in the fifteenth century to master the Italian Renaissance type of hendecasyllable, with a great measure of success on the part of the Marqués de Santillana in his sonnets. It was not, however, until the beginning of the sixteenth century that the Italian metres and verse forms became acclimatized in Spain. This was mainly due to two poets, Juan Boscán, a Catalan, and Garcilaso de la Vega, a Castilian. Boscán took the initiative but Garcilaso attained greater perfection. The hendecasyllable in his hands attained the fluent ease of his models, Petrarch, Tasso, and Bembo. Garcilaso, though an imitator, was a true poet, and his exquisite *églogas*, *canciones*, and *sonetos* were the main factors in establishing the vogue of Italianate poetry in Spain.

Boscán and Garcilaso both used what is considered the "proper" Renaissance line with stresses on the second, sixth, and tenth syllables, but also frequently the "improper" line with stresses on the fourth and eighth syllables, and even blended the two, as can be tested by examining any group of their hendecasyllables. The stresses may be shifted to the first or third syllables, and there are even cases of a stress on the seventh syllable. Generally speaking the rhythm is what some call iambic and others trochaic, showing a tendency to alternate stressing. Synalepha was more regularly observed by Garcilaso than by Boscan but in both one notices some hesitation when a word begins with an *h* derived from a Latin *f* which might be slightly aspirated. Boscán is rather inclined to follow the Catalan fashion of ending a line on a stressed syllable, *terminación aguda*, but Garcilaso is more faithful to his Italian models in using the *terminación grave*. The following are the main verse forms, introduced in imitation of Italian poetry:

Soneto

Of these verse forms the sonnet is the one which has attained the most lasting popularity in Spain as elsewhere. Spanish poets preferred the usual Italian form composed of two hendecasyllabic quatrains generally rhymed *abba abba* followed by two tercets rhymed variously *cde cde*, *dcd cdc*, etc., unlike the Elizabethans, who preferred the scheme of three quatrains with alternate rhyme and a final couplet.

Octava real

The hendecasyllable is also the basic line of the *ottava rima* called in Spanish *octava rima* but also more frequently *octava real*. Boscán wrote a poem in praise of love in this stanza in imitation of one by Bembo. The rhyme scheme, as will be seen from the following example, is *abababcc*. It begins:

En el lumbroso y fértil Oriente
adonde más el cielo está templado,
vive una sosegada y dulce gente,
la cual en solo amar pone el cuidado.
Esta jamás padece otro accidente
sino es aquel que amores han causado
aquí gobierna y siempre gobernó
aquella reina que en la mar nació.

Tercetos

Hendecasyllabic tercets were introduced into Spain by certain Catalan poets, but Boscán was the first to compose them in Castilian. They rhyme *aba bcb cdc* etc., and here is an example from the beginning of Garcilaso's second eclogue:

En medio del invierno está templada
el agua dulce desta clara fuente,
y en el verano más que nieve helada.
¡ Oh claras ondas, como veo presente,
en viéndoos, la memoria de aquel día,
de que el alma temblar y arder se siente !
En vuestra claridad vi mi alegría
escurecerse toda y enturbiarse;
cuando os cobré, perdí mi compañía.

In the same eclogue we find a long passage in hendecasyllables with internal rhyme of which the following is an example:

Nuestro ganado pace; el viento *espira*;
Filomena *sospira* en dulce *canto*,
y en amoroso *llanto* se *amancilla*;
gime la *tortolilla* sobre el *olmo*;
preséntanos a *colmo* el prado flores. . . .

Verso suelto

The *verso suelto*, unrhymed or blank verse as we call it in English, was used by both Boscán and Garcilaso, but it never had the vogue in Spain that it had in England. A good specimen is found in Garcilaso's *Epístola a Boscán*.

'*Silva*' and '*lira*'

The hendecasyllable was combined with a heptasyllable in a stanza of varying length called in Spanish *silva* or sometimes *estancia*, which is the Spanish form of the Italian *stanza*. Some of Garcilaso's most beautiful poetry was composed in this metre, notably the first eclogue, a selection from which appears in the Anthology. This eclogue has stanzas of fourteen lines, three *canciones* have stanzas of thirteen and the fourth *canción* stanzas of twenty lines. Special mention must be made of a short stanza employed by Garcilaso in the well-known *Canción a la Flor de Gnido* in imitation of a poem by Bernardo Tasso. This stanza has five lines, three of seven and two of eleven, arranged as follows:

> Si de mi baja lira
> tanto pudiese el son, que en un momento
> aplacase la ira
> del animoso viento,
> y la furia del mar y el movimiento . . .

This verse came to be called *lira* from the last word in the first line and was brought to the highest perfection by Fray Luis de León and San Juan de la Cruz.

Fernando de Herrera used the *silva* in his stirring *canciones* on Don Juan de Austria's victory at Lepanto and the defeat and death of Don Sebastián, King of Portugal, at Alcazarquivir. Góngora has stanzas of varying length in his descriptive poem, *Las soledades*, reserving the stanza of thirteen lines for a set piece like the bridal song of the rustic choir, and Lope de Vega makes extensive use of the *silva* in many of his *Rimas humanas* and *sacras* and in the poems scattered through his novels. The sonnet cultivated in the sixteenth and seventeenth centuries by Herrera, Góngora, Lope de Vega, and many others has maintained its popularity throughout the ages and is not excluded from the repertoire of the twentieth-century poets, who are inclined to eschew set metres of any kind. Tercets make heavier going, but Lope de Vega handled them with his usual ease in epistles in *La Circe* and *La Filomena* and even used this metre in a poem in lighter vein like his *Epístola a Gaspar de Barrionuevo* in *Rimas humanas*.

Definitely classical in style and inspiration are the tercets of the anonymous *Epístola a Fabio* and the *silvas* of Rodrigo Caro's *Canción a las ruinas de Itálica.* Fray Luis de León not only imitated the odes of Horace but actually translated some of them in varied combinations of hendecasyllables and heptasyllables. In the early seventeenth century Esteban Manuel de Villegas produced an ode definitely labelled Sapphic, composed of quatrains of three lines of eleven syllables followed by one of five syllables.

Survival of Pre-Renaissance Metres

All this goes to show that the imitation of classical models was now established and held an important place in Spanish poetry. One has only to look into the tomes of the *Biblioteca de Autores Españoles* to realize how large a place it is. This does not mean that the older verse forms and metres have disappeared; the subject matter may change, but the forms persist. We find the most obvious example of this in the *romance.* The great vogue of the narrative ballads was followed by a period when the so-called *romances artísticos* became the vehicle for the poet's account of his own love affairs. Lope de Vega wrote a series of *romances* in pastoral style to his mistress, Elena Osorio, and his wife, Isabel de Urbina, under the names of Filis and Belisa, and another of *romances moriscos* in which Filis is disguised as Zaida and the poet himself as Zaide.

Cristobal de Castillejo, a contemporary of Garcilaso, voiced the opposition to the Renaissance styles in poetry and advocated the continuation of the metres and style of the *cancioneros* of the fifteenth century. He mocked Garcilaso and Boscán in both *soneto* and *décimas.* The question passed out of the phase of controversy and examples of earlier metres continually appear throughout the sixteenth century. Garcilaso and Boscán wrote *villancicos* and *coplas*; Fray Luis de León wrote a *décima* on the occasion of his leaving prison. Santa Teresa, hardly affected by the classical vogue of her day, wrote rustic *villancicos* on the birth of Christ and a *glosa* in seven-lined octosyllabic stanzas on the theme:

> Vivo sin vivir en mí,
> y tan alta vida espero,
> que muero porque no muero.

in which the last line serves as a refrain. San Juan de la Cruz developed this theme in the same metre and wrote several others in typical *villancico* form. In his poem, *Pastorcico*, though using hendecasyllables, he arranged them in *cuartetos* rhyming like the *redondilla, abba*. Baltasar del Alcázar, Pedro Espinosa, and others represented in *Flores de poetas ilustres de España* wrote occasional *redondillas, quintillas*, and *octavillas*, but it was Lope de Vega who cultivated with the greatest enthusiasm and success the older types of verse. He not only combined the style and versification of the fifteenth-century court poets but he fell under the spell of genuine folk-poetry. His occupational songs, *canciones de velador, de siega*, and *de vendimia*, his *canciones de boda* and *de bautizo* are hardly distinguishable from the traditional songs of the country folk. *Letras para cantar, bailes*, and *seguidillas* flow with equal facility from his ready pen. Góngora, too, famed for his ultra-classical *Polifemo* and *Las soledades*, could produce delightful *villancicos* and *letrillas* in traditional style. His baroque tendencies are often shown even in his *romancillos* and *letrillas*, and his *romance, Angélica y Medoro*, is couched in that learned and elaborate language that has made the epithets *culterano* and *gongorista* identical. In many poems the blending of the two styles has produced results of real lyric beauty. Francisco de Quevedo preferred the Renaissance metres for his more serious compositions such as the famous *Epístola al Conde-Duque de Olivares* and numerous sonnets, but for gay satirical verses he could use the shorter metres to good effect as in the sprightly *décimas* of *Punto en boca* and in the *sextillas* of *Poderoso caballero es don Dinero* with its repetitive refrain which bears comparison with Góngora's *Dineros son calidad*.

Metre in the Drama of the Golden Age

It is not only in purely lyrical poetry that we find these varied metrical forms. Metrical variety characterizes the very texture of the dramatic presentation in the theatre of the Golden Age. Lope de Vega, who laid down the main lines for the drama in Spain from his own times onwards, unlike the Elizabethans used both pre-Renaissance and Renaissance metres with the balance in favour of the former, preferring the lively octosyllable to the more stately hendecasyllable. Lope in his *Arte nuevo de hacer comedias* gave rules for the use of certain verse forms which he does not consistently observe. The *romance* metre is the most commonly used of all these, especially appropriate for narrative speeches. Next in frequency is the *redondilla*, the octosyllabic quatrain rhymed *abba* which Lope considered most suitable for lovers' colloquies. The *quintilla* is not mentioned by Lope in this connexion, but may be included under the name of *redondilla* which seems to have been variously applied to either the single *quintilla* or the *copla real*, a combination of two *quintillas*, as in the case of the poems dedicated by Cervantes to Isabel de Valois on the occasion of her death. Lope uses both the single and double *quintillas* in his plays, and the latter with notable effect in the pathetic farewell of Don Alonso to Doña Inés in *El caballero de Olmedo*. *Décimas* Lope finds suitable for complaints and we may recall as a striking example the lament of Segismundo in the first act of Calderón's play *La vida es sueño*. Lope throws out the suggestion that the *octava* might rival the *romance* as a vehicle for narrative, but in practice the latter holds the field.

Of the Renaissance metres Lope preferred the sonnet for soliloquies and the tercets for serious matters though for these he has occasionally recourse to *verso suelto*, the Spanish blank verse. The *silva* is also used for various purposes and gives particular dignity and charm to the love duo of Abindarráez and Jarifa at the beginning of *El remedio en la desdicha*. In the *sextina*, a six-lined stanza, and in the *pareado* or couplet the hendecasyllable is used either alone or in combination with the heptasyllable. The *pareado* may be used independently for dialogue, as in Act II of Calderón's *El príncipe constante*, or to wind up a stanza or a scene as in the examples quoted below. These quotations taken mainly from Lope de Vega's better-known plays will serve to illustrate the above remarks:

Pre-Renaissance metres:

Romance

Por la tarde salio Inés
a la feria de Medina,

tan hermosa, que la gente
pensaba que amanecía:
rizado el cabello en lazos,
que quiso encubrir la liga,
porque mal caerán las almas
si ven las redes tendidas . . .

El caballero de Olmedo, Act I

Redondilla (cuarteta)

¡Dichosa tú, casadilla,
que en tan buen estado estás!
Ea, ya no falta más
sino salir a la villa.

Peribáñez y el comendador de Ocaña, Act I, Sc. 13

Quintilla

Reina, pues que tan dichosa
te hará el cielo, dulce esposa,
que te diga quien te vea:
La ventura de la fea
pasóse a Casilda hermosa.

Peribáñez y el comendador de Ocaña, Act I, Sc. I

Copla real (dos quintillas)

Tener de tu esposo el nombre
amor y favor ha sido;
pero es justo que me asombre
que amado y favorecido,
tenga tal tristeza un hombre.
Parto a morir, y te escribo
mi muerte, si ausente vivo,
porque tengo, Inés, por cierto
que si vuelvo, será muerto,
pues partir no puedo vivo.

El caballero de Olmedo, Act II

Décima

Nobles campos de Galicia,
que a sombras destas montañas,
que el Sil entre verdes cañas
llevar la falda codicia,

dais sustento a la milicia
de flores de mil colores;
aves que cantáis amores,
fieras que andáis sin gobierno,
¿habeis visto amor más tierno
en aves, fieras y flores?
El mejor alcalde el Rey, Act I

Renaissance metres:

Silva

ABINDARRÁEZ. Verdes y hermosas plantas,
que el sol con rayos de oro y ojos tristes
ha visto veces tantas,
cuantas ha que de un alma el cuerpo fuistes;
laureles que tuvistes
hermosura y dureza:
si no es el alma agora
como fué la corteza,
enternézcaos de un hombre la tristeza,
que un imposible adora.
El remedio en la desdicha, Act I

Sextina

COMENDADOR. Hermosa labradora,
más bella, más lucida,
que ya del sol vestida
la colorada aurora;
sierra de blanca nieve,
que los rayos de amor vencer se atreve.
Peribáñez y el comendador de Ocaña, Act I, Sc. XI

Octava real

SANCHO. Yo solo labrador en la campaña,
y en el gusto del alma caballero,
y no tan enseñado a la montaña
que alguna vez no juegue el limpio acero,
oyendo nueva tan feroz y estraña,
no fuí ni pude, labrador grosero;
sentí el honor con no haberlo tocado,
que quien dijo de sí, ya era casado.
El mejor alcalde el Rey, Act II

Tercetos

ALBORÁN. ¡ Oh ilustre y generoso descendiente
de aquellos malogrados Bencerrajes
por su valor y envidia juntamente !
¡ Oh reliquia de aquellos dos linajes !
¡ Oh fénix de su muerte a sangre y fuego,
porque mejor de los aromas bajes !
En este punto de Granada llego,
y el traer sangre tuya en la memoria
(que casi te la doy en llanto ciego)
ha hecho que te obligue con su historia,
que ya la sabes por ajena fama,
a restaurar su antiguo nombre y gloria.

El remedio en la desdicha, Act I

Verso suelto ending with *pareado*

COMENDADOR. Di que entre ; que del modo que a quien ama,
la calle, las ventanas y las rejas
agradables le son, y en las criadas
parece que ve el rostro de su dueño,
así pienso mirar en su marido
la hermosura por quien estoy perdido.

Peribáñez y el comendador de Ocaña, Act I, Sc. XVI

Pareado used in conjunction with *verso de romance*

ESTRELLA. No importa que esté partida ;
que es bien que las piedras sientan
mis contentos y alegrías.
¡ Ay venturoso día !
Esta, amigos, ha sido estrella mía !

La estrella de Sevilla, Act II, Sc. XVIII

Soneto

Una moza de cántaro y del río,
más limpia que la plata que en él lleva,
recién herrada de chinela nueva,
honor del delantal, reina del brío,
con manos de marfil, con señorío
que no hay tan gran señor que se le atreva,
pues donde lava dice amor que nieva,
es alma ilustre al pensamiento mío.

Por estrella, por fe, por accidente,
viéndola henchir el cántaro, en despojos
rendí la vida al brazo transparente.
Y envidiosos del agua mis enojos
dije: ¿Por qué la coges de la fuente,
si la tienes, más cerca, de mis ojos?

La moza de cántaro, Act II, Sc. III

Metre in Poetry of the Eighteenth and Nineteenth Centuries

The seventeenth century had brought the use of Renaissance and earlier metres to such a pitch of perfection that there seemed little for the eighteenth-century poets to do but to follow their example within the limits of their period and inspiration. A French king was on the throne and the influence of French ideas was strong, so we are not surprised to find a number of long poems on moral, social, and political themes couched in hendecasyllables. Towards the end of the century the patriotic motive inspires lengthy diatribes against Napoleon and appeals calling on the Spaniards to defend their liberty and take vengeance for their wrongs. These subjects demanded a resounding rhetorical style which found a fitting vehicle in the classical *silva*. The writers of fables, Samaniego and Iriarte, influenced no doubt by La Fontaine, are lighter in their manner and display a welcome sense of humour. They employ in many cases the short-lined metres which Iriarte uses with particular gaiety and liveliness. Even the longer metres are less solemn and portentous in their hands.

The *romance* is still in favour as a metrical form. Juan Meléndez Valdés, the best lyric poet of his age, gives us one entitled *La mañana de San Juan*, which though it has not the magic of the older ballads has a pleasant descriptive style. Nicasio Álvarez de Cienfuegos shows a preference for the shorter metres, and the prolific Alberto Lista, though he has forty-five sonnets and sixty-three *silvas* in his repertoire, has also fifty *romances* and seventeen *seguidillas* as well as a number of poems in lines of five, six, seven, and eight syllables. Nicolas Fernández de Moratín's famous *Fiesta de toros en Madrid* is in *quintillas* and he also wrote *romances*, but he is represented in the Anthology by a *lira*. A selection that would give any idea of the vast production of these eighteenth-century poets would be over-lengthy. The Anthology can only touch the fringe, but suggests as far as possible in the space at our disposal the variety of content and form.

The Romantic Poets

With Quintana, Lista, and Nicasio Gallego we pass the dividing line between the two centuries and approach the Romantic period. The full effect of the Romantic movement which had already begun abroad was not felt in Spain until the third decade of the nineteenth century, when the political exiles, including the poets, returned home. The new spirit which burned in the work of such writers as the Duque de Rivas and José María Heredia is one which affects the content rather than the form of their poetry. The ballad form, as we have seen, had never gone out of fashion, but the Duque de Rivas went back to the old tradition of the ballad as an historic narrative. On the other hand, he took the legend of the *Siete infantes de Lara* and rewrote the story that had been in the past so vividly presented in lively octosyllables in rather heavy hendecasyllables. His famous *Faro de Malta* is an ode in the Horatian style such as was cultivated by his predecessors in the seventeenth and eighteenth centuries. Heredia's poem on the Niagara Falls, vivid and eloquent as it is, is composed in *silvas*.

It is not until we come to José de Espronceda that we discover any great originality in the handling of metre. He can write a sonnet, compose a ballad and turn the *silva* to good effect in his forceful and picturesque *Himno al sol*. His originality is really seen in his varied use of standard forms and in the way he combines different verse forms in one poem, *polimetría* as it is now called. He composes *cuartetas* and *cuartetos* of four, six, eight, and eleven-syllabled lines with alternate rhyme or assonance. In the *Canción del pirata* variety is produced by using stanzas of four-syllabled lines alternating with an octosyllabic stanza or one with *pie quebrado*. In *El verdugo* the poet combines lines of ten or twelve syllables with shorter ones of five. The change of metre keeps the reader's attention alert and often marks a change of tone in the treatment of the theme. The twelve-syllabled line is the basis of the *cuartetos* of the *Canto del cruzado*.

An almost bewildering variety of metre is found in the fantastic narrative poem, *El estudiante de Salamanca*. In Part I the conventional ballad metre in which the poem begins is soon interrupted by a series of trisyllables and tetrasyllables and later come *cuartetos* of dodecasyllables followed by *octavillas* and these again by the melancholy *octavas reales*, which introduce the tragic figure of the beautiful ill-fated Elvira. In Part II, octosyllabic *cuartetas* are followed by *quintillas* and these by hendecasyllabic *cuartetos* describing Elvira's madness, and finally come the solemn *octavas reales* of her death-bed letter. In Part III, the scene of Don Felix and the gamesters gives an opportunity for a dialogue in *redondillas* in true Lope style, only interrupted by five hendecasyllabic *cuartetos* for the entrance of Elvira's angry brother. Part IV displays an even greater variety, a continuing series of metrical changes, but the most striking effect is produced in the description of the final catastrophe. One after another the *octavas* are graded in diminishing lines from the hendecasyllabic, passing through *octavas* of ten, nine, eight, seven, six, five, four, and three-syllabled lines to the final gasp of three disyllables: *leve/breve/son*, giving the impression of the libertine's gradual passage from excitement, wonder, fear, delirium to unconsciousness and his inevitable doom. The calm of morning which follows this dreadful night is described in serene classical hendecasyllables.

This recalls *La noche de insomnio y el alba* by Gertrudis Gómez de Avellaneda in which she passes from disyllables in a series of lines increasing in length until the final quatrains in lines of sixteen syllabes.

Zorrilla too followed Espronceda's lead in the use of varied metre and explored all the possible combinations of *cuartetas*, *quintillas*, *sextillas*, etc. In *La azucena silvestre* he emulated Espronceda's *tour de force* in his description of the penitence of the crime-stained hermit, Juan Guarino, as he wanders through the wilds of Montserrat. Here he graduates his metres from Alexandrines, hendecasyllables, etc., down to disyllables and then works his way back to dodecasyllables, hendecasyllables, and

Alexandrines, a striking example of *polimetría*. In the resuscitation of the Alexandrine, Zorrilla anticipated the *poetas modernistas*. The Alexandrine is the basis of the stanzas of four, six, and eight lines in a poem written by Zorrilla on the occasion of his ceremonial coronation at Granada; and a greater novelty still, in his poem *A Colón* we find continuous unrhymed Alexandrines. In *La siesta* he combines Alexandrine *quatrains* with dodecasyllabic couplets interrupted by the short-lined triplets of the troubadour's song. In the more usual current metres Zorrilla excelled in the *romance* and is seen at his best in such ballads as *A buen juez, mejor testigo* and *Justicias del Rey Don Pedro*. He made effective use of the *octavilla*, amid a variety of other metres, in his colourful poem *Granada*, but though a prolific and facile verse writer he lacks Espronceda's vigour and dramatic power.

Gertrudis Gómez de Avellaneda, perhaps under Zorrilla's influence, also cultivated the Alexandrine, but she gave it an original turn and considerable fluidity by her treatment, omitting the cæsura or making pauses anywhere but after the seventh syllable. This will be seen in the stanzas quoted in the Anthology from her poem *Soledad del alma*. She took liberties too with the hendecasyllable and in her poem *A Él* she interrupts the smooth flow of the line by a sudden colon, an exclamation mark or a question. The following will serve as a sample:

¡ Quísolo Dios y fué : gloria a su nombre !
Todo se terminó : recobro aliento :
¡ Angel de las venganzas ! ya eres hombre . . .
Ni amor ni miedo al contemplarte siento.

Gustavo Adolfo Bécquer had a magic touch, and whatever metre he used he changed from a formal arrangement of lines to something alive which responds to the inspiration of each thought and emotion. Generally speaking the verse group he prefers is the quatrain in which the lines vary from ten to twelve, from eleven to seven or five or from eight to five according to the poet's whim. Bécquer on the whole prefers assonance to perfect rhyme as having less artificial precision. Besides the more usual combinations of lines of seven and eleven syllables, Bécquer combined lines of ten and twelve syllables as in *Rima I, Yo sé un himno gigante y extraño . . .* or of ten and six syllables as in

Rimas VII and *VIII*. He varies the arrangement of lines in different stanzas and often adds a line or a single word as a kind of *estrambote*. His apparently effortless metrical skill can only be appreciated by studying his *Rimas* at first hand.

Bécquer's contemporaries, Ramón de Campoamor and Gaspar Núñez de Arce, combine a certain freedom in line grouping with conventional syllabic regularity.

Even more of an innovator than Bécquer was the great Galician poetess, Rosalía de Castro. The metrical forms in her first poems in Galician, *Cantares gallegos*, derive mainly from folk-song and ballad and are usually based on a *copla* or short *estribillo*. We hear the beat of the bagpipe in *As de cantar*, and *Miña santiña* is quick with dance rhythm. It is interesting to note that Rosalía has included an *alba* in traditional style beginning, *Cantan os galos pr' ọ dia*. In her later volumes, *Follas novas*, in Galician, and in *En las orillas del Sar*, in Castilian, she makes definite experiments in metre, as can be seen in the examples given in the Anthology. Like Bécquer she prefers assonance to perfect rhyme and like him she too omits any titles to her poems, so that her changes of metre might lead us to think we were reading separate compositions when each is really a part of a larger unity. This is the case with the first poem from *En las orillas del Sar*, quoted in the Anthology, where the theme of the hope of life after death binds the whole series of different types of stanzas together. Rosalía also combined lines of ten and sixteen and made more daring combinations like those of eleven and eight syllables which were considered very harsh by the critics of her day. She also made occasional use of the regular Alexandrine and combined it with the seven-syllabled half-line. She gave a passionate intensity to the long lines of sixteen and eighteen syllables in the poems beginning *Dicen que no hablan las plantas ni las fuentes ni los pájaros*, and *Su ciega y loca fantasía corrió arrastrada por el vértigo*.

Modernismo

Towards the end of the nineteenth century there arose a movement known as *modernismo*, a rather inadequate word applied to the work of a younger generation desirous of change and seeking fresh fields for inspiration. In this case the leader and inspirer of the movement was the Nicaraguan, Rubén Darío, who, coming to Europe in the 1890's, stayed for some time there, mainly in France and Spain, and who was acclaimed in Spain as a great Spanish poet. He invaded Spain through France and brought with him some of the ideas and modes of the French *Parnassiens* and *Symbolistes*. He was however not a mere importer of foreign modes, but a vigorous and original personality who introduced fresh colour and sound into Spanish poetry and encouraged the younger poets to strike out a line of their own.

Rubén Darío essayed an enormous variety of poetic forms, and stimulated by direct contact with Spain, explored the resources of Spanish literature from the Middle Ages onwards. The influence of the French schools of the nineteenth century is most evident in *Azul* (1881) and *Prosas profanas* (1896), but in *Cantos de vida y esperanza* (1905) the influence of Spain predominates. Even in *Azul*, Rubén Darío was already experimenting in the use of the Alexandrine and the dodecasyllable and he produced an unusual sonnet, *Venus*, in seventeen-syllabled lines. In *Prosas profanas* there are a few *Dezires, layes y canciones* in imitation of the fifteenth-century poets and an interesting *Elogio de la seguidilla*.

We have seen that Zorrilla, La Avellaneda, and Rosalía Castro made occasional use of the Alexandrine: it was Darío who developed its possibilities to the full. He claimed Berceo as his prototype, but he is far from imitating Berceo's even regularity. The cæsura is sometimes omitted and on the other hand the line is often broken up by three or even four pauses. A good example of the Alexandrine with a regular mid-line pause is the romantic *Sonatina* in stanzas of six lines. But Rubén Darío's greatest innovation in the use of the Alexandrine was to apply it to the sonnet, and he claimed that *Caupolicán* (*Azul*) was the first Spanish sonnet to be written in this metre.[1] *Caracol* and *Dulzura del Angelus* are composed altogether in Alexandrines, in the sonnet *Melancolía* we find Alexandrines mixed with hendeca-

[1] In this connexion, Henríquez Ureña states that Pedro de Espinosa had already in the seventeenth century composed a sonnet in Alexandrines. *La Versificación Española*, p. 318, note.

syllables. Another metre line which had fallen out of use since the fifteenth century, the enneasyllable, was reintroduced into Spanish poetry by Rubén Darío, probably under French influence. At any rate, in the case of *Responso a Verlaine* where it appears in combination with the Alexandrine, José Montesinos shows how this specific verse form is similar to that of *Plus de Sang* by François Coppée. Darío used the nine-syllabled line in the regular quatrains of one of his most popular poems, *Canción de otoño en primavera*, and in the rather freakish *Soneto de trece versos*, both of which appear in *Cantos de vida y esperanza* (1905). In *Canto a la Argentina* (1910) the lines vary from eight to nine syllables as in the thirteenth-century *Razón d'Amor*.

In *Azul* and *Prosas profanas* we find dodecasyllables divided into hemistiches of six syllables or of seven and five. An example of the former is found in *Era un aire suave de pausados giros* with its smooth undulating rhythm, and of the second in *Elogio de la seguidilla*. This latter recalls the type of *seguidilla* used by Cervantes on various occasions, though here the dodecasyllables are arranged in quatrains instead of couplets.

Rubén Darío handled the hendecasyllable with the same ease and freedom as the Alexandrine, varying the main stresses and using enjambement. In *Pórtico*, dedicated to Salvador Rueda, he regularly stressed the fourth and the seventh syllables in a manner reminiscent of the *verso de gaita gallega*, while in *Divagación* there is greater variety of stressing and rhythm.

An interesting attempt to reproduce the rhythm of the Latin hexameter is seen in *Salutación del optimista*, which begins:

Inclitas razas ubérrimas, sangre de Hispania fecunda,
espíritus fraternos, luminosas almas, salve!

And now we come to the greatest innovation of all, free verse, as in *Marcha triunfal* with lines varying from three to twenty-one syllables and whose only element of conventional metre is the retention of rhyme and a musical rhythm based as Henríquez Ureña points out on a trisyllabic prosodic group with the stress on the second syllable. This rhythm is also apparent in *Salutación a Leonardo*, as is seen in the line:

Sonrisa mas dulce no sabe Gioconda

while in *La canción de los osos*, the group is mainly tetrasyllabic.

In *El país del sol* the medium is manifestly rhythmic prose arranged in paragraphs whose only traces of resemblance to poetic verses lie in the rhymes at the beginning and end of each section and the refrain *en el país del sol*.

In the use of free verse based mainly on a prosodic group of four syllables Rubén Darío had a predecessor in the Colombian poet José Asunción Silva. An example of this is seen in one of his *Nocturnos* in which the length of the printed line varies from four to twenty-four syllables, but the rhythm is based on a prosodic group of four syllables:

> Una noche,
> una noche toda llena de murmullos, de perfumes y de musicas de alas;
> Una noche
> en que ardían en la sombra nupcial y húmeda las luciérnagas fantásticas,
> a mi lado lentamente, contra mí ceñida toda, muda y pálida,
> como si un presentimiento de amarguras infinitas
> hasta el secreto fondo de las fibras te agitara,
> por la senda florecida que atraviesa la llanura
> caminabas;
> y una luna llena
> por los cielos azulosos, infinitos y profundos esparcía su luz blanca;

Here there is alternate assonance in the even lines of only the stressed syllable of the ending whether *grave* or *esdrújula*. In *Día de difuntos*, Silva is more successful in attaining a musical rhythm in tune with the changing bells which provide an unheard but suggested accompaniment. The rhythm is emphasized by the rhyme scheme—perfect rhyme in this case, not mere assonance.

Salvador Rueda, born in Málaga in 1861 and so also somewhat older than Rubén Darío, was an innovator in his own way in the use of metre before the latter appeared on the scene. He wished to preserve the rhythm—*el ritmo* had a very special meaning for him—of the older poetry but made experiments in the application of certain lines. He became one of the chief supporters of the modernist movement and an admirer of its leader. He was addicted to the dodecasyllable, divisible like that of Dario into hemistiches of six and six or seven and five syllables, reminiscent of the *seguidilla*. He even applied dodecasyllables of the latter type in his sonnet *Los pavos reales*. In *Ascua* he combined dodecasyllables with hexasyllables in a modern version of the classical *silva*. Elsewhere he used eighteen-syllabled lines divided into prosodic groups of six syllables, unlike those of Rosalía Castro which were divided into regular hemistiches of nine syllables. His most daring innovation is seen in the quatrains of seventeen-syllabled lines of *Idilio* :

> Entre el sopor de la siesta que duerme Galicia lozana,
> junto a la fuente que ronda zumbando clamante el abejorro,
> medio entreabierta la boca encendida de olor de manzana
> bebe una moza las gotas del arco movible del chorro.

At the turn of the century there is a poet, José Gabriel y Galán, who stands rather outside the modernist movement and who is essentially traditional in feeling and to a great extent in form. He is a regional poet including in his scope two regions, that round Salamanca and Extremadura. In his poems in Castilian and Extremaduran dialect we find *redondillas*, *quintillas*, *sextillas*, these mainly in Castilian, but in both there are poems in ballad metre, and also in more modern style combinations of ten- and six-syllabled lines. In *La jurdana*, an extract from which is quoted in the Anthology, composed in lines of twelve and eight syllables, there is a noticeable tendency to divide each line into tetrasyllabic groups. This division into prosodic groups is even more marked in *Las canciones de la noche*, which begins :

> Una noche rumorosa y palpitante

and also in the well-known *Los pastores de mi abuelo*, beginning :

> He dormido en la majada sobre un lecho de lentiscos

Henríquez Ureña, who notices this tendency, ascribes it to the influence of Silva, but used as in these cases in lines of regular length the effect becomes very monotonous with little of Silva's free-flowing rhythm. In the unfinished dramatic sketch of country life *La Majada* the poet's free use of metre is due to the fact that the lines are meant to be sung, for the play was to have appeared as a *zarzuela*.

Miguel de Unamuno, a contemporary of Silva and the modernist school, does not follow them in metrical innovations.

Rebellious and individual in many of his ideas, he is on the whole conservative in regard to metre. He produced a *Rosario de sonetos* and a *Romancero del destierro*, and his most ambitious poem, *El Cristo de Velázquez*, is composed in unrhymed hendecasyllables, *verso suelto*, with the small peculiarity of ending each section with a *terminación aguda*. In *La catedral vieja de Salamanca* he used a free arrangement of lines of eleven, seven, and five syllables, a variant of the *silva*, while in *Castilla* and *La hora de Dios* he produced classical Sapphic odes reminiscent of Villegas and the seventeenth century. In his introduction to *Teresa* he gives his considered opinion that perfect rhyme is superior to assonance.

The impulse given to originality and free experimentation by the modernist movement was apparent in the first decades of the twentieth century in the poetry of Ramón del Valle-Inclán and of the brothers Manuel and Antonio Machado. The critics are inclined to exclude Antonio Machado from the circle of the *modernistas* because he avoided the sonorous rotundity of Rubén Darío and cultivated a style less exuberant, yet full of beauty and profound emotion. He handled his varied verse forms with ease and dignity, and though he used assonance in many of his poems he showed in others a liking for the restraint of perfect rhyme. Ramón Pérez de Ayala is a poet of transition and has his own individual way of treating metre, conventional or otherwise. Juan Ramón Jiménez is *modernista* in some aspects of his earlier work. He is the most prolific in production and varied in style of all this group and has charmed several generations of readers throughout many different phases. Many of his delicate poems recall the ethereal touch of Bécquer, whose search for elusive beauty may have been a contributory element in the cult of pure poetry, expressed by Juan Ramón in his poem *Vino primero, pura*. As he progresses in power and skill he follows the line of ever greater freedom in line and arrangement that characterizes the period known as *postmodernismo*.

'*Postmodernismo*' *in the Twentieth Century*

In the disillusionment of the post-war period following the Treaty of Versailles, there arose in Europe a revolt against accepted cultural standards. This revolt is expressed in movements such as futurism, cubism, creationism, and surrealism, based on the theory of the paramount importance of the subconscious in creative work. These tendencies were represented in Spain by the movements of *ultraísmo*, whose chief spokesman was Guillermo de la Torre, and *creacionismo*, advocated by the Chilean poet Vicente Huidobro. The *ultraístas* produced verse which displayed a complete disregard for set forms and even for rhythm of any kind. A poem might be reduced to a couple of exclamatory phrases or presented like a diagram on a blackboard. The essence of pure poetry was sought in its bare bones. These extravagances had only a passing vogue, though the theories behind them affected such serious and talented poets as Gerardo Diego and Juan Larrea. The quest for pure poetry continued and its spirit was sought in the allusive phrase and subtle metaphor and in the avoidance of explicit statement.

A remarkable renovation of essentially Spanish poetry was fostered by the work of such poets as Jorge Guillén, Pedro Salinas, and Dámaso Alonso, who were also professors of literature and acquainted with the poetic treasures of the Spanish past. They revealed the beauty of this older poetry both by precept and example and they were ably seconded by Gerardo Diego, who published in 1932 his anthology, *Antología 1915–1931*. This is a collection of modern poetry in which the selection has been made by the authors themselves. The traditional poetry of the *romances* and of the anonymous lyrics collected in the *cancioneros* which had provided inspiration for Gil Vicente and Lope de Vega came into its own again. The period studied with most appreciation was that of the Golden Age. Garcilaso de la Vega, Herrera, Fray Luis de León, San Juan de la Cruz, Lope de Vega, and Góngora became a real part of the national cultural background. The tercentenary of Góngora's death was celebrated in 1927 and was marked by the publication of an anthology in his honour compiled by Gerardo Diego and, more important still, a critical edition of Góngora's *Soledades* edited by Dámaso Alonso. One result of this revival of the past was the renewed interest in formal metre. Jorge Guillén has written a series of seventeen *décimas* of which the first is dedicated to Góngora and the last to

Juan Ramón Jiménez. Vicente Aleixandre, a contemporary poet who affects in general the greatest freedom in line and structure, devotes to Fray Luis de León a correct Renaissance sonnet. Rafael Alberti's *Elegía a Garcilaso* is conceived in completely modern style, yet on the other hand his *Corrida de toros* on a contemporary theme is composed in hendecasyllabic tercets.

Two poets often quoted as exemplifying the revival of the spirit of traditional popular poetry, Federico García Lorca and Rafael Alberti, are both Andalusians but otherwise very different in temperament and achievement.

García Lorca was the most striking poet of his generation and his fame has spread far beyond the bounds of his own country. He drew much of his inspiration from his native region, Andalusia, its life, its dance and song rhythms, and its gipsy lore. His scope is however not limited to poems of popular inspiration but covers a wide field including classical and romantic elements as well as those of symbolism and surrealism. He even wrote an ode to Walt Whitman in true Whitmanesque manner. He transmutes whatever matter or manner he chooses with his genius for extracting music from words and infusing them with emotion. He can write a simple poem with exquisite charm, and he can present violent passion and tragedy with dramatic force, as is shown in some of his gipsy ballads and in his verse dramas.

Rafael Alberti lacks the passionate depth of García Lorca, but his touch, if cool, is sure. In *Marinero en tierra*, his first book, he cultivates a gay popular vein. *Cal y canto* which followed is impregnated with neo-gongorism and we find sonnets, tercets, and ballads on modern subjects in imitation of Góngora's abstruse metaphorical style. There is even an unfinished *Soledad tercera* which is presumably meant to be a continuation of Góngora's *Soledades*. However, in spite of homage paid to such earlier poets as Garcilaso and Góngora, free verse prevails in Alberti's poems.

It would take up too much space in an essay of this kind to make a critical examination of every type of verse in use by the poets of our day. Each poet is free to take from what the centuries have bequeathed and give it his own interpretation. The general tendency is to seek for essential expression and avoid redundancy and exaggeration. Enough has been said, we hope, to help the curious reader to distinguish the elements due to a cultural past and those which reflect the poet's individual relation to his art or merely the mode of the moment.

Further light on literary and artistic aspects of Spanish poetry, apart from the purely metrical element, will be found in the books listed for reference. Gerald Brenan's *Literature of the Spanish People* is particularly interesting as written from the English point of view. With keen pleasure, which he communicates to us as we read, he traces the influence of traditional verse from Medieval times to the present day, giving a special section to modern popular poetry in his chapter on the nineteenth century. His analysis of Góngora's inspiration and achievement is masterly, not merely illuminating the subtle artificialities of his style but explaining his attitude to nature—his Arcadia, an undiscovered paradise. G. Díaz-Plaja in the latter part of his *Historia de la poesía lírica española* deals in great detail with the various trends of contemporary poetry. In an interesting essay recently published on the poetry of Jorge Guillén, J. M. Blecua makes a careful analysis of the very original use made by the poet of metric lines and stanzas.

It has not been thought necessary to include biographical notes on the individual poets as they are available in the usual manuals

ANÓNIMO

(twelfth century)

Cantar de mio Cid

[Rodrigo Díaz, el Cid Campeador, goes into exile. In Burgos all refuse him hospitality for fear of King Alfonso's wrath. A little girl appeals to him to pass on and he leaves after saying a prayer in the church of Santa María.]

El Campeador adeliñó a su posada,
assí commo llegó a la puerta, fallóla bien cerrada,
por miedo del rey Alfons, que assí lo pararan: [1]
que si non la quebrantás', que non gela [2] abriessen por nada.
Los de mio [3] Cid a altas vozes llaman,
los de dentro non les querien tornar palabra.
Aguijó mio Cid, a la puerta se llegava,
sacó el pie del estribera, una feridal dava;
non se abre la puerta, ca [4] bien era cerrada.
Una niña de nuef [5] años a ojo se parava: [6]
"Ya Campeador, en buena [7] cinxiestes espada!
El rey lo ha vedado, anoch dél entró su carta,
con grant recabdo [8] e fuertemente seellada.
Non vos osariemos abrir nin coger por nada;
si non, perderiemos los averes [9] e las casas,
e aun demás los ojos de las caras.
Cid, en el nuestro mal vos non ganades nada;
mas el Criador vos vala [10] con todas sus vertudes santas."
Esto la niña dixo [11] e tornós pora su casa.
Ya lo vede [12] el Cid que del rey non avie gracia.[13]
Partiós de la puerta, por Burgos aguijava,
llegó a Santa María, luego descavalgava.
fincó los inojos,[14] de coraçon rogava.

La oración fecha, luego cavalgava;
salió por la puerta e Arlançón passava.

Cantar del destierro

Note: The weakened forms of the imperfect and conditional endings, *ie, iemos ien,* etc., with or without an accent on the *í*, are common in Medieval Spanish *Avíe* = *había, avíemos* = *habíamos,* etc.

[1] *pararan* = *habían dispuesto* [2] *gela* = *se la*

[3] *mio* = *mi.* This is the usual unaccented masculine form of the possessive adjective in old Spanish.

[4] *ca* = for [5] *nuef* = *nueve* [6] *a ojo se parava* = *se presentó*

[7] *en buena* = *en buena hora* [8] *recabdo* = *precaución*

[9] *averes* = *bienes* [10] *vala* = *valga* [11] *dixo* = *dijo*

[12] *vede* = *ve* [13] *avie gracia* = *tenía favor*

[14] *fincó los inojos* = *hincó de rodillas*

[Mio Cid rides out from Valencia on his steed, Babieca, to welcome his wife Jimena and his daughters. Then from a tower of the Alcázar he shows them the city he has won from the Moors.]

En cabo del cosso [1] mio [2] Cid descavalgava,
adeliñó a su mugier e a sus fijas amas; . . .

A la madre e a las fijas bien las abraçava,
del gozo que avíen de los sos ojos lloravan . . .

Oíd lo que dixo el que en buena cinxo [3] espada:
" Vos doña Ximena, querida mugier e ondrada,
e amas mis fijas mio coraçón e mi alma,
entrad comigo en Valencia la casa,[4]
en esta heredad que vos yo he ganada."
Madre e fijas las manos le besavan.
A tan grand ondra ellas a Valencia entravan.

Adeliñó mio Cid con ellas al alcácer,
allá las subie en el más alto logar.
Ojos vellidos [5] catan [6] a todas partes,
miran Valencia commo yaze la cibdad,

e del otra parte a ojo han [7] el mar,
miran la huerta, espessa [8] es e grand,
e todas las otras cosas que eran de solaz;
alçan las manos pora Dios rogar,
desta ganancia cómmo es buena e grand.

Cantar de las bodas

[1] *En cabo del cosso* = at the end of his run. The *cosso* or *corrida* was a display of horsemanship common among knights from the time of Charlemagne.

[2] *mio* = *mi*. This is the usual unaccented masculine form of the possessive adjective in old Spanish. *Cf.* masc. *sos* for *sus* a few lines down.

[3] *cinxo* = *ciñó* [4] *casa* = *ciudad* [5] *vellidos* = *bellos*

[6] *catan* = *miran* [7] *a ojo han* = *tienen a la vista*

[8] *espessa* = thickly grown

[Félez Muñoz finds his cousins, the daughters of the Cid, in the oakwood of Corpes where they had been ill-treated and left for dead by their cruel and cowardly husbands, the Infantes de Carrión.]

Vansse los infantes, aguijan a espolón.
Por el rastro tornós Félez Muñoz,
falló [1] sus primas amortecidas amas a dos. . . .

Partiéronsele las telas de dentro del coraçón,[2]
llamando: " ¡ Primas, primas, don Elvira e doña Sol!
Despertedes, primas, por amor del Criador!
mientra es el día, ante que entre la noch,
los ganados [3] fieros non nos coman en aqueste mont! "
Van recordando don Elvira e doña Sol,
abrieron los ojos e vieron a Félez Muñoz.
" Esforçadvos,[5] primas, por amor del Criador!
De que non me fallaren [6] infantes de Carrión,
a grant priessa [7] seré buscado yo;
si Dios non nos vale, aquí morremos [8] nos."
Tan a grant duelo fablava doña Sol:
" sí vos lo meresca, mio primo, nuestro padre el Campeador,[9]
dadnos del agua, sí vos vala el Criador." [10]

Con un sombrero que tiene Félez Muñoz,
nuevo era e fresco, que de Valencial' sacó,
cogió del agua en elle [11] e a sus primas dió;
mucho son lazradas [12] e amas las fartó.

Cantar de Corpes

[1] *falló* = *halló*. *Cf.* initial *f* with *fallaren*, *fablava*, and *fartó*. [2] *partiéronse . . . coraçón* = his heartstrings were torn [3] *ganados* = *bestias* [4] *mont*[*e*] = *bosque*, here an oakwood [5] *esforçadvos* = take courage [6] *de que non me fallaren* = as soon as they miss me [7] *priessa* = *prisa* [8] *morremos* = *moriremos* [9] *sí vos lo meresca . . . el Campeador* = as our father may reward you [10] *sí vos vala el Criador* = as the Creator may help you [11] *elle* = *él* [12] *lazradas* = *maltratadas*

[El Cid puts on his gala clothes to attend the Cortes that King Alfonso has called together at Toledo to try the Infantes de Carrión for their wicked conduct towards their wives Doña Elvira and Doña Sol in the oakwood of Corpes]

Nos' detiene por nada el que en buen ora nació:
calças de buen paño en sus camas [1] metió,
sobrellas unos çapatos que a grant huebra [2] son.
Vistió camisa de rançal [3] tan blanca como el sol,
con oro e con plata todas las presas [4] son,
al puño bien están, ca él se lo mandó;
sobrella un brial primo de çiclatón,[5]
obrado es con oro, parecen por o son.
Sobresto una piel vermeja, las bandas d'oro son,
siempre la viste mio Cid el Campeador.
Una cofia sobre los pelos d'un escarín de pro,[6]
que nol' contalassen [7] los pelos al buen Cid Campeador;
la barba avie luenga e prísola con el cordón,
por tal lo faze esto que recabdar [8] quiere todo lo so.
De suso cubrió un manto que es de grant valor,
en elle abríen que veer quantos que i son.
Con aquestos ciento que adobar [9] mandó,

apriessa cavalga, de San Serván salió;
assí iva [10] mio Cid adobado a la cort.

Cantar de Corpe

[1] *camas* = legs. *Cf.* French *jambes.*
[2] *a grant huebra* = with fine embroidery
[3] *rançal* = linen [4] *presas* = loops, fasteners
[5] *un brial primo de çiclatón* = a fine gown of brocaded silk
[6] *escarín de pro* = fine linen [7] *contalar* = tear, pull out
[8] *recabdar* = keep safe [9] *adobar* = prepare, get ready
[10] *iva* = *iba*

ANÓNIMO

(thirteenth century)

'*Estonz* [1] *alçó los ojos . . .*'

[Charlemagne laments over the dead body of Roland on the field of battle.]

Estonz [1] alçó los ojos, cató cabo adelante,[2]
vido [3] a don Roldán acostado a un pilare,
como se acostó a la ora de finare.
El rey cuando lo vido, oít lo que faze:
arriba alçó las manos, por las barbas tirare,
por las barbas floridas bermeja sallía la sangre;
essa ora [4] el buen rey oít lo que diráde,
diz': " Muerto es mio sobrino, el buen de don Roldáne!
Aquí veo atal cosa que nunca vi tan grande:
¡yo era para morir, e vos pora escapare!
¡Tanto buen amigo vos me solíades ganare!
por vuestra amor arriba muchos me solían amare;
pues vos sodes muerto, sobrino, buscarme han todo male.
Asaz veo una cosa que sé que es verdade:
que la vuestra alma bien sé que es en buen logare;
mas atal viejo mezquino, ¿agora [5] qué faráde?
Oy he perdido esfuerço con que solía ganare.
¡Ay, mi sobrino, non me queredes fablare!

Non vos veo colpe nin lançada porque oviésedes male,
por esso non vos creo que muerto sodes, don Roldáne. . . .

¡ Con tal duelo estó,[6] sobrino, agora non fués' bivo !
¡ Agora ploguiés' al Criador, a mi señor Jesuchristo,
que finase en este logar, que me levase [7] contigo ! . . ."

El rey quando esto dixo, cayó esmortecido.

Cantar de Roncesvalles

[1] *estonz'* = *entonces* [2] *cabo adelante* = straight ahead
[3] *vido* = *vió* [4] *essa ora* = then [5] *agora* = now
[6] *estó* = *estoy* [7] *levase* = *llevase*

ANÓNIMO (*c.* 1300)

' " *Señor Almonçor, por mis pecados* " . . . '

[Gonzalo Gustios, a prisoner of the great Almanzor in Cordova, laments over the severed heads of his sons and that of their tutor, Nuño Sabido.]

—" Señor Almonçor, por mis pecados
conozco estas cabeças, que de mis fijos son ;
esta otra es de Nuño Sabido, su amo que los crió. . . ."

—" Sálvevos Dios, Nuño Sabido, mi compadre e mi amigo ;
dadme agora cuenta de mis fijos, que en vuestras manos ove [1] metido, . . .
Cataríades [2] los agüeros como amo y padrino ;
no vos querría creer Gonçalo Gonçales, mi fijo,
ca se doldría [3] de mí que estava cativo.
Perdonadme, compadre e mi buen amigo,
que mucha falsedad sobre vos he dicho."

La cabeça de Nuño Sabido tornóla en su lugar
e la de Diego Gonçales fué a tomar,
mesando sus cabellos e las barbas de su faz :

—“ ¡ Viejo so, mesquino, para estas bodas bofordare! [4]
Fijo Diego Gonçales, a vos quería yo máse:
fazíalo con derecho, ca vos naciérades ante. . .
desque vos moristes, fijo, lo poblado se despoblaráve.”
Cada uno como nació así las iva tomare.

La cabeça de Martín Gonçales en brazos la tomava.
—“ Fijo Martín Gonçales, vos avíades persona honrada, . . .
Tal jugador de tablas [5] no lo avié en toda España . . .
La cabeça de Martín Gonçales luego la dejava
e la de Suer Gonçales en braços la tomava.

—“ Fijo Suer Gonçales, cuerpo tan leale,
de las vuestras buenas costumbres un rey se devía pagare:
de aves érades maestro, en España no avié vuestro pare.
¡Malas bodas vos guisó vuestro tío, hermano de vuestra madre!:
a mí dexó en cativerío, e a vos llevó a descabeçare . . .

La de Fernán Gonçales en braços la tomóve:
—“ Fijo, cuerpo honrado e nombre de buen señore,
del conde Fernán Gonçales que vos bautizó.
Matador de oso e de puerco e de cavalleros señore;
¡ Vuestro tío don Rodrigo malas bodas vos guisó! . . .

La cabeça de Ruy Gonçales en braços la priso:
—“ Fijo Ruy Gonçales, cuerpo tan sabido, . . .
leal para señore e bueno para amigo,
mejor cavallero de armas que nunca ome [6] vido . . .

La cabeça de Gucios Gonçales en braços la tomava . . .
faziendo fiero [7] duelo los ojos le besava:
—“ Fijo Gucios Gonçales, avíadas buena maña:
no dixérades una mentira por cuanto avía en España;
cavallero de buena guisa, buen feridor d'espada,
nunca ninguno feristes con ella que no perdiese el alma . . .

La cabeça de Gonçalo Gonçales   en braços la fué tomare,
mesando sus cabellos,   faziendo duelo grande:
—" Fijo Gonçalo Gonçales   a vos amava vuestra madre.
Las vuestras buenas costumbres   ¿ quién las podrié contare?
Buen amigo para amigos   e para señor leale,
conocedor de derecho,   amávades lo juzgar;
en armas esforçado,   a los vuestros franquear;
alançador a tablado [8]   nunca ome lo vido tale;
en cámara con dueñas   sabíades muy bien fablar,
a las unas proveíades vos   e a las otras dávades;
menester avía agudeza   quien con vos razonase,
mucho sería agudo   si lo peor no llevase.
Los que me temían por vos,   enemigos me serán,
aunque yo torne a Lara   nunca valdré un pan;
non he pariente ni amigo   que me pueda vengar,
¡ más me valdría la muerte   que esta vida tal! "
La cabeça de las manos   sobre las otras se le cae;
amortescióse e cayó en tierra   de sí no sabía parte.
Pesó mucho a Almonçore   e comenςó de llorare.

Cantar de los infantes de Lara

[1] *ove* = *hube*   [2] *catariades* = you would observe   [3] *doldría* = *dolería*   [4] *bofordare* = *bohordar*, to throw a lance (*bohordo*) in sport, to show skill in bringing down a framework of planks, a frequent practice in the celebration of a wedding as in this case   [5] *tablas* = tables, a game similar to backgammon (*tablas reales*)   [6] *ome* = *hombre*, used like the French *on*   [7] *fiero* = great, awful   [8] *alançador a tablado* = skilled in throwing a lance at a framework of planks (*tablado*)

GONZALO DE BERCEO

(thirteenth century)

' *Fué a Sancta María . . .*'

[St Dominic helps a poor religious house.]

Fué a Sancta María el varón benedicto,
non falló pan en ella nin otro ningún victo,[1]
demandaba almosna [2] commo romero fito,[3]
todos le daban algo, qui media, qui zatico [4] . . .

El varón de buen seso por la ley complir,
queriendo de lacerio [5] de sus manos vevir,
empeçó a labrar [6] por dexar de pedir
ca era grave cosa para él de sofrir.

Mejoró en las casas, e ensanchó heredades.
Compuso la eglesia, esto bien lo creades,
de libros e de ropas e de muchas bondades:
sufrió en este comedio [7] muchas adversidades.

Yo Gonzalo, que fago esto a su amor
yo la vi, assí veya [8] la faz del Criador,
una chica cocina asaz poca labor,
y escriben que la fizo esse buen confessor.

Fué en pocos de años la casa arreada,[9]
de labor [10] de ganados asaz bien aguisada,[11]
ya trovaban en ella los mezquinos posada,[12]
por él fué, Deo gracias, la eglesia sagrada.

Vida de Santo Domingo de Silos

[1] *victo* = food [2] *almosna* = *limosna*
[3] *romero fito* = persistent pilgrim or beggar
[4] *qui media . . . zatico* = one a half (loaf) and one a bit of bread
[5] *lacerio* = *trabajo* [6] *labrar* = *trabajar*
[7] *en este comedio* = in the meantime [8] *assí veya* = as I may see
[9] *arreada* = adorned, furnished [10] *labor* = *labranza*
[11] *aguisada* = equipped, prepared
[12] *trovaban . . . posada* = found lodging

'*Yo maestro Gonzalvo de Berceo nomnado . . .*'

[The poet going on a pilgrimage finds himself in a meadow gay with flowers, fruit-trees, fountains, and singing birds. The meadow is the Virgin Mary.]

Yo maestro Gonzalvo de Berceo nomnado,
yendo en romería caecí [1] en un prado
verde e bien sencido [2] de flores bien poblado,
logar cobdiciaduero [3] pora omne cansado.

Daban olor sobejo [4] las flores bien olientes,
refrescaban en omne las caras e las mientes,
manaban cada canto [5] fuentes claras corrientes,
en verano bien frías, en ivierno calientes.

Avié í [6] grand abondo [7] de buenas arboledas,
milgranos [8] e figueras, peros [9] e manzanedas,[10]
e muchas otras frutas de diversas monedas; [11]
mas non avié ningunas podridas nin acedas. . . .

Yaciendo a la sombra perdí todos cuidados,
odí [12] sones de aves dulces e modulados:
nunca udieron [13] omnes órganos tan temprados,[14]
nin que formar pudiessen sones más acordados. . . .

El prado que vos digo, avié otra bondat:
por calor nin por frío non perdié su beldat,
siempre estaba verde en su entegredat,
non perdié la verdura por nulla tempestat.

Milagros de Nuestra Señora. Introducción

[1] *caecí = me encontré* [2] *sencido = intacto*
[3] *cobdiciaduero = deseable* [4] *sobejo = excelente*
[5] *cada canto = por todas partes* [6] *Avié í = había allí*
[7] *abondo = abundancia* [8] *milgranos = granados* [9] *peros = perales*
[10] *manzanedas = manzanos* [11] *monedas = valores* [12] *odí = oí*
[13] *udieron = oyeron* [14] *temprados = templados*

ANÓNIMO

(thirteenth century)

'*Dixo la buena duenya . . .*'

[Tarsiana, lost daughter of Apollonius, King of Tyre, askes her evil master for permission to earn money as a *juglaresa* (a woman minstrel) rather than live a life of shame. Her playing and singing delight all hearers. She finally sings a ballad relating to her own sad adventures.]

Dixo la buena duenya un sermón [1] tan temprado,
" Senyor, si lo oviesse [2] de ti condonado,[3]
otro mester [4] sabía que es más sin pecado,
que es ganancioso, e es más ondrado.

Si tú me lo condonas por la tu cortesía,
que meta yo estudio en essa maestría,
quanto tú me demandares yo tanto te daría,
tu avriés gran ganancia e yo non pecaría. . . ."

Luego el otro día de buena madrugada
levantóse la duenya ricamente adobada.[5]
priso [6] una viola [7] buena e bien temprada,
e sallió al mercado violar [8] por soldada.[9]

Començó unos viesos [10] e unos sones tales,
que traién grant dulçor e eran naturales,
finchíense [11] de omnes apriesa los portales,
non les cabié en las plazas, subiense a los poyales.

Quando con su viola hovo bien solazado,
a sabor de los pueblos hovo asaz cantado,
tornóles a rezar [12] un romance bien rimado,
de la su razón [13] misma por o avía pasado.[14]

Libro de Apolonio

[1] *sermón = discurso* [2] *oviesse = hubiese*
[3] *condonado = permitido* [4] *otro mester* = another trade
[5] *adobada = adornada* [6] *priso = tomó*
[7] *viola = vihuela*, a stringed instrument, a forerunner of the violin
[8] *violar* = to play the viola [9] *soldada = dinero*
[10] *viesos = versos* [11] *finchíense = se henchían* [12] *rezar = recitar*
[13] *razón = relato* [14] *por o . . . pasado* = all she had gone through

'Tierra es muy temprada . . .'

[In praise of Spain, and especially of Castile.]

Tierra es muy temprada, sin grandes callenturas;
non faze en ivierno destempradas friuras;
non es tierra en el mundo que aya tales pasturas,
árboles pora fruta, siquier de mil naturas.

Sobre todas las tierras, mejor es la montaña,
de vacas e de ovejas non hay tierra tamaña,[1]
tantos ay de puercos que es fiera fazaña: [2]
sírvense muchas tierras de las cosas de España. . . .

Buena tierra de cera e buena de venados,
de río, de mar, muchos buenos pescados,
quien los quiere recientes, quien los quiere salados:
son de estas cosas tales pueblos muy abastados.

De panes e de vinos tierra muy comunal,
non fallarían en el mundo otra mejor nin tal,
muchas de buenas fuentes e mucho buen río cabdal,
e otras muchas mineras de que fazen la sal.

Ay muchas venas de fierro e de plata,
ay venas de oro, que son de mejor barata.[3]
Ay sierras e valles e mucha de buena mata,
todas llenas de grana [4] pora fazer escarlata. . . .

Pero de toda España, Castilla es mejor,
porque fué de los otros el comienço mayor,
guardando e temiendo siempre a su señor,
quiso acrecentar ansí [5] el nuestro Señor.

Poema de Fernán González

[1] *tamaña = tan grande, tan buena*
[2] *fiera fazaña = cosa extraordinaria*
[3] *barata = precio, valor*
[4] *grana = cochinilla*
[5] *ansí = así*

JUAN LORENZO DE ASTORGA

(thirteenth century)

' El mes era de mayo . . .'

[A description of Spring, introducing the marriage of Alexander the Great with the daughter of King Darius of Persia.]

El mes era de mayo, un tiempo glorïoso,
quando fazen las aves un solaz deleitoso,
son vestidos los prados de vestido fremoso,[1]
da suspiros la duenna, la que non ha [2] esposo.

Tiempo dolce e sabroso por bastir [3] casamientos,
ca lo tempran las flores e los sabrosos vientos,
cantan las donzelletas, son muchas a convientos,[4]
fazen unas a otras buenos pronunciamentos.

Caen en el serano [5] las bonas rociadas,
entran en flor las miesses ca son ya espigadas,
fazen las duenyas triscas [6] en camisas delgadas:
¡ entón [7] casan algunos que pues [8] messan las barvas !

Andan moças y viejas cobiertas en amores,
van coger por la siesta [9] a los prados las flores,
dizen unas a otras: —" Bonos son los amores ! "
Y aquellos plus tiernos tiénense por mejores.

Los días son grandes, los campos reverdidos,
son los passariellos [10] del mal pelo exidos,
los távanos que muerden non son aún venidos,
luchan los monagones [11] en bragas [12] sen vestidos.

Libro de Alexandre

[1] *fremoso = hermoso* [2] *ha = tiene* [3] *bastir = construir, arreglar*
[4] *convientos = reuniones* [5] *serano = atardecer* [6] *triscas = danzas*
[7] *enton = entonces* [8] *pues = después* [9] *siesta = tarde*
[10] *son los passariellos . . . exidos* = the little birds have lost their ugly feathers.
[11] *monagones = muchachos* [12] *bragas* = short breeches

JUAN RUIZ, ARCIPRESTE DE HITA

(fourteenth century)

Ensienplo del águila e del caçador

[The fable of the eagle and the hunter, addressed to Don Amor.]

El águila cabdal canta sobre la haya;
todas las otras aves, de allí las atalaya;
non ay péndola [1] della, que en la tierra caya:
si ballestero la falla, préciala más que saya.

Saetas e quadrillos, que trae amolados,
con péndolas de águila los ha empendolados; [2]
fué, com' avía usado, a ferir los venados;
al águila cabdal dióle por los costados.

Cató contra sus pechos el águila ferida,
e vido que sus péndolas la avían escarnida;
dixo contra sí mesma una razón temida:
"De mí mesma salió quien me tiró [3] la vida."

El loco, el mesquino, que su alma non cata,[4]
usando tu locura e tu mala barata,[5]
destruye a su cuerpo e a·su alma mata:
que de sí mesmo sale quien su vida desata.

Ome, ave o bestia, a que amor retiente,[6]
desque cumple luxuria, luego se arrepiente:
entristécese en punto, luego flaqueça siente;
acórtase la vida: quien lo dixo non miente.

Libro de buen amor

[1] *péndola = pluma* [2] *empendolados = emplumados*
[3] *tiró = quitó* [4] *cato = mira por* [5] *barata = maña, engaño*
[6] *retiente = re-tienta,* tempts repeatedly

Historia de doña Endrina e don Melón

[The poet tells the goddess, Venus, of his love for the fair lady, Doña Endrina, and describes her beauty.]

" Señora doña Venus, muger de don Amor,
noble dueña, omíllome yo, vuestro servidor:
de todas cosas sodes vos e el Amor señor,
todos vos obedescen como a su facedor.

Reys, duques e condes e toda criatura
vos temen e vos serven como a vuestra fechura:
complit los mis deseos, datme dicha è ventura;
non me seades escasa nin esquiva nin dura. . . .

Doña Endrina, que mora aquí en mi vezindat,
de fermosura, donaire, de talla e de beldat,
sobra e vence a todas quantas ha en la cibdat: [1]
si el amor no m' engaña, yo vos digo la verdat.

Esta dueña me ferió de saet' enarbolada,
atravesó 'l coraçón, en él la trayo [2] fincada;
con toda la mi grant fuerça non puede ser arrancada,
la llaga más va cresciendo, del dolor non mengua nada. . . .

¡ Ay ! ¡ quán fermosa viene doñ' Endrina por la plaça !
¡ Qué talle, qué donaire, qué alto cuello de garça !
¡ Qué cabellos, qué boquilla, qué color, qué buen andança ! [3]
Con saetas d'amor fiere, quando los sus ojos alça. . . .

Libro de buen amor

[1] *cibdat = ciudad* [2] *trayo = traigo*
[3] *andança = modo de andar*

Cómo dize el Arcipreste que se ha de entender su libro

Qualquier ome que l'oya,[1] si bien trobar [2] sopiere,
puede más añadir e enmendar si quisiere;
ande de mano en mano a quienquier que lo pidiere,
como pella [3] las dueñas, tómelo quien podiere.

Pues es de *Buen amor*, emprestadlo de grado,[4]
nol' neguedes su nombre nil' dedes refertado,[5]
nol' dedes por dineros vendido nin alquilado;
ca non ha grado nin gracias [6] el *Buen amor* comprado.

Fizvos [7] pequeño libro de texto, mas la glosa
non creo que es pequeña, ante es muy gran prosa:
que sobre cada fabla [8] s'entiende otra cosa,
sin la que se alega en la razón fermosa.

De la santidad mucha es bien grand licionario;[9]
mas de juego e de burla es chico breviario;
por ende fago punto e cierro mi armario:
seavos chica fabla, solaz [10] e letuario.[11]

Señores, hevos servido con poca sabiduría;
por vos dar solaz a todos fablévos en juglaría;
yo un galardón [12] vos pido que por Dios en romería
digades un *Pater noster* por mí e *Ave María*.

Libro de buen amor

[1] *oya = oiga* [2] *trobar = hacer versos* [3] *pella = pelota*
[4] *de grado = de buena gana*
[5] *refertado = de mala gana* [6] *non ha grado nin gracias = no se agradece*
[7] *fizvos = híceos* [8] *fabla = manera de hablar, lectura*
[9] *licionario = leccionario* [10] *solaz = placer*
[11] *letuario = electuario* [12] *galardón = premio, recompensa*

Cántica de serrana

Dó la casa del Cornejo,
primer día de semana,
en comedio del vallejo
encontré una serrana
vestida de buen bermejo,
e buena cinta de lana;
díxel' : " Dios te salve, hermana."

Diz : " ¿ Qué buscas por la sierra ?
¿ Cómo andas descaminado ? "
Dixe : " Ando por esta tierra,
do querría casar de grado."
Ella dixo : " Non lo yerra
el que aquí es casado,
busca e fallarás recado.

" Mas, pariente, tú te cata,
si sabes de sierra algo."
Dixe : " Bien sé guardar mata [1]
e yegua en cerro cabalgo,
sé el lobo cómo se mata ;
quando yo en pos dél salgo,
antes lo alcanço que el galgo." . . .

Diz : " Aquí avrás casamiento
tal qual tu demandudieres :
casarme he de buen talento
contigo, si algo dieres,
harás buen entendimiento."
Díxel' : " Pid' lo que quisieres,
e darte he lo que pidieres.

Diz : " Dame un prendedero,[2]
que sea de bermejo paño,
e dame un bel pandero,
e seis anillos de estaño,

un zamarrón disantero,[3]
garnacho [4] para entre el año,
e non fables en engaño.

" Dame zarcillos [5] e hevilla
de latón bien reluciente,
e dame toca amarilla
bien listada en la frente,
zapatas hasta rodilla ;
e dirá toda la gente :
¡ Bien casó Menga Lloriente ! "

Yol' dixe : " Darte he esas cosas
e aun más, si más comides,[6]
bien loçanas e fermosas ;
Luego fagamos las bodas,
a tus parientes conbides,
e esto non lo olvides,
ca yo voy por lo que pides."

Libro de buen amor

[1] *guardar mata* = watch the undergrowth (for game and birds). Proverb : *De mala mata, nunca buena caza.*

[2] *prendedero* = usually a hook to catch up a skirt, etc., but here apparently a ribbon for the same purpose

[3] *zamarrón disantero* = a Sunday-best sheepskin coat

[4] *garnacho* = a close-fitting jerkin or corselet

[5] *zarcillos* = earrings

[6] *comides* = you think of

Del Ave María de Santa María

Ave María gloriosa,
Virgen Santa, preciosa,
¡ Cómo eres piadosa
todavía !

Gratia plena,
abogada sin mancilla,
por la tu merced, Señora,

haz esta maravilla
señalada.
Por la tu bondad agora
guárdame toda ora
de muerte vergoñosa,
porque loé a ti, fermosa,
noche e día.

Dominus tecum,
estrella resplandeciente,
melecina de cuidados,
catadura muy bella,
reluciente;
sin mancilla de pecados,
por los tus gozos preciados
te pido, virtuosa,
que me guardes, limpia rosa,
de folía. . . .

Libro de buen amor

Cántica de loores a Santa María

Quiero seguir a ti, flor de las flores,
siempre dezir, cantar de tus loores,
non me partir de te servir,
mejor de las mejores.

Grand fiança he yo en ti, Señora,
la mi esperança en ti es toda hora,
de tribulança sin tardança,
¡venme librar agora!

¡Virgen santa! yo paso atribulado
pena atanta con dolor atormentado,
e me espanta coita atanta,
que veo ¡mal pecado!

Estrella del mar, puerto de folgura,
de dolor complido e de tristura,
¡ venme librar e conortar,
Señora del altura !

Nunca fallece la tu merced complida.
siempre guarece de coitas e da vida,
nunca perece nin entristece
quien a ti non olvida.

Sufro grand mal sin merecer, a tuerto,
esquivo tal porque pienso ser muerto ;
¡ mas tú me val, que non veo ál
que me saque a puerto !

Libro de buen amor

PERO LÓPEZ DE AYALA

(1332–1407)

De los mercadores

[A satirical description of the tricks practised by the merchants.]

Pues ¿ qué de los mercadores aquí podría dezir ?
si tienen tal oficio para poder fallir,[1]
jurar e perjurar, en todo siempre mentir,
olvidan Dios e alma, nunca cuidan [2] morir. . . .

Una vez pidrán [3] cinquenta doblas [4] por un paño,
si vieren que estades duro e entendedes vuestro daño,
diz' : —" Por treinta vos lo do,[5] mas nunca él cumpla el año,[6]
si non le costó quarenta ayer de un omne estraño.[7]

Diz' : —" Yo tengo escarlatas de Brujas [8] e de Mellinas,[9]
veinte años ha que non fueron en esta tierra tan finas ;
diz' : —" Tomadlas vos, señor, antes que unas mis sobrinas
las lieven de mi casa, que son por ellas caninas.[10]

" Si vos tenedes dineros, sinon yo tomar he de plata,
ca en mi tienda fallaredes toda buena barata."
El cuitado qué lo cree e una vez con él se ata,
a través yaze caído si delante non se cata. . . .[11]

Las varas e las medidas, Dios sabe quáles serán,
una mostrarán luenga [12] e con otra medirán;
todo es mercaduría,[13] non entienden que en esto han
ellos pecado ninguno, pues que siempre así lo dan.

Rimado de Palacio

[1] *fallir* = *engañar* [2] *cuidan* = *piensan* [3] *pidrán* = *pedirán*
[4] *dobla* = a gold coin worth about eight shillings [5] *do* = *doy*
[6] *mas nunca . . . año* = may he die within the year ! (a change to indirect speech)
[7] *estraño* = *extraño, forastero* [8] *Brujas* = Bruges
[9] *Mellinas* = Malines [10] *caninas* = hungry, ravenous
[11] *si delante . . . cata* = if he doesn't mind his step
[12] *luenga* = long [13] *mercaduría* = business

Cantar

Sennor, si tú has dado
tu sentencia contra mí,
por merced te pido aquí
que me sea revocada.

Tú, Sennor, tienes judgado por tu alta providencia,
que emendando el pecador se mude la tu sentencia:
por ende con penitencia e con voluntad quebrantada,
ha mi vida ordenada, por complir lo que fallí:
Sennor, si tú has dada
tu sentencia contra mí,
por merced te pido aquí
que me sea revocada.

Con tu ayuda, Sennor, e de la Sennora mía,
podré yo muy pecador emendarme todavía,
e tu servicio será en cobrar esta vegada,
una oveja muy errada, que en el yermo me perdí.
Sennor, si tú has dada, etc.

Non sea yo desechado de la tu merced muy grande,
e a siervo tan errado con sanna [1] non le demande,
e con crueça non ande por juicio tu espada,
e seame otorgada piedat si fallescí. . . .
Sennor, si tú has dada, etc.

Después deste cantar, finqué [2] más espaciado,
teniendo en Dios mi juicio de ser por él librado,
e por estar más firme, fize otro deytado,[3]
a Dios me confesando, como siervo culpado.

Rimado de Palacio

[1] *sanna* = *saña* [2] *finqué* = *quedé*
[3] *deytado* = *dictado*, a poetical composition

Deytado del cisma de la eglesia[1]

La nave de sant Pedro pasa grande tormenta,
e non cura ninguno de la ir a acorrer:
de mill e tresientos e ocho con setenta
así la veo fuerte padescer:
e quien lo puede non quiere valer,
e así está en punto de ser anegada,
si Dios non acorre aquesta vegada,
por su misericordia segunt suele faser.

Veo grandes ondas, e ola espantosa,
el piélago grande, el mastel fendido,
seguro non falla el puerto de posa,
el su governalle está enflaquecido

de los marineros e puesto en olvido,
las áncoras fuertes non le tienen provecho,
sus tablas por fuerça quebradas de fecho,
acorro de cables parece perdido.

La nave es la eglesia católica santa
e el governalle es nuestro prelado:
el mastel fendido que a todos espanta,
es el colegio muy noble e onrrado
de los cardenales, que está devisado [2]
por muchos pecados en muchos desmanos: [3]
las áncoras son los reyes christianos
que la sostienen e la han dexado.

Las tablas resias es la unidat
que todos juntos un cuerpo es nombrado!
Los cables fuertes creo por verdat
que son los prelados que han poco cuidado
de aqueste fecho, que está, mal pecado,
tan luengo, tan malo, esquivo tan fuerte,
do muchos christianos peligran de muerte
en mar deste mundo breve ocasionado.

Rimado de Palacio

[1] This is an early example of *octavas de arte mayor.*
[2] *devisado = dividido* [3] *desmanos = desmanes*

Cantar a la Virgen

Sennora estrella lusiente
que a todo el mundo guía,
guía a este tu sirviente
que su alma en ti fía.

A canela bien oliente
eres, Sennora, conparada,
de la tierra del oriente
es olor muy apreciada.

A ti faz clamor la gente
en sus cuitas todavía,
quien por pecador se siente
llamando Santa María.

Sennora, estrella lusiente
que a todo el mundo guía,
guía a este tu sirviente
que su alma en ti fía.

Al cedro en la altura
te compara Salomón,
eguala tu fermosura
al ciprés del monte Sion.
Palma fresca en verdura,
fermosa e de grant valía,
oliva la Escriptura
te llama, Sennora mía.

Sennora, estrella lusiente
que a todo el mundo guía,
guía a este tu sirviente
que su alma en ti fía.

De la mar eres estrella,
del cielo puerta lumbrosa,
después del parto donsella,
de Dios Padre fija, esposa.
Tú amansaste la querella
que por Eva a nos venía,
e el mal que fizo ella
por ti ovo mejoría.

Sennora, estrella lusiente
que todo el mundo guía,
guía a este tu sirviente
que su alma en ti fía.

Rimado de Palacio

ANÓNIMO

ROMANCES CAROLINGIOS

Romance de Durandarte

Muerto queda Durandarte al pie de una gran montaña.
un canto por cabecera, debajo una verde haya,
todas las aves del monte alrededor le acompañan,
llorábale Montesinos, que a su muerte se hallara,
hecha le tiene la fuesa en una peñosa cava;
quitándole estaba el yelmo, desciñéndole la espada,
desarmábale los pechos, el corazón le sacaba,
para enviarlo a Belerma como él se lo rogara,
y desque le hubo sacado su rostro al suyo juntaba,
tan agramente llorando mil veces se desmayaba,
y desque volvió en sí estas palabras hablaba:
—" Durandarte, Durandarte, Dios perdone la tu alma
" y a mí saque deste mundo para que contigo vaya."

Romance de Rosaflorida

En Castilla está un castillo que se llama Rocafrida;
al castillo llaman Roca, y a la fonte llaman Frida.
El pie tiene de oro, y almenas de plata fina;
entre almena y almena está una piedra zafira;
tanto relumbra de noche como el sol a mediodía.
Dentro estaba una doncella que llaman Rosaflorida:
siete condes la demandan, tres duques de Lombardía;
a todos les desdeñaba, tanta es su lozanía.
Enamoróse de Montesinos de oídas que no de vista.
Una noche estando así, gritos da Rosaflorida;
oyérala un camarero, que en su camara dormía.
" ¿Qué es aquesto, mi señora? ¿qué es esto, Rosaflorida?
o tenedes mal de amores, o estáis loca sandía.
" Ni yo tengo mal de amores, ni estoy loca sandía,
mas llevásesme estas cartas a Francia la bien guarnida;
diéseslas a Montesinos, la cosa que yo más quería;

dile que me venga a ver para la Pascua Florida;
darle he yo este mi cuerpo, el más lindo que hay en Castilla,
si no es el de mi hermana, que de fuego sea ardida;
y si de mí más quisiere yo mucho más le daría:
darle he siete castillos los mejores que hay en Castilla."

Romance de Gerineldo

Levantóse Gerineldo que al Rey dejara dormido:
fuése para la infanta donde estaba en el castillo.
—" Abráisme ", dijo, " señora, abráisme, cuerpo garrido."
—" ¿ Quién sois vos, el caballero, que llamáis a mi postigo ? "
—" Gerineldo soy, señora, vuestro tan querido amigo."
Tomárala por la mano, en un lecho la ha metido,
y besando y abrazando Gerineldo se ha dormido.
Recordado había el Rey, de un sueño despavorido;
tres veces lo había llamado, ninguna le ha respondido.
—" Gerineldo, Gerineldo, mi camarero polido,
" si me andas en traición, trátasme como a enemigo.
O dormías con la infanta, o me has vendido el castillo."
Tomó la espada en la mano, en gran saña va encendido:
fuérase para la cama donde a Gerineldo vido.
El quisiéralo matar; mas crióle de chiquito.
Sacara luego la espada, entre entrambos la ha metido,
porque desque recordase viese cómo era sentido.
Recordado había la infanta, e la espada ha conocido.
—" Recordados, Gerineldo, que ya érades sentido,
que la espada de mi padre yo me la he bien conocido."

Romance de la batalla de Roncesvalles

Domingo era de Ramos, la Pasión quieren decir,
cuando moros y cristianos todos entran en la lid.
Ya desmayan los franceses, ya comienzan de huir.
!Oh cuán bien los esforzaba ese Roldán paladín!
¡ Vuelta, vuelta, los franceses, con corazón, a la lid!

¡ más vale morir por buenos, que deshonrados vivir!
Ya volvían los franceses con corazón a la lid;
a los encuentros primeros mataron sesenta mil.
Por Roncesvalles arriba huyendo va el rey Marsín,
caballero en una cebra, no por mengua de rocín.
La sangre que dél corría las yerbas hace teñir;
las voces que iba dando al cielo quieren subir.
¡ Reniego de ti, Mahoma, y de cuanto te serví!
Hícete cuerpo de plata, pies y manos de marfil;
hícete casa de Meca donde adorasen en ti,
y por más te honrar, Mahoma, cabeza de oro te fiz.
Sesenta mil caballeros a ti te los ofrecí;
mi mujer la reina mora te ofreció treinta mil.
de todos estos, Mahoma, tan solo me veo aquí."

Romance de la muerte de Roldán

Por muchas partes herido sale el viejo Carlo Magno,
huyendo de los de España porque le han desbaratado:
los once deja perdidos sólo Roldán ha escapado,
que nunca ningún guerrero llegó a su esfuerzo sobrado,
y no podía ser herido ni su sangre derramado.
Al pie estaba de una cruz por el suelo arrodillado:
los ojos vueltos al cielo, desta manera ha hablado:
" Animoso corazón, ¿ cómo te has acobardado
en salir de Roncesvalles sin ser muerto o bien vengado?
¡ Ay amigos y señores! ¡ cómo os estaréis quejando
que os acompañé en la vida, y en la muerte os he dejado!"
Estando en esta congoja vió venir a Carlo Magno
triste, solo, y sin corona, con el rostro ensangrentado.
Desque así lo hubo visto cayó muerto el desdichado.

ROMANCES HISTÓRICOS

Romance del reino perdido

Las huestes de don Rodrigo desmayaban y huían
cuando en la octava batalla sus enemigos vencían.
Rodrigo deja sus tiendas y del real se salía:

solo va el desventurado, sin ninguna compañía.
El caballo de cansado ya mudar no se podía:
camina por donde quiere, que no le estorba la vía.
El rey va tan desmayado, que sentido no tenía;
muerto de sed y hambre, que de velle era gran mancilla;
iba tan tinto de sangre, que una brasa parecía.
Las armas lleva abolladas, que eran de gran pedrería;
la espada lleva hecha sierra de los golpes que tenía;
el almete de abollado en la cabeza se le hundía;
la cara lleva hinchada del trabajo que sufría.
Subióse encima de un cerro el más alto que veía;
desde allí mira su gente cómo iba de vencida.
De allí mira sus banderas, y estandartes que tenía,
cómo están todos pisados que la tierra los cubría;
mira por los capitanes que ninguno parescía;
mira el campo tinto en sangre, la cual arroyos corría.
El triste de ver aquesto gran mancilla en sí tenía;
llorando de los sus ojos de esta manera decía:
—Ayer era rey de España, hoy no lo soy de una villa;
ayer villas y castillos, hoy ninguno poseía;
ayer tenía criados, hoy ninguno me servía,
hoy no tengo ni una almena que pueda decir que es mía.
¡Desdichada fué la hora, desdichado fué aquel día
en que nací y heredé la tan grande señoría,
pues lo había de perder todo junto y en un día!
¡Oh muerte! ¿por qué no vienes y llevas esta alma mía
de aqueste cuerpo mezquino, pues se te agradecería?

Romance del conde Fernán González

"Buen conde Fernán González, el rey envía por vos,
que vayades a las cortes que se hacían en León;
que si vos allá vais, conde, daros han buen galardón,
daros han a Palenzuela y a Palencia la mayor,
daros han las nueve villas, con ellas a Carrión;
daros han a Torquemada, la torre de Mormojón,
daros han a Tordesillas, y a Torre de Labatón.

Buen conde, si allá non ides, daros han por traidor."
Allí respondiera el conde y dijera esta razón:
" Mensajero eres, amigo, non mereces culpa, non;
que yo no he miedo al rey, ni a cuantos con él son.
Villas y castillos tengo, todos a mi mandar son,
dellos me dejó mi padre, dellos me ganara yo;
los que me dejó mi padre poblélos de ricos hombres,
las que me hube ganado poblélas de labradores;
quien no tenía más que un buey dábale otro que eran dos;
al que casaba su hija dábale muy rico don,
al que faltaban dineros también se los presto yo;
cada día que amanece por mí hacen oración;
no la hacían por el rey, que no la merece, non;
él les puso muchos pechos, y quitáraselos yo."

Romance de Bernardo del Carpio

Las cartas y mensajeros del rey a Bernardo van,
que vaya luego a las cortes para con él negociar.
Bernardo, como es discreto, mal recelado se ha,
las cartas echó en el fuego los suyos mandó juntar:
" Cuatrocientos sois, los míos, los que coméis el mi pan,
nunca fuisteis repartidos, agora os repartirán:
en el Carpio quedan ciento para el castillo guardar;
los ciento por los caminos, que a nadie dejéis pasar;
doscientos iréis conmigo para con el rey hablar;
si mala me la dijere, peor se la he de tornar.
Con esto luego se parte y comienza a caminar;
por sus jornadas contadas a la corte fué a llegar.
De los doscientos que lleva los ciento mandó quedar
para que tengan segura la puerta de la ciudad;
con los ciento que le quedan se va al palacio real:
cincuenta deja a la puerta que a nadie dejen pasar,
treinta deja a la escalera para el subir y el bajar,
con solamente los veinte a hablar con el rey se va" . . .

—Dios vos mantenga, buen rey, y a los que con vos están.
—Bernardo, mal seas venido, traidor hijo de otro tal;
dite yo el Carpio en tenencia tú tómaslo en heredad.
—Mentides, buen rey, mentides, que no decides verdad,
que nunca yo fuí traidor, ni en mi linaje lo hay.
Acordársevos, debiera de aquello del Encinal,
cuando gentes enemigas allí os trataron tan mal,
que os mataron el caballo, y aun a vos querían matar;
Bernardo como traidor el suyo vos fuera a dar;
con una lanza y adarga de entre ellos os fué a sacar.
El Carpio entonces me distes por juro y por heredad;
prometísteme a mi padre, no me guardastes verdad.
—Prendedlo, mis caballeros, que atrevido se me ha.
Todos le estaban mirando, nadie se le osa llegar.
Revolviendo el manto al brazo la espada fuera a sacar.
—¡ Aquí, aquí, los mis doscientos, los que comedes mi pan,
que hoy era venido el día que honra habedes de ganar!
El rey, como aquesto vido, procuróle de amansar;
—Malas mañas has, sobrino, no las puedes olvidar;
lo que hombre te dice en burla de veras vas a tomar.
Yo te do el Carpio, Bernardo, por juro y por heredad.
—Aquesas burlas, el rey, no son burlas de burlar.
El castillo está por mí, nadie me lo puede dar;
quien quitármelo quisiere yo se lo sabré vedar.

Duelo de Gonzalo Gustios ante las cabezas de sus hijos

Pártese el moro Alicante víspera de San Cebrián;
ocho cabezas llevaba, todas de hombres de alta sangre.
Sábelo el rey Almanzor, a recibírselo sale;
aunque perdió muchos moros piensa en esto bien ganar.
Mandara hacer un tablado para mejor los mirar;
mandó traer un cristiano que estaba en captividad,
como ante sí lo trujeron empezóle de hablar;
díjole:—Gonzalo Gustios, mira quién conocerás;
que lidiaron mis poderes en el campo de Almenar,
sacaron ocho cabezas, todas son de gran linaje.

Respondió Gonzalo Gustios: —Presto os diré la verdad.
Y limpiándoles la sangre asaz se fuera a turbar;
dijo llorando agramente; —¡Conózcolas por mi mal!
La una es de mi carillo; las otras me duelen más,
de los infantes de Lara son, mis hijos naturales.
Así razona con ellas como si vivos hablasen:
—¡Sálveos Dios, Nuño Salido, el mi compadre leal!
¿Adónde son los mis hijos que yo os quise encomendar?
Mas perdonadme, compadre, no he por qué os demandar;
muerto sois como buen ayo, como hombre muy de fiar.
Tomara otra cabeza, del hijo mayor de edad:
—Oh, hijo Diego González, hombre de muy gran bondad,
del conde Garci Fernández, alférez el principal,
a vos amaba yo mucho, que me habíades de heredar!
Alimpiándola con lágrimas volviérala a su lugar.
Y toma la del segundo, don Martín que se llamaba:
—¡Dios os perdone, el mi hijo, hijo que mucho preciaba;
jugador de tablas erais el mejor de toda España;
mesurado caballero, muy bien hablábais en plaza!
Y dejándola llorando la del tercero tomaba:
—¡Suero González, todo el mundo os estimaba;
un rey os tuviera en mucho sólo para la su caza!
Ruy Velázquez, vuestro tío, malas bodas os depara;
a vos os llevó a la muerte, a mí en cautivo dejaba!
Y tomando la del cuarto lasamente la miraba:
—¡Oh, hijo Fernán González (nombre del mejor de España
del buen conde de Castilla, aquél que vos baptizara),
matador de oso y de puerco, amigo de gran compaña;
nunca con gente de poco, os vieran en alianza!
Tomó la de Ruy González, al corazón la abrazaba;
—¡Hijo mío, hijo mío, quién como vos se hallara;
gran caballero esforzado, muy buen bracero a ventaja;
vuestro tío, Ruy Velázquez tristes bodas ordenara!
Y tomando otra cabeza, los cabellos se mesaba:
—¡Oh, hijo Gustios González, habíades buenas mañas,
no dijerades mentira ni por oro ni por plata;
animoso, buen guerrero, muy gran heridor de espada,
que a quien dábades de lleno, tullido o muerto quedaba!

Tomando la del menor   el dolor se le doblaba:
—¡Hijo Gonzalo González,   los ojos de doña Sancha!
¡Qué nuevas irán a ella,   que a vos más que a todos ama!
¡Tan apuesto de persona,   decidor bueno entre damas,
repartidor de su haber,   aventajado en la lanza!
¡Mejor fuera la mi muerte   que ver tan triste jornada!
Al duelo que el viejo hace,   toda Córdoba lloraba,
El rey Almanzor, cuidoso,   consigo se lo llevaba
y mandaba a una morica   lo sirviese muy de gana.
Esta le torna en prisiones   y con amor le curaba;
hermana era del rey,   doncella moza y lozana;
con ésta Gonzalo Gustios   vino a perder la su saña,
que de ella le nació un hijo   que a los hermanos vengara.

Romances de los siete infantes de Lara

La Venganza de Mudarra

A caza va don Rodrigo,   ése que dicen de Lara:
perdido había el azor,   no hallaba ninguna caza;
con la gran siesta que hace   arrimado se ha a una haya,
maldiciendo a Mudarrillo,   hijo de la renegada,
que si a las manos le hubiese   que le sacaría el alma.
El señor estando en esto,   Mudarrillo que asomaba:
—Dios te salve, buen señor,   debajo de la verde haya.
—Así te haga a ti, caballero;   buena sea tu llegada.
—Dígasme, señor, tu nombre,   decirte he yo la mi gracia.
—A mí llaman don Rodrigo,   y aun don Rodrigo de Lara,
cuñado de don Gonzalo,   hermano de doña Sancha;
por sobrinos me los hube   los siete infantes de Lara.
Maldigo aquí a Mudarrillo,   hijo de la renegada;
si delante lo tuviese,   yo le sacaría el alma.
—Si a ti dicen don Rodrigo,   y aun don Rodrigo de Lara,
a mí Mudarra González,   hijo de la renegada,
de Gonzalo Gustios hijo   y alnado de doña Sancha;
por hermanos me los hube   los siete infantes de Lara;
tú los vendiste, traidor,   en el val de Arabiana.

Mas si Dios ahora me ayuda   aquí dejarás el alma.
—Espéresme, don Mudarra,   iré a tomar las armas.
—El espera que tú diste   a los infantes de Lara;
aquí morirás, traidor,   enemigo de doña Sancha.

Romances de los siete infantes de Lara

Romance de Jimena Gómez

En Burgos está el buen rey   asentado a su yantar,
cuando la Jimena Gómez   se le vino a querellar;
cubierta paños de luto,   tocas de negro cendal;
las rodillas por el suelo,   comenzara de fablar:
—Con mancilla vivo, rey;   con ella vive mi madre;
cada día que amanece   veo quien mató mi padre
caballero en un caballo   y en su mano un gavilán;
por hacerme más enojo   cébalo en mi palomar;
con sangre de mis palomas   ensangrentó mi brial.
¡Hacedme, buen rey, justicia,   no me la queráis negar!
Rey que non face justicia   non debía de reinar,
ni comer pan a manteles,   ni con la reina folgar.
El rey cuando aquesto oyera   comenzara de pensar:
"Si yo prendo o mato al Cid,   mis cortes revolverse han;
pues, si yo lo dejo de hacer,   Dios me lo demandará."
Allí habló doña Jimena   palabras bien de notar:
—"Yo te lo diría, rey,   cómo lo has de remediar.
Mantén tú bien las tus cortes,   no te las revuelva nadie,
y al que mi padre mató   dámelo para casar,
que quien tanto mal me hizo   sé que algún bien me fará."
—"Siempre lo he oído decir,   y ahora veo que es verdad,
que el seso de las mujeres   no era cosa natural:
hasta aquí pidió justicia,   ya quiere con él casar.
Mandaré una carta al Cid,   mandarle quiero llamar."
Las palabras no son dichas,   la carta camino va;
mensajero que la lleva   dado la había a su padre.

Romances del Cid

Romance del cerco de Zamora

Sobre el muro de Zamora vide un caballero erguido;
al real de los castellanos decía con grande grito:
—¡ Guarte, guarte, rey don Sancho, no digas que no te aviso,
que del cerco de Zamora un traidor había salido:
Vellido Dolfos se llama, hijo de Dolfos Vellido;
si gran traidor fué su padre, mayor traidor es el hijo;
cuatro traiciones ha hecho, y con ésta serán cinco!
Si te engaña, rey don Sancho, no digas que no te aviso.
Gritos dan en el real: ¡ A don Sancho han mal herido!
¡ Muerto le ha Vellido Dolfos; gran traición ha cometido!
Desque le tuviera muerto metióse por un postigo;
por las calles de Zamora va dando voces y gritos:
—¡ Tiempo era, doña Urraca, de cumplir lo prometido!

Romances del Cid

Romance de la jura de Santa Águeda

En Santa Águeda de Burgos do juran los hijos de algo
allí toma juramento el Cid al rey castellano,
si se halló en la muerte del rey don Sancho su hermano;
las juras eran tan recias, el rey no las ha otorgado:
—" Villanos te maten, Alfonso, villanos que no hidalgos,
de las Asturias de Oviedo, que no sean castellanos;
si ellos son de León, yo te los do marcados;
caballeros vayan en yeguas, en yeguas que no en caballos;
las riendas traigan de cuerda, y no con frenos dorados; . . ."
Allí respondió el buen Rey, bien oiréis lo que ha hablado:
—" Mucho me aprietas, Rodrigo, Rodrigo mal me has tratado,
mas hoy me tomas la jura, cras me besarás la mano."
Allí respondió el buen Cid como hombre muy enojado:
—" Aqueso será, buen Rey, como fuere galardonado;
que allá en las otras tierras dan sueldo a los hijosdalgo.
Por besar mano de rey no me tengo por honrado;
porque la besó mi padre me tengo por afrentado."
" Vete de mis tierras, Cid, mal caballero probado,

vete, no me entres en ellas hasta un año pasado."
" Que me place," dijo el buen Cid, " que me place de buen grado
por ser la primera cosa que mandas en tu reinado:
tú me destierras por uno, yo me destierro por cuatro."
Ya se partía el buen Cid de Vivar y esos palacios,
las puertas deja cerradas, los alamudes echados,
las cadenas deja llenas de podencos y de galgos.
Con él lleva sus halcones, los pollos y los mudados.
Con él van cien caballeros, todos eran hijos de algo,
los unos iban a mula y los otros a caballo.
Por una ribera arriba al Cid van acompañando;
acompañándolo iban mientras él iba cazando.

Romances del Cid

Romance de los condes de Carrión

" Yo me estando en Valencia, en Valencia la mayor,
buen rey, vi yo vuestra seña y vuestro honrado pendón.
Saliera yo a recibirlo como vasallo a señor;
enviásteme una carta con un vuestro embajador:
que en la villa de Requena con vos me avistara yo.
Allí os convidé a comer, buen rey, tomástelo vos;
y al alzar de los manteles, dijistes esta razón:
que diese yo las mis hijas a los condes de Carrión.
No quería Jimena Gómez, la madre que las parió;
por cumplir vuestro mandado, otorgáraselas yo.
Un día estando en las bodas soltárase un león;
los condes fueron cobardes. Luego piensan la traición:
pidiéranme las mis hijas para volver a Carrión;
como eran sus mujeres entregáraselas yo;
¡ ay en medio del camino cuán mal paradas que son! "
Allí dijeron los condes una muy mala razón:
—" Mentides, el Cid, mentides, no somos traidores nos.
Nos somos fijos de reyes, sobrinos de emperador;
¿ merescimos ser casados con fijas de un labrador? "

Levantóse Per Bermúdez, el que las damas crió,
y al conde que así había hablado diérale un gran bofetón.
Alborotóse la corte, y el rey los apaciguó:
—" Afuera, Pero Bermúdez, no me revolváis quistión."
—" ¡ Otórganos campo, rey, otórganoslo, señor,
que con muy gran dolor vive la madre que las parió ! "
Los condes, como lo oyeron, no consienten campo, non.
Hablara el rey a los condes, bien oiréis lo que allí habló:
—" Si vos no otorgáis el campo, yo he de hacer justicia hoy."
Entonces habló un criado de los condes de Carrión:
—" Ellos otorgan el campo mañana en saliendo el sol."
Otro día de mañana todos en el campo son:
por el Cid va Nuño Gustos, hombre de muy gran valor:
con él va Pero Bermúdez, el ayo que las crió.
Los condes vienen de negro, y los del Cid de color;
repentidos van los condes, de vellos es gran dolor.
Ya los meten en el campo, ya les partían el sol;
luego abajaban las lanzas, ¡ cuán bien combatidos son !
A los primeros encuentros los condes vencidos son;
quedaron ante la corte culpados de traición;
a Gustios y Per Bermúdez el rey cabe sí asentó.

Romances del Cid

Romance de la muerte del rey don Pedro

Los fieros cuerpos revueltos entre los robustos brazos
están el cruel don Pedro y don Enrique su hermano.
No son abrazos de amor los que los dos se están dando,
que el uno tiene una daga y otro un puñal acerado.
El rey tiene a Enrique estrecho y Enrique al rey apretado,
uno en cólera encendido y otro de rabia abrasado:
y en aquesta fiera lucha sólo un testigo se ha hallado,
paje de espada de Enrique que de afuera mira el caso.
Después de luchar vencidos ¡ o suceso desgraciado !
que ambos vinieron al suelo, y Enrique cayó debajo.
Viendo el paje a su señor en tan peligroso caso,
por detrás al rey se allega, reciamente de él tirando,

diciendo ;—" No quito rey ni pongo rey de mi mano,
pero hago lo que debo al oficio de criado."
Y dió con el rey de espaldas y Enrique vino a lo alto,
hiriendo con un puñal en el pecho del rey falso,
donde a vueltas de la sangre, el vital hilo cortando,
salió el alma más cruel que vivió en pecho cristiano.

Romances del rey don Pedro

Romance de la pérdida de Antequera

La mañana de San Juan, al tiempo que alboreaba,
gran fiesta hacen los moros por la vega de Granada.
Revolviendo sus caballos y jugando de las lanzas,
ricos pendones en ellas broslados por sus amadas,
ricas marlotas vestidas, tejidas de oro y grana,
el moro que amores tiene señales de ello mostraba,
y el que no tenía amores allí no escaramuzaba.
Las damas moras los miran de las torres del Alhambra ;
también se los mira el rey de dentro de la Alcazaba.
Dando voces vino un moro, sangrienta toda la cara :
" —¡ Con tu licencia, buen rey, diréte una nueva mala :
el infante don Fernando tiene a Antequera ganada ;
muchos moros deja muertos, yo soy quien mejor librara,
y siete lanzadas traigo, la menor me llega al alma ;
los que conmigo escaparon en Archidona quedaban ! "
Cuando el rey oyó tal nueva la color se le mudaba.
Mandó tocar sus trompetas y sonar todas al arma ;
mandó juntar a los suyos, para hacer gran cabalgada.

Romances fronterizos

Álora la bien cercada

Álora, la bien cercada, tú que estás en par del río,
cercóte el adelantado una mañana en domingo,
de peones y hombres de armas el campo bien guarnecido ;
con la gran artillería hecho te había un portillo.

Viérades moros y moras todos huir al castillo;
las moras llevaban ropa, los moros harina y trigo,
y las moras de quince años llevaban el oro fino,
y los moricos pequeños llevaban la pasa y el higo.
Por cima de la muralla su pendón llevan tendido.
Entre almena y almena quedado se había un morico
con una ballesta armada, y en ella puesto un cuadrillo.
En altas voces, decía, que la gente lo había oído:
"¡Treguas, treguas, adelantado, por tuyo se da el castillo!"
Alza la visera arriba, por ver el que tal le dijo:
asestárale a la frente, salido le ha al colodrillo.
Sacólo Pablo de rienda, y de mano Jacobillo,
estos que había criado en su casa desde chicos.
Lleváronle a los maestros por ver si será guarido;
a las primeras palabras el testamento les dijo.

Romances fronterizos

Romance del rey moro que perdió Alhama

Paseábase el rey moro por la ciudad de Granada
desde la puerta de Elvira hasta la de Vivarrambla.
"¡Ay de mi Alhama!"
Cartas le fueron venidas que Alhama era ganada:
Las cartas echó en el fuego, y al mensajero matara.
"¡Ay de mi Alhama!"
Descabalga de una mula, y en un caballo cabalga;
por el Zacatín arriba subido se había al Alhambra.
"¡Ay de mi Alhama!"
Como en el Alhambra estuvo, al mismo punto mandaba
que se toquen sus trompetas, sus añafiles de plata.
"¡Ay de mi Alhama!"
Y que las cajas de guerra apriesa toquen al arma,
porque lo oigan sus moros, los de la Vega y Granada.
"¡Ay de mi Alhama!"
Los moros que el son oyeron que al sangriento Marte llama,
uno a uno y dos a dos juntado se ha gran batalla.
"¡Ay de mi Alhama!"

Allí habló un moro viejo,   desta manera hablara:
" ¿ Para qué nos llamas, rey,   para qué es esta llamada?"
" ¡ Ay de mi Alhama!"
" Habéis de saber, amigos,   una nueva desdichada:
que cristianos de braveza   ya nos han ganado Alhama."
" ¡ Ay de mi Alhama!"
Allí habló un alfaquí   de barba crecida y cana:
" ¡ Bien se te emplea, buen rey!   ¡ Buen rey, bien se te empleara!"
" ¡ Ay de mi alhama!"
" Mataste los Abencerrajes,   que eran la flor de Granada;
cogiste los tornadizos   de Córdoba la nombrada."
" ¡ Ay de mi Alhama!"
" Por eso mereces, rey,   una pena muy doblada;
que te pierdas tú y el reino,   y aquí se pierda Granada."
" ¡ Ay de mi Alhama!"

Romances fronterizos

Romance de Abenamar

Por Guadalquivir arriba   el buen rey don Juan camina:
encontrara con un moro   que Abenámar se decía.
El buen Rey desque lo vido   desta suerte le decía:
" Abenámar, Abenámar,   moro de la morería,
hijo eres de un moro perro   y de una cristiana cativa.
Tu padre llaman Halí   y a tu madre Catalina.
Cuando tú naciste, moro,   la luna estaba crecida,
y la mar estaba en calma,   viento no la rebullía.
Moro que en tal signo nace   no debe decir mentira:
preso tengo un hijo tuyo,   yo le otorgaré la vida,
si me dices la verdad   de lo que preguntaría.
Moro, si no me la dices,   a ti también mataría."
" Yo te la diré, buen Rey,   si tú me otorgas la vida."
" Dígasmela tú, el moro, que otorgada te sería.
¿ Qué castillos son aquellos,   que altos son y relucían?"
" El Alhambra era, señor,   y la otra es la Mezquita;
los otros los Alijares   labrados a maravilla.

El moro que los labró cien doblas ganaba al día,
y el día que no los labra de lo suyo las perdía;
desque los tuvo labrados, el rey le quitó la vida
porque no labre otros tales al rey del Andalucía.
La otra era Granada, Granada la noblecida
de los muchos caballeros y de gran ballestería."
Allí habla el rey Don Juan, bien veréis lo que diría:
"Granada, si tú quisieses contigo me casaría:
darte he yo en arras y dote a Córdoba y a Sevilla,
y a Jérez de la Frontera, que cabe sí la tenía.
Granada, si más quisieses, mucho más yo te daría."
Allí hablara Granada, al buen Rey le respondía:
"Casada soy, el rey Don Juan, casada, que no viuda;
el moro que a mí me tiene bien defenderme querría." . . .

Romances fronterizos

ROMANCES DEL CICLO BRETÓN

Romance de Lanzarote

Nunca fuera caballero de damas tan bien servido,
como fuera Lanzarote cuando de Bretaña vino,
que dueñas curaban dél, doncellas del su rocino.
Esa dueña Quintañona, ésa le escanciaba el vino,
la linda reina Ginebra se lo acostaba consigo;
y estando al mejor sabor, que sueño no había dormido,
la reina toda turbada un pleito ha conmovido.
—"Lanzarote, Lanzarote, si antes hobieras venido
no hablara el orgulloso las palabras que había dicho,
que a pesar de vos, señor, se acostaría comigo."
Ya se arma Lanzarote de gran pesar comovido.
despídese de su amiga, pregunta por el camino,
topó con el orgulloso debajo de un verde pino,
combátense de las lanzas, y a las hachas han venido.
Ya desmaya el orgulloso, ya cae en tierra tendido,
cortárale la cabeza, sin hacer ningún partido;
vuélvese para su amiga, donde fué bien recibido.

Romance de don Tristán

Herido está don Tristán de una muy mala lanzada,
diérasela el rey su tío con una lanza herbolada.
Diósela desde una torre, que de cerca non osaba.
Que el hierro tiene en el cuerpo, de fuera le tiembla el asta
valo a ver la reina Iseo, la su linda enamorada,
cubierta de un paño negro, que de luto se llamaba.
Viéndole tan mal parado dice así la triste dama:
—" Quien vos hirió, don Tristán, heridas tenga de rabia,
que no hallase maestro que sopiese de sanallas."
Júntanse boca con boca como palomillas mansas,
llora el uno, llora el otro, la cama bañan en agua;
allí nace un arboledo que azucena se llamaba,
cualquier mujer que la come luego se siente preñada.
¡ Así hice yo, mezquina, por la mi ventura mala!

ROMANCES NOVELESCOS

Romance de la mora Moraima

Yo me era mora Moraima, morilla de un bel catar;
cristiano vino a mi puerta, cuitada por me engañar.
Hablóme en algarabía, como aquel que la bien sabe:
—Ábrasme la puerta, mora, sí Alá te guarde de mal.
—¿ Cómo te abriré, mezquina, que no sé quién te serás?
—Yo soy el moro Mazote, hermano de la tu madre,
que un cristiano dejó muerto, tras mí venía el alcalde:
si no me abres tú, mi vida, aquí me verás matar.
Cuando esto oí, cuitada, comencéme a levantar;
visitiérame una almejía, no hallando mi brial,
fuérame para la puerta y abríla de par en par.

Romance del conde Arnaldos

¡ Quién hubiese tal ventura sobre las aguas de mar,
como hubo el conde Arnaldos la mañana de San Juan!
Con un falcón en la mano la caza iba a cazar,

vió venir una galera que a tierra quiere llegar.
Las velas traía de seda, la jarcia de un cendal,
marinero que le manda diciendo viene un cantar
que la mar facía en calma, los vientos hace amainar,
los peces que andan n'el hondo arriba los hace andar,
las aves que andan volando 'nel mástel las faz posar:
allí fabló el conde Arnaldos, bien oiréis lo que dirá:
—"Por Dios te ruego, marinero, dígasme ora ese cantar."
Respondióle el marinero, tal respuesta le fué a dar:
—"Yo no digo esta canción sino a quien conmigo va."

La ermita de San Simón

En Sevilla está una ermita cual dicen de San Simón,
adonde todas las damas iban a hacer oración.
Allá va la mi señora, sobre todas la mejor,
saya lleva sobre saya, mantillo de un tornasol,
en la su boca muy linda lleva un poco de dulzor,
en la su cara muy blanca lleva un poco de color,
y en los sus ojuelos garzos lleva un poco de alcohol,
a la entrada de la ermita relumbrando como el sol.
El abad que dice la misa no la puede decir, non,
monacillos que le ayudan no aciertan responder, non.
Por decir "amén, amén," decían "amor, amor."

La mañanica de San Juan

Yo me levantara, madre mañanica de Sant Juan:
vide estar una doncella riberica de la mar:
sola lava y sola tuerce, sola tiende en un rosal;
mientras los paños se enjugan, dice la niña un cantar:
"¿Dó los mis amores, dó los? ¿Dónde los iré a buscar?"
Mar abajo, mar arriba, diciendo iba un cantar,
peine de oro en las sus manos por sus cabellos peinar.
"Dígasme tú, el marinero, que Dios te guarde de mal,
si los viste, a mis amores, si los viste allá pasar."

ANÓNIMO

Razón d'amor

(thirteenth century)

Qui triste tiene su coraçón
venga oír esta razón.
Odrá razón acabada,
feita d' amor e bien rimada.
Un escolar la rimó
que siempre dueñas amó;
mas siempre ovo criança
en Alemania y en Francia;
moró mucho en Lombardía
pora aprender cortesía.

En el mes de abril, después yantar,
estava so un olivar.
Entre cimas de un mançanar
un vaso de plato vi estar.
Pleno era de un claro vino
que era vermejo e fino;
cubierto era de tal mesura
no lo tocas' la calentura. . . .

Qui de tal vino oviesse
en la mañana cuan comiesse,
e dello oviesse cada día
nunca más enfermaría.
Arriba del mançanar
otro vaso vi estar;
pleno era de un agua frida
que en el mançanar se nacía.
Beviera d' ela de grado,
mas ovi miedo que era encantado,
Sobre un prado pus' mi tiesta
que no me fiziese mal la siesta;
partí de mí las vistiduras

que no me fiziese mal la calentura.
Plegué a una fuente perenal,
nunca fué omne que viese tal;
tan grant virtud en sí avía,
que de la fridor que d'í ixía,
cient pasadas a derredor
non sintríades la calor.
Todas yerbas que bien olíen
la fuent cerca sí las teníe:
í es la salvia, í son las rosas,
í el lirio e las violas;
otras tantas yerbas í avía,
que sol' nombrar no las sabría.
Mas el olor que d'í ixía
a omne muerto ressucitaría.
Pris' del agua un bocado
e fuí todo esfriado.
En mi mano pris' una flor,
sabet non toda la peyor,
e quis' cantar de fin amor.
Mas vi venir una doncella,
pues nací non vi tan bella:
blanca era e bermeja,
cabellos cortos sobr' el oreja,
fruente blanca e loçana,
cara fresca como maçana; . . .

De las flores viene tomando,
en alta voz d' amor cantando,
e decía:—" ¡ Ay, meu amigo,
si me veré ya más contigo!
Améte siempre e amaré
quanto que viva seré.
Porque eres escolar
quisquiere te devría más amar.
Nunqua odí de omne decir
que tanta bona manera ovo en sí. . . ."

Quant la mia señor esto dizía,
sabet a mí non vidía;
pero sé que no me conocía,
que de mí non foiría.
Yo non fiz aquí como villano;
levéme e pris 'la por la mano. . . .

Dix'le yo:—" dezit, la mia señor,
si supiestes nunca d'amor?"
Diz ella:—" A plan con grant amor ando,
mas non conozco mi amado;
pero dízeme un su mensajero,
qu'es clérigo e non cavallero,
sabe muito de trobar,
de leyer e de cantar; . . ."

—" Por Dios, que digades, la mia señor,
¿qué donas tenedes por la su amor?"
—" Estas luvas y es' capiello,
est' oral y est' aniello
embió a mí es' meu amigo,
que por la su amor trayo conmigo."
Yo conocí luego las alfayas
que yo gelas avía embiadas.
Ela conoció una mi cinta man a mano,
que ela la fiziera con la su mano. . . .

—" ¡Dios señor, a ti loado
quant conozco meu amado!
¡Agora he tod' bien comigo
quant' conozco meu amigo!"
Una gran pieça alí estando,
de nuestro amor ementando,
ela dixo:—" El mio señor,
ora me sería de tornar

si a vos non fuese en pesar,"
Yo le dix' :—" It, la mia señor,
pues que ir queredes,
mas de mi amor pensat, fe que devedes." . . .

La mia señor se va privado,
dexa a mí desconortado. . . .

Mocedades de Rodrigo

(fourteenth century)

[The marriage of El Cid and Ximena.]

Allí cavalgó Ximena Gómez, tres doncellas con ella van,
e otros escuderos que la avían de guardar.
Llegava a Zamora, do la corte del rey está,
llorando de los ojos e pidiéndol' piedat:
—" Rey, dueña so lazrada, e áveme piedat.
Orphanilla finqué pequeña, de la condessa mi madre.
Fijo de Diego Laínez fízome mucho mal:
príssome mis hermanos, e matóme a mi padre.
A vos que sodes rey véngome a querellar.
Señor, por merced, derecho me mandat dar."
Mucho pessó al rey, e començó de fablar:
—" En grand cuita son mis reinos; Castilla alçárseme ha:
e si se me alçan castellanos, fazerme han mucho mal."
Cuando lo oyó Ximena Gómez, las manos le fué bessar.
—" Merced," " señor, non lo tengades a mal.
Mostrarvos he assosegar a Castilla e a los reinos otro tal:
datme a Rodrigo por marido, aquel que mató a mi padre." . . .

Essas horas dixo el rey al conde don Ossorio, su amo:
—" Datme vos acá essa doncella, despossaremos este lozano."
Aun no lo creyó don Diego, tanto estava espantado.
Salió la doncella, e tráela el conde por la mano.
Ella tendió los ojos, e a Rodrigo comenzó de catarlo.

Dixo :—" Señor, muchas mercedes, ca éste es el conde que yo demando."
Allí despossavan a doña Ximena Gómez con Rodrigo el castellano.

ALFONSO XI

(*c.* 1314–50)

Cantiga

En un tiempo cogí flores
del muy noble paraíso,
cuitado de mis amores
e d' el su fremoso riso!
e siempre vivo en dolor,
e ya no lo puedo sofrir,
mas me valerá la muerte
que en el mundo vivir.
Yo con cuidado d' amores
vol'o vengo ora dizer.
que he d' aquesta mi senhora
que mucho desejo aver.

En el tiempo en que solía
yo coger d' aquestas flores,
d'al cuidado non avía
desque vi los sus amores;
e non sé por quál ventura
me vino a defalir,
si lo fiz' el mi pecado,
si lo fizo el mal dizir.
Yo con cuidado de amores
vol'o vengo ora dizer,
que he d' aquesta mi senhora
que mucho desejo aver.

No creades, mi senhora,
el mal dizer de las gentes,
ca la muerte m' es llegada

si en ello parades mentes;
ay, senhora, noble rosa,
mercede vos vengo pidir,
avede de mí dolor
e no me dexedes morir.
Yo con cuidado de amores
vol'o vengo ora dizer,
que he d' aquesta mi senhora
que mucho desejo aver.

Yo cogí la flor das frores
de que tú coger solías,
cuitado de mis amores
bien sé lo que tú querías;
Dios lo pueste por tal guisa
que te lo pueda fazer,
ant' yo quería mi muerte
que te así veja a morrer.
Yo con cuidado d' amores
vol'o vengo ora dizer,
que he d' aquesta mi senhora
que mucho desejo aver.

SANTOB DE CARRIÓN

(early fourteenth century)

'*Por nàscer en espino . . .*'

[The poet reflects that nothing can be judged by appearance.]

Por nascer en espino   non val la rosa cierto
menos, nin el buen vino   por salir de sarmiento.

Non val el açor menos   por nascer de mal nido,
nin los enxemplos buenos   por los dezir judío. . . .

E razón muy granada   se diz en pocos versos
e cinta muy delgada   sufre costados gruesos.

E mucho omne entendido por seer vergonçoso,
es por torpe tenido e llamado astroso;

e si viese sazón mejor y más apuesta
diría su razón que al que lo denuesta.

Proverbios morales

RODRIGO YÁÑEZ

(*c.* 1350)

'*Non querrá Santa María . . .*'

[The battle of Salado.]

. . . Non querrá Santa María
abogada de los cristianos,
que se alaben deste día
estos moros africanos.

Oy será desbaratada
Africa con su compaña,
e por siempre será honrada
la cavallería de España.

" Agora, amigos; ¡ Santiago !
¡ Pensad de me seguir,
adelante, fijos dalgo,
non temades de morir ! "

Muy aprisa cavalgó
el buen rey, sin detenencia,
las espuelas allegó
al su cavallo Valencia.

Salió por una ladera,
aqueste buen rey sin miedo,
ívase en costanera
el arçobispo de Toledo,

que lo aguardava sin arte
por complir su penitencia;
don Johan, a la otra parte,
el obispo de Palencia.

Los de Tarifa salieron,
todos carrera les dan,
e por el real ferieron,
como fuego de alquitrán. . . .

El pendón adelantaron
por cima de la montaña,
e muy acerca fallaron
el muy noble rey de España.

Que iva sin fallemiento
los puertos atravesando,
commo un león fambriento
en los moros derribando, . . .

e el buen rey bien lidiando,
faziendo grand mortandad,
españoles esforçando,
e loando su bondad.

Dezían:—" ¡ Qué buen señor,
e qué noble cavallero!
¡ Val Dios, qué buen lidiador!
¡ Val Dios, qué real bracero!"

De aquesta fincó necia
Africa, sin toda falla,
Alixandre, rey de Grecia,
non ferió mejor batalla.

Nin Pepinos, rey de Francia,
con la su cavallería,
non fizo mayor matança,
de la que fué aquel día.

África perdió ventura,
España quedó honrada :
una legua de andadura,
aturó la arrancada.

Poema de Alfonso XI

MEENDIÑO, JUGLAR GALLEGO

(thirteenth century)

Cantiga de amigo

Sedia m'eu na ermida de San Simón
e cercaronmi as ondas que grandes son ;
eu atendend' o meu amigo.

Estando na ermida ante o altar,
cercaronmi as ondas grandes do mar ;
eu atendend' o meu amigo.

E cercaronmi as ondas que grandes son,
e non ei barqueiro nen remador ;
eu atendend' o meu amigo.

Cercaronmi as ondas do alto mar,
e non ei barqueiro nen sei remar.
eu atendend'o meu amigo.

Non ei barqueiro nen remador,
e morrer ei, fremosa, no mar mayor.
eu atendend'o meu amigo.

Non ei barqueiro nen sei remar,
e morrer ei, fremosa, no alto mar;
eu atendend'o meu amigo.

[Castilian version without refrain:]

Cercaronme las ondas que grandes son,
no tengo barquero ni remador . . .

Cercaronme las olas altas del mar,
no tengo barquero ni sé remar. . . .

No tengo barquero ni remador,
he de morir, hermosa, en el mar mayor . . .

No tengo barquero ni sé remar;
he de morir, hermosa, en el alto mar . . .

EL ALMIRANTE DON DIEGO FURTADO DE MENDOZA

(† 1404)

Cossante

A aquel árbol que mueve la foxa
algo se le antoxa.

Aquel árbol del bel mirar
face de manyera flores quiere dar:
algo se le antoxa.

Aquel árbol de bel veyer
face de manyera quiere florecer;
algo se le antoxa.

Face de manyera flores quiere dar:
ya se demuestra; salidlas mirar:
algo se le antoxa.

Face de manyera quiere florecer:
ya se demuestra; salidlas a ver:
algo se le antoxa.

Ya se demuestra; salidlas mirar:
vengan las damas las fructas cortar:
algo se le antoxa.

GARCI FERNÁNDEZ DE JERENA

(late fourteenth century)

Cantiga

Despedida del Amor:

Por una floresta estraña,
yendo triste muy pensoso
oí un grito pavoroso,
voz aguda con gran saña:
—" Montaña ",
iba esta voz diziendo,
" ora a Deus te encomiendo
que non curo más de España."

De la voz fuí espantado
e miré con gran pavor,
e vi que era el Amor
que se chamava cuitado.
De grado
o seu grand planto fazía,
segund entendí dezía:
—" Alto prez veo abajado."

Desque vi que se quexava,
por saber de su querella
pregunté a una donzella
que por la floresta andava;

falava
a donzella sin plazer:
" Plázeme de vos dezer
por qué Amor tan triste estava:

amigo, saber devedes
que Amor vive en manzela,
e se va ya de Castela
e nunca mientra bivedes
sabredes
ónde faze su morada;
por una que foy loada
de quexa porfazaredes."

Cantiga

Por manera de desfecha de la otra:

De la montaña, montaña,
de la montaña partía
o Amor e su compaña
maldiziendo todavía
a bondad e cortesía.
De la montaña partía
o Amor e su compaña.

De la montaña espaciosa,
al partir de aquesta gente,
una que chamavan Rosa
maldiziendo de talente:
—" Tal nombrar non osaría."
De la montaña partía
o Amor e su compaña.

Vi fazer esquivo planto
e guayas muy dolorosas,
con dolor fillar quebranto

a las donzellas cuitosas,
diziendo :—" ¡ Qué negro día ! "
De la montaña partía
o Amor e su compaña.

Dolorosas vozes davan
las que de aquí partían,
unas donzellas choravan,
otras grand planto fazían,
chamando :—" ¡ Qué negra vía ! "
De la montaña partía
o Amor e su compaña.

MACÍAS EL ENAMORADO

(late fourteenth century)

Cantiga para su amiga

Señora, en que fiança
he por cierto, sin dubdança
tú non ayas por vengança
mi tristura.

En ti adoro agora
e todavía
de todo lealmente :
miémbrate de mí, señòra,
por cortesía,
e siempre te venga emiente,
e non dexes tu serviente
perder por olbidança,
e tú farás buenestança
e mesura. . . .

Non sé lugar tan forte
que me defenda
de la tu muy grant beldad ;

en ti traigo yo la morte
sin contenda,
si me non vale tu bondad;
e porque esto es verdad,
¡ay! amor, en remembrança
en meu cor tengo tu lança
de amargura. . . .

FERNÁN PÉREZ DE GUZMÁN

(*c.* 1376–1460)

Algunas de las cient trinadas a loor de la Virgen María

Alma mía,
noche e día
loa la Virgen María.
Ésta adora,
ésta onora,
désta su favor implora.
Ésta llama,
a ésta ama,
que sobre todos derrama.
beneficios
sin servicios
e nos libra de los vicios.
Esta estrella
es aquélla
la qual, Virgen e donzella,
concibió,
parió e crió
al gran Rey que nos salvó. . . .

clara aurora
más decora
que la luna, por mí ora
al divino
uno e trino,

cuyo espíritu en ti vino;
e tú guía
el alma mía
a la celestial vía. Amen.

Pregunta que fizo a Alfonso Álvarez de Villasandino

Abril ya pasado aquende
e llegando el mes de mayo,
mi coraçón con desmayo
como quien plazer atiende,
quando el sol más se enciende,
de un árbol dixo un gayo:
" Aunque uno cuida el bayo,
quien lo ensilla al entiende."

Commo ferido e llagado
mi coraçón sin sospecha,
más triste dixo que endecha
es tu cantar desdonado.
" Dí, gayo de mi cuidado,
quál injuria te fué fecha
por que tu muy cruel flecha
ha mi gozo así turbado?"

Nunca talé tu floresta
ni corté tus nuevas flores,
a gayos nin a ruiseñores
nunca lancé con ballesta:
mi deseo e mi requesta
siempre fué servir amores;
a todos sus servidores
mi voluntad es muy presta.

Los laureles he por vicio,
los rosales por estrena;
las flores de la açucena
ya sintieron mi servicio:

a vezes por este oficio
he plazer, a vezes pena;
por menor que Policena
nunca mi puerta desquicio.

Debatiéndose e cantando
voló e fuése su vía,
yo que vi con alegría
quedé triste e sospirando:
así vivo imaginando
la fin deste quál sería,
si será de qual solía
ser la que sirvo mudando.

FINIDA

Pues fuestes siempre del bando
de amor en su compañía,
amigo, por cortesía
idme aquesto declarando.

ALFONSO ÁLVAREZ DE VILLASANDINO

(*c.* 1340–*c.* 1428)

Por amor e loores de una señora

Visso enamoroso,
duélete de mí,
pues vivo pensoso
desseando a ti.

La tu fermosura
me puso en prisión;
por la cual ventura
del mi coraçón
nos' parte tristura
en toda sazón:
porén tu figura
me entristece assí.

Todo el mi cuidado
es en te loar,
quel tiempo passado
non posso olvidar:
farás aguissado
de mí te membrar,
pues siempre de grado
leal te serví.

Estoy cada día
triste sin plazer;
si tan sólo un día
te pudiesse ver,
yo confortar me ía
con tu parecer:
porén cobraría
el bien que perdí.

Razonando en tal figura
las aves fueron volando;
yo aprés de una verdura
me fallé triste cuidando:
e luego en aquella ora
me membró gentil señora
a quien noche e día adora
mi coraçón sospirando.

Cantiga por amor e loores de unas lindas donzellas que andavan con la señora reina de Navarra

Por una floresta oscura,
muy cerca de una presa,
vi dueña fazer mesura
e danzar a la francesa:
Teresa
era d'esta compañía,
e otra que non diría,
que mi vida tiene presa.

Andavan por la floresta,
todas cercadas de flores,
en su dança muy onesta,
que fazían por sus tenores
discores;
melodía muy estraña
que fazía esta compaña,
me fizo perder dolores.

Vilas andar de tal guisa
de que yo fuí muy pagado
d'ellas; traían devisa
de flores en su tocado:
de grado
me llegara a su dança
mas ove grant recelança
de ser d'ellas profazado.

Pero díxeles:—" Señoras,
gozo e plazer ayades."
Respondieron esas oras:
" E vos más si lo buscades.
¿ Amades
entre nos alguna dueña?
Non vos embargue vergueña;
dezidlo, non vos temades."

Respondíles muy sin arte,
por les contar mi deseo:
" Todo mi coraçón parte
una de vos, en que creo
e veo
su figura todavía;
mas su nombre non diría,
que dezir me sería feo."

" Amigo, Dios te consuele
e te dé consolación,

e se duelen que se duele
de la tu tribulación.
Perdición
es aquesta en que andas.
Dios te dé lo que demandas,
e cumpla tu entención."

JUAN RODRÍGUEZ DEL PADRÓN

(mid fifteenth century)

Canción

Vive leda si podrás,
y no penes atendiendo,
que según peno partiendo,
ya no espero que jamás
te veré ni me verás.

¡ O dolorosa partida !
¡ O triste amador que pido
licencia, que me despido
de tu vista y de mi vida !
El trabajo perderás
en aver de mí más cura :
según que mi gran tristura,
ya no espero que jamás
te veré ni me verás.

FRANCISCO IMPERIAL

(fifteenth century)

' *Era cercado todo aquel jardín . . .* '

. . . Era cercado todo aquel jardín
de aquel arroyo a guissa de cava,
e por muro muy alto jazmín,
que todo a la redonda lo cercava.

El son del agua en dulçor passava
harpa, dulçaina, vihuela de arco,
e non me digan que mucho abarco
que non sé si dormía o si velava.

En mí dezía:—" Mucho me maravillo
que non veo aquí ninguna entrada;
non veo puente, puerta nin portillo."
Esto diziendo vi una puerta alçada
entre el jazmín, non tabla labrada,
mas de robí más vivo que centella:
commo movíme a ir derecho a ella
non vi de quién luego fué abaxada.

Muy a vagar passé allén la puente,
oliendo del jardín los dulces olores,
porque de entrar ove mayor talente
e fize entrada entre flores e flores.
Ante que entrase, ove muchos suores;
de que fuí entrado ¡ oyd qué aventura!
vi toda blanca la mi vestidura,
e luego conoscí los mis errores.

Desque volví a mano diestra el rostro,
vi por la yerva pissadas de omne,
onde alegre fuíme por el rastro,
el qual derecho a un rossal llevóme;
e commo quando entre árboles asome
alguno que, ante, los ramos mesce,
e poco a poco todo assí paresce,
tal vi un omne; muy cortés salvóme.

Era en vista benigno e suave,
e en color era la su vestidura
ceniza o tierra que seca se cave;
barva e cabello alvo sin mesura;
traía un libro de poca escriptura
escripto todo con oro muy fino,

e començava : " *En medio del camino,*"
e del laurel corona e cintura.

De grant autoridad avía semblante,
de poeta de grant excelencia.
onde omilde enclinéme delante,
faciéndole devida reverencia,
e díxele con toda obediencia :
—" Afectuosamente a vos me ofresco,
e maguer tanto de vos non meresco,
sea mi guía vuestra alta ciencia."

Dióme respuesta en puro latín :
—" A mi plaze lo que tu desseas."
E, desí, dixo en lengua florentín :
—" E porque cierto tú más de mí seas,
buelve comigo, e quiero que veas
las siete estrellas que en el cielo relumbran,
e los sus rayos que al mundo alumbran ;
e esto, fijo, ciertamente creas."

Tomóme la mano e bolvió por do vino
e yo siguiendo siempre sus pisadas,
e los ojos baxos por no perder tino,
non fueran ciento aun bien contadas,
que oí bozes muy asossegadas,
angelicales, e musicado canto ;
mas eran lexos de mí aun tanto
que las non entendí a las vegadas. . . .

Dezir a las siete Virtudes

Por amor e loores de una fermosa muger de Sevilla que llamó él Estrella Diana

Non fué por cierto mi carrera vana,
passando la puente de Guadalquivir,
atan buen encuentro que yo vi venir
ribera del río, en medio Triana,

a la muy fermosa Estrella Diana,
qual sale por mayo al alva del día,
por los santos passos de la romería:
muchos loores aya Santa Ana.

E por galardón demostrar me quiso
la muy delicada flor de jasmín,
rosa novela de oliente jardín,
e de verde prado gentil flor de liso,
el su gracioso e onesto riso,
semblante amoroso e viso suave,
propio me paresce al que dixo: *Ave*,
quando enviado fué del paraíso.

Callen poetas e callen autores,
Omero, Oracio, Vergilio e Dante,
e con ellos calle Ovidio *D'amante*
e cuantos escrivieron loando señores,
que tal es aquesta entre las mejores,
commo el lucero entre las estrellas,
llama muy clara a par de centellas,
e commo la rosa entre las flores. . . .

MARQUÉS DE SANTILLANA

(1398–1458)

Serranilla

Después que nascí,
non vi tal serrana
como esta mañana.

Allá a la veguela,
a Mata el Espino,
en esse camino
que va a Loçoyuela,
de guisa la vi
que me fizo gana
la fructa temprana.

Garnacha traía
de oro, presada
con broncha dorada
que bien relucía.
A ella volví
diziendo :—" Loçana,
¿ e sois villana ? "

—" Sí soy, cavallero ;
si por mí lo avedes,
dezid, ¿ qué queredes ?
Fablad verdadero."
Yo le dixe así :
" —Juro por Santana
que non sois villana."

Serranilla de Bores

Moçuela de Bores,
allá do la Lama,
púsome en amores.

Cuidé que olvidado
amor me tenía,
como quien se avía
grand tiempo dexado
de tales dolores,
que más que la llama
queman amadores.

Mas ví la fermosa
de buen continente,
la cara plaziente,
fresca como rosa,
de tales colores
cual nunca vi dama
nin otra, señores.

Por lo cual :—" Señora "
(le dixe), " en verdad
la vuestra beldad
saldrá desde agora
dentre estos alcores,
pues meresce fama
de grandes loores."

Dixo :—" Cavallero,
tiradvos afuera :
dexad la vaquera
pasar al otero ;
ca dos labradores
me piden de Frama,
entrambos pastores."

—" Señora, pastor
seré si queredes :
mandarme podedes,
como a servidor :
mayores dulçores
será a mí la brama
que oír ruiseñores."

Así concluímos
el nuestro processo
sin fazer excesso,
e nos avenimos.
E fueron las flores
de cabe Espinama
los encobridores.

Canción

Deseando ver a vos,
gentil señora,
non he reposo por Dios
punto nin ora.

Deseando aquel buen día
que vos vea,
el contrario de alegría
me guerrea.
Del todo muero por vos
e non mejora
mi mal, júrovos a Dios;
mas empeora.

Bien digo a mi corazón
que non se quexe;
mas sirva toda sazón
e non se dexe
de amar e servir a vos,
a quien adora;
pues recuérdevos por Dios
piedad agora.

Villancico

(*A unas tres fijas suyas*)

Por una gentil floresta
de lindas flores e rosas,
vide tres damas fermosas
que de amores han recuesta.
Yo, con voluntad muy presta,
me llegué a conoscellas;
començó la una de ellas
esta canción tan honesta:

"Aguardan a mí:
nunca tales guardas vi."

Por mirar su fermosura
destas tres gentiles damas,
yo cobríme con las ramas,
metíme so la verdura.

La otra con grand tristura
començó de sospirar
e dezir este cantar
con muy honesta mesura:

" La niña que amores ha,
sola, ¿ cómo dormirá? "

Por non les fazer turbança
non quise ir más adelante.
A las que con ordenança
cantavan tan consonante,
La otra con buen semblante
dixo:—" Señoras de estado,
pues las dos avéis cantado,
a mí conviene que cante ":

" Dejadlo al villano pene;
véngueme Dios delle."

Desque ya hovieron cantado
estas señoras que digo,
yo salí desconsolado,
como ome sin abrigo.
Ellas dixeron:—" Amigo,
non sois vos el que buscamos
mas cantad, pues que cantamos ":

" Sospirando iva la niña
e non por mí,
que yo bien se lo entendí."

La comedieta de Ponça

Descripción del tiempo:

Los campos e miesses ya descoloraban,
e los deseados tributos rendían;
los vientos pluviosos las nuves bogavan,
e las verdes frondes del aire tremían.

Dexado el estilo de los que fingían
metáforas vanas con dulce locuela,
diré lo que priso mi última cela;
e cómicos oyan, si bien los oían.

Al tiempo que al pasto salen de guarida
las fieras silvestres, e humanidad
descansa e reposa, e la fembra ardida
libró de Oloferne la sacra cibdad;
forçada del sueño la mi libertad,
diálogo triste e fabla llorosa
firió mis orejas, e tan pavorosa
que sólo en pensarlo me vence piedad.

Así recordado, miré do sonava
el clamoso duelo, e vi quatro donas,
cuyo aspecto e fabla muy bien denotava
ser quasi deesas o magnas personas;
vestidas de negro, e a las coronas,
llamando la muerte con tantas querellas,
que dubdo si fueron tan grandes aquellas,
que Ovidio tocó de las tres Gorgonas. . . .

Micer Johan Bocacio de Certaldo, ilustre poeta florentino:

Aprés de las quales vi más un varón
en hábito honesto, mas bien arreado,
e non se ignorava la su perfección,
ca de verde lauro era coronado.
Atento escuchava, cortés, inclinado
a la más antigua, que aquella fablava:
quien vió las sus quexas e a quien las narrava,
de cómo ya vive soy maravillado.

Exhortación de la reina doña Leonor:

Aquella muy manso fablava, diziendo:
" Eres tú Bocacio, aquél que trató
de tantas materias, ca yo non entiendo

que otro poeta a ti se egualó?
Eres tú, Bocacio, el que compiló
los casos perversos del siglo mundano?
Señor, si tú eres, apresta la mano
que non fué ninguna semblante que yo. . . .

Soneto

Lexos de vos e cerca de cuidado,
pobre de goço e rico de tristeça,
fallido de reposo e abastado
de mortal pena, congoxa e braveça;
desnudo de esperança e abrigado
de inmensa cuita e visto de aspereça,
la mi vida me fuye, mal mi grado,
la muerte me sigue sin pereça.
Nin son bastantes a satisfazer
la sed ardiente de mi grand deseo
Tajo al presente, nin me socorrer
la enferma Guadiana, nin lo creo:
sólo Guadalquevir tiene poder
de me guarir e sólo aquél deseo.

Soneto

Doradas ondas del famoso río
que baña en torno la noble ciudad,
do es aquélla, cuyo más que mío
soy e posee la mi voluntad:
pues que en el vuestro lago y poderío
es la mi barca veloce, cuytad
con todas fuerças e curso radío
e presentadme a la su beldad.
Non vos empida dubda nin temor
de daño mío, ca yo non lo espero;
e si viniere, venga toda suerte.
E si muriere, muera por su amor:
murió Leandro en el mar por Ero:
partido es dulce al aflicto muerte.

JUAN DE MENA

(1411–56)

'. . . *Luego resurgen tamaños clarores* . . .'

[Divine Providence guides the poet.]

. . . Luego resurgen tamaños clarores
que fieren la nube dexándola enxuta,
en partes pequeñas assí resoluta,
que toda la fazen bolar en vapores,
e resta en el medio cubierta de flores
una donzella tan mucho fermosa,
que ante su gesto es loco quien osa
otras beldades loar de mayores.

Luego del todo ya restituída
ovieron mis ojos su virtud primera,
ca por la venida de tal mensagera
se cobró la parte que estava perdida:
e puesto que fuesse assí descogida,
más provocava a bueno e onesto
la gravedad de su claro gesto
que non por amores a ser requerida.

Desque sentida la su proporción
de umana forma non ser discrepante,
el miedo pospuesto, prosigo adelante
en umil estilo tal breve oración:
" O más que seráfica clara visión,
suplico me digas de dónde veniste;
e quál es el arte que tú más seguiste,
e cómo se llama la tu discreción."

Respuso: " Non vengo a la tu presencia
de nuevo, mas antes soy en todas partes,
segundo te digo que sigo tres artes
de donde depende muy grand ecelencia:
las cosas presentes ordeno en essencia,

e las por venir dispongo a mi guisa,
las fechas revelo ; si esto te avisa,
divina me puedes llamar Providencia. . . .

E contra do vido mostrarse la puerta
se iva, llevándome ya de la mano ;
notar la entrada me manda temprano,
de cómo era grande e a todos abierta.
" Mas una cautela yaze encubierta,"
dixo, " que quema muy más que la brasa,
que todos los que entran en esta grand casa
han la salida dubdosa e non cierta." . . .

Assí razonando la puerta passamos
por do confluía tamaño gentío,
que allí do el ingresso más era vazío
unos a otros estorvo nos damos,
ca por la cosa que mucho andamos
quando deseo común más se esfuerça,
más nuestra priessa nos daña e nos fuerça,
e lo que queremos menos acabamos. . . .

El laberinto de Fortuna

GÓMEZ MANRIQUE

(*c.* 1415–90)

Canción

De guisa vuestro deseo
  me atormenta,
que nada de quanto veo
  me contenta.

Deziembre paresce mayo,
e noches los claros días ;
mis mayores alegrías
pasan más rezias que rayo ;

e si mugeres oteo
de gran cuenta,
ninguna de quantas veo
me contenta.

Canción

Con la belleza prendés,
donzella, quantos miráis,
e con la fonda matáis
e ferís los que querés.

Nunca vi tal desmesura,
prender los ombres seguros,
e ferir desde los muros
con fonda de fermosura.
No puede ningún arnés
defensar al que miráis,
pues que mirando matáis
e ferís los que querés.

La representación del nacimiento de Nuestro Señor

Para callar al niño

Callad fijo mío chiquito.

Callad vos, Señor,
nuestro redentor,
que vuestro dolor
durará poquito.

Ángeles del cielo,
venid dar consuelo
a este moçuelo
Jesús tan bonito . . .

Este santo dino
niño tan benino,
por redemir vino
el linaje aflito.

Cantemos gozosas,
ermanas graciosas,
pues somos esposas
del Jesú bendito.

JORGE MANRIQUE

(1440–79)

Coplas que fizo por la muerte de su padre

Recuerde el alma dormida,
avive el seso y despierte,
contemplando
cómo se passa la vida,
cómo se viene la muerte
tan callando;
cuán presto se va el plazer,
cómo después de acordado
da dolor,
cómo a nuestro parescer,
qualquiera tiempo passado
fué mejor.

Pues si vemos lo presente
cómo en un punto se es ido
y acabado,
si juzgamos sabiamente,
daremos lo no venido
por passado.
No se engañe nadie, no,
pensando que ha de durar
lo que espera

más que duró lo que vió,
pues que todo ha de passar
    por tal manera.

Nuestras vidas son los ríos
que van a dar en el mar
    que es el morir :
allí van los señoríos
derechos a se acabar
    y consumir ;
allí los ríos caudales,
allí los otros, medianos
    y más chicos,
allegados son iguales,
los que viven por sus manos
    y los ricos.

Dexo las invocaciones
de los famosos poetas
    y oradores ;
no curo de sus ficciones,
que traen yervas secretas
    sus sabores.
Âquel solo me ençomiendo,
âquel solo invoco yo
    de verdad,
que en este mundo viviendo,
el mundo no conosció
    su deidad.

Este mundo es el camino
para el otro, que es morada
    sin pesar ;
mas cumple tener buen tino
para andar esta jornada
    sin errar.
Partimos cuando nascemos,

andamos mientra vivimos,
y llegamos
al tiempo que fenescemos;
assí que quando morimos
descansamos.

Este mundo bueno fué
si bien usássemos dél
como devemos,
porque, según nuestra fe,
es para ganar aquel
que atendemos.
Y aun aquel fijo de Dios
para sobirnos al cielo
descendió
a nascer acá entre nos,
y a vivir en este suelo
do murió.

Si fuesse en nuestro poder
tornar la cara fermosa
corporal,
como podemos fazer
el ánima gloriosa
angelical,
¡qué diligencia tan viva
tovieramos toda hora,
y tan presta,
en componer la cativa,
dexándonos la señora
descompuesta!

Ved de quán poco valor
son las cosas tras que andamos
y corremos,
que, en este mundo traidor,
aun primero que muramos
las perdemos:

dellas desfaze la edad,
dellas casos desastrados
que acaescen,
dellas, por su calidad,
en los más altos estados
desfallescen.

Dezidme, la fermosura,
la gentil frescura y tez
de la cara,
la color y la blancura,
quando viene la vejez,
¿ quál se para ?
Las mañas y ligereza
y la fuerça corporal
de joventud,
todo se torna graveza
quando llega al arrabal
de senectud.

Pues la sangre de los godos,
y el linaje, y la nobleza
tan crescida,
¡ por quántas vías y modos
se sume su grand alteza
en esta vida !
Unos, por poco valer,
¡ por quán baxos y abatidos
que los tienen !
Y otros, por no tener,
con oficios no devidos
se mantienen.

Los estados y riqueza,
que nos dexan a desora,
¿ quién lo duda ?
No les pidamos firmeza,

pues son de una señora
    que se muda;
que bienes son de Fortuna
que revuelve con su rueda
    presurosa,
la qual no puede ser una,
ni estar estable ni queda
    en una cosa.

Pero digo que acompañen
y lleguen hasta la huessa
    con su dueño:
por esso no nos engañen,
pues se va la vida apriessa
    como sueño.
Y los deleites de acá
son, en que nos deleitamos,
    temporales,
y los tormentos de allá,
que por ellos esperamos,
    eternales.

Los plazeres y dulçores
desta vida trabajada
    que tenemos,
¿qué son sino corredores,
y la muerte la celada
    en que caemos?
No mirando nuestro daño,
corremos a rienda suelta
    sin parar;
desque vemos el engaño
y queremos dar la vuelta,
    no hay lugar.

Essos reyes poderosos
que vemos por escrituras
    ya passadas,

con casos tristes llorosos
fueron sus buenas venturas
　　trastornadas;
assí que no hay cosa fuerte,
que a papas y emperadores
　　y prelados
assí los trata la Muerte
como a los pobres pastores
　　de ganados. . . .

¿Qué se fizo el rey don Juan?
Los infantes de Aragón,
　　¿qué se fizieron?
¿Qué fué de tanto galán?
¿Qué fué de tanta invención
　　como truxieron?
Las justas y los torneos,
paramentos, bordaduras,
　　y cimeras,
¿fueron sino devaneos?
¿qué fueron sino verduras
　　de las eras?

¿Qué se fizieron las damas,
sus tocados, sus vestidos,
　　sus olores?
¿Qué se fizieron las llamas
de los fuegos encendidos
　　de amadores?
¿Qué se fizo aquel trobar,
las músicas acordadas
　　que tañían?
¿Qué se fizo aquel dançar,
aquellas ropas chapadas
　　que traían?

Pues el otro su heredero,
don Enrique, ¡qué poderes
　　alcançava!

¡ Quán blando, quán falaguero
el mundo con sus plazeres
se le dava !
Mas veréis quán enemigo,
quán contrario, quán cruel
se le mostró,
aviéndole sido amigo,
¡ quán poco duró con él
lo que le dió !

Las dádivas desmedidas,
los edificios reales
llenos de oro,
las vaxillas tan febridas,
los enriques y reales
del tesoro,
los jaezes, los cavallos
de su gente, y atavíos
tan sobrados,
¿ dónde iremos a buscallos ?
¿ qué fueron sino rocíos
de los prados ? . . .

Pues aquel grand condestable,
maestre que conoscimos
tan privado,
no cumple que dél se fable,
sino sólo que lo vimos
degollado.
Sus infinitos tesoros,
sus villas y sus lugares,
su mandar,
¿ qué le fueron sino lloros ?
¿ fuéronle sino pesares
al dexar ? . . .

Aquel de buenos abrigo,
amado por virtuoso

de la gente,
el maestre don Rodrigo
Manrique, tanto famoso
y tan valiente,
sus grandes fechos y claros
no cumple que los alabe,
pues los vieron,
no los quiero fazer caros,
pues el mundo todo sabe
quáles fueron.

¡ Qué amigo de sus amigos !
¡ Qué señor para criados
y parientes !
¡ Qué enemigo de enemigos !
¡ Qué maestro de esforçados
y valientes !
¡ Qué seso para discretos !
¡ Qué gracia para donosos !
¡ Qué razón !
¡ Qué benigno a los subjetos,
y a los bravos y dañosos,
un león ! . . .

No dexó grandes tesoros,
ni alcançó grandes riquezas
ni vaxillas,
mas fizo guerra a los moros,
ganando sus fortalezas
y sus villas ;
y en las lides que venció,
muchos moros y cavallos
se perdieron,
y en este oficio ganó
las rentas y los vassallos
que le dieron. . . .

Después de puesta la vida
tantas vezes por su ley
al tablero,
después de tan bien servida
la corona de su rey
verdadero,
después de tanta hazaña
a que no puede bastar
cuenta cierta,
en la su villa de Ocaña
vino la Muerte a llamar
a su puerta,

diziendo :—" Buen cavallero,
dexad el mundo engañoso
y su halago :
vuestro corazón de azero
muestre su esfuerço famoso
en este trago ;
y pues de vida y salud
fezistes tan poca cuenta
por la fama,
esfuérçese la virtud
para sofrir esta afruenta
que vos llama.

" No se os faga tan amarga
la batalla temerosa
que esperáis,
pues otra vida más larga
de fama tan gloriosa
acá dexáis.
Aunque esta vida de onor
tampoco no es eternal
ni verdadera,
mas con todo es muy mejor
que la otra temporal
perescedera.

" El vivir que es perdurable
no se gana con estados
mundanales,
ni con vida deleitable,
en que moran los pecados
infernales;
mas los buenos religiosos
gánanlo con oraciones
y con lloros,
los cavalleros famosos
con trabajos y aflicciones
contra moros.

" Y pues vos, claro varón,
tanta sangre derramastes
de paganos,
esperad el galardón
que en este mundo ganastes
por las manos;
y con esta confiança,
y con la fe tan entera
que tenéis,
partid con buena esperança,
que estotra vida tercera
ganaréis."

—" No gastemos tiempo ya
en esta vida mezquina
por tal modo,
que mi voluntad está
conforme con la divina
para todo;
y consiento en mi morir
con voluntad plazentera
clara y pura,
que querer ombre vivir
quando Dios quiere que muera
es locura.

"Tú, que por nuestra maldad
tomaste forma servil
y baxo nombre,
Tú, que a tu divinidad
juntaste cosa tan vil
como el ombre,
Tú, que tan grandes tormentos
sofriste sin resistencia
en tu persona,
no por mis merescimientos,
mas por tu sola clemencia
me perdona."

Assí con tal entender,
todos sentidos umanos
conservados,
cercado de su muger,
de sus fijos y hermanos
y criados,
dió el alma a quien gela dió,
el qual la ponga en el cielo
en su gloria,
y aunque la vida murió,
nos dexó harto consuelo
su memoria.

Canción

No tardes, muerte, que muero;
ven, porque viva contigo;
quiéreme, pues te quiero,
que con tu venida espero
no tener guerra comigo.

Remedio de alegre vida
no lo hay por ningún medio,
porque mi grave herida

es de tal parte venida,
que eres tú sola remedio.
Vén aquí, pues, ya que muero;
búscame, pues que te sigo;
quiéreme, pues que te quiero,
e con tu venida espero
no tener vida comigo.

Canción

Por vuestro gran merecer
amor me pone tal grado,
que me pierdo por perder
de las angustias cuidado.

Pues que se acabe la vida
con dolor tan lastimero,
yo contento si lo quiero,
si ella queda servida;
porque quiere mi querer
muy contento e no forçado,
que me pierdo por perder
de las angustias cuidado.

GARCI SÁNCHEZ DE BADAJOZ

(*c.* 1460–*c.* 1526)

Un sueño que soñó

La mucha tristeza mía
que causó vuestro desseo,
ni de noche ni de día,
quando estoy donde no os veo,
no olvido mi compañía.

Yo los días no los vivo,
velo las noches cativo,
y si alguna noche duermo,
suéñome muerto en un yermo
en la forma que aquí escrivo.

Yo soñava que me iva
desesperado de amor
por una montaña esquiva
donde sino un ruiseñor,
no hallé otra cosa viva:
y del dolor que llevava,
soñava que me finava,
y el amor que lo sabía,
y que a buscarme venía
y al ruiseñor preguntava:

" Dime, lindo ruiseñor,
¿ viste por aquí perdido
un muy leal amador
que de mí viene herido ? "
—" ¿ Cómo ! Sois vos el amor ? "
—" Sí, yo soy a quien seguís,
y por quien dulces vivís
todos los que bien amáis."
—" Ya sé por quién preguntáis,
por Garci Sánchez dezís.

" Muy poco ha que passó
solo por esta ribera,
y como le vi y me vió,
yo quise saber quién era,
y él luego me lo contó,
diciendo " :—" Yo soy aquel
a quien más fué amor cruel,
cruel que causó el dolor,
qu'a mí no me mató amor,
sino la tristeza dél."

Yo le dixe :—" ¿ Si podré
a tu mal dar algún medio ? "
Díjome :—" No, y el por qué
es porque aborrí el remedio
quando dél desesperé."
Y estas palabras diciendo
y las lágrimas corriendo,
se fué con dolores graves ;
yo con otras muchas aves
fuemos empós dél siguiendo,

hasta que muerto cayó
allí entre unas acequias,
y aquellas aves y yo
le cantamos las obsequias,
porque d'amores murió :
y aun no medio fallecido,
la tristeza y el olvido
le enterraron de crueles,
y en estos verdes laureles
fué su cuerpo convertido.

D'allí nos quedó costumbre
las aves enamoradas
de cantar sobre su cumbre
las tardes, las alboradas,
cantares de dulcedumbre."
—" Pues yo os otorgo indulgencia
de las penas quel ausencia
os dará, amor y tristura,
a quien más su sepoltura
servirá con reverencia."

FIN

Vime alegre, vime ufano
de estar con tan dulce gente,
vime con bien soberano

enterrado honradamente,
y muerto de vuestra mano:
allí, estando en tal concierto,
creyendo que era muy cierto
que veía lo que escrivo,
recordé y halléme vivo,
de la qual causa soy muerto.

FLORENCIA PINAR

(fifteenth century)

Canción (a unas perdices que la enviaron vivas)

Destas aves su nación
es cantar con alegría,
y de vellas en prissión
siento yo grave passión,
sin sentir nadie la mía.

Ellas lloran que se vieron
sin temor de ser cautivas,
y a quien eran más esquivas
essos mismos las prendieron:
sus nombres mi vida son
que va perdiendo alegría,
y de vellas en prissión
siento yo grave passión,
sin sentir nadie la mía.

CARVAJALES

(fifteenth century)

Villancete

Saliendo de un olivar,
más fermosa que arreada,
vi serrana que tornar
me fizo de mi jornada.

Tornéme en su compañía
por faldas de una montaña,
suplicando sil' plazía
de mostrarme su cabaña;
dixo:—" Non podéis librar,
señor, aquesta vegada,
que superfluo es demandar
a quien non suele dar nada."

Si lealtad non me acordara
de la más linda figura,
del todo me enamorara:
tanta vi su fermosura;
dixe:—" ¿ Qué queréis mandar,
señora, pues sois casada,
que vos non quiero enojar,
ni ofender mi enamorada?"

Replicó:—" Id en buen hora,
non curés de amar villana:
pues servís a tal señora,
non troqués seda por lana
nin queráis de mi burlar,
pues sabéis que so enajenada."
Vi serrana, que tornar
me fizo de mi jornada.

FRAY AMBROSIO MONTESINO

(fifteenth century)

La noche santa

No la debemos dormir
la noche santa,
no la debemos dormir.

La Virgen a solas piensa
qué hará
quando al Rey de luz inmensa
parirá,
si de su divina esencia
temblará,
o qué le podrá decir.
No la debemos dormir
la noche santa,
no la debemos dormir.

JUAN ÁLVAREZ GATO

(*c.* 1433–96)

Cantar a lo divino

El cantar que dizen: "Quita allá, que no quiero, falso enemigo, quita allá, que no quiero que huelgues comigo", endereçado a lo espiritual.

Quita allá, que no quiero,
mundo enemigo,
quita allá, que no quiero
pendencias contigo.

Ya sé lo que quieres,
ya sé tus dulçores:
prometes plazeres,
das cien mil dolores:
de los favoridos,
de tus amadores,
el mejor librado
es el más perdido.

No quiero tus ligas
más en mi posada,
y aunque me persigas
no se me da nada;

que estonces se gana
la gloria doblada,
cuanto más te huyo
y menos te sigo.

Quita allá, que no quiero,
falso enemigo,
quita allá, que no quiero
pendencias contigo.

Letra

Venida es, venida,
al mundo la vida.

Venida es al suelo
la gracia del cielo
a darnos consuelo
y gloria complida.

Nacido ha en Belén
el que es nuestro bien;
venido es en quien
por él fué escogida.

En un portalejo,
con pobre aparejo,
servido d'un viejo,
su guarda escogida.

La piedra preciosa,
ni la fresca rosa,
no es tan hermosa
como la parida.

Venida es, venida,
al mundo la vida.

LOPE DE ESTÚÑIGA

(fifteenth century)

Canción

Gentil dama esquiva
de ti doy querella:
fázesme que viva
triste con mansiella.

Andaré llorando
por tierras extrañas;
mi cuerpo rasgando
fasta las entrañas;
a todos mostrando
mis cuitas tamañas
e cómo me dañas
en edad novela.

Gemido profundo
mi lloro despierte:
en todo me fundo
sobre triste suerte,
tal nascí en el mundo
que codicio fuerte
pasar ya la muerte
por mucho que duela.

Libertad estava
conmigo segura:
amor la dexava
vivir en folgura.
Porque te mirava
vino fermosura,
púsola en tristura
a do la encarcela . . .

FRAY ÍÑIGO DE MENDOZA

(*c.* 1482)

Prueva como muchos tienen por su dios al dinero

. . . Lo que más temes perder
o que más amas hallar,
lo que más te da plazer
en lo aver y poseer
se deve tu dios llamar;
lo que más te manda y vieda
es el más proprio dios tuyo,
de la qual sentencia queda
que resciben la moneda
muchos ombres por dios suyo.

No sé qué más adorar
ni qué más dar sacrificio
que mentir y trafagar,
perjurar y renegar
cada día en su servicio,
nunca dormir sin temor,
nunca vevir sin sospecha:
puedo te jurar, lector,
que aunque soy fraire menor,
no es mi regla tan estrecha. . . .

Vita Christi

Al niño Jesús

Eres niño y has amor:
¿qué farás cuando mayor?

Pues que en tu natividad
te quema la caridad,
en tu varonil edad
¿quién sufrirá su calor?

Eres niño y has amor:
¿qué farás cuando mayor?

Será tan vivo su fuego,
que con importuno ruego,
por salvar el mundo ciego,
te dará mortal dolor.

Eres niño y has amor:
¿qué farás cuando mayor?

Arderá tanto tu gana,
que por la natura humana
querrás pagar su mançana
con muerte de malhechor.

Eres niño y has amor:
¿qué farás cuando mayor?

¡O amor digno de espanto!
pues que en este niño sancto
has de pregonarte tanto,
cantemos a tu loor:

Eres niño y has amor:
¿qué farás cuando mayor?

COMENDADOR ESCRIVÁ

(*c.* 1497)

Canción

Ven muerte tan escondido,
que no te sienta comigo,
porqu'el gozo de contigo
no me torne a dar la vida.

Ven como rayo que hiere,
que hasta que ha herido
no se siente su rüido,
así sea tu venida,
si no, desde aquí me obligo
qu'el gozo que habré contigo
me dará de nuevo vida.

Canción

Vos me matáis de tal suerte
y con pena tan gloriosa,
que no sé más dulce cosa
que los trances de mi muerte.

E della soy tan ufano,
tan penado e tan contento,
que no trocaré un tormento
por mil bienes de otra mano.
Y, pues que quiso mi suerte
darme pena tan gloriosa,
no quiero más dulce cosa
que los trances de mi muerte.

GUEVARA
(late fifteenth century)

Esparsa

Las aves andan volando
contando canciones ledas,
las verdes hojas temblando,
las aguas dulces sonando,
los pavos hacen las ruedas:
yo, sin ventura amador,
contemplando mi tristura,
deshago por mi dolor
la gentil rueda de amor
que hice por mi ventura.

Otras suyas

Consuélame desconsuelo,
pena triste no descansa,
la tormenta menos mansa
me da vida en este suelo:
lloros son mis buenos sones,
es mi muerte no morir,
danme gozo mis passiones
porque son las opiniones
que dan fin a mi vivir.

Mi morir que va llegando
esclaresce mis clamores
que la muerte no penando,
fueran muertos mis dolores:
y partido para el cielo,
si quién soy queréis oir
yo diré: "Qué desconsuelo
yo vestido con un duelo,
que morí por no morir!"

JUAN DEL ENCINA

(*c.* 1468–*c.* 1529)

Villancico

Anda acá, pastor,
a ver al Redemptor.

Anda acá, Minguillo,
deja tu ganado,
toma el caramillo,
zurrón e cayado:
vamos sin temor
a ver al Redemptor.

No nos aballemos
sin llevar presente;
mas ¿qué llevaremos?
Dílo tú, Llorente.
¿Qué será mejor
para el Redemptor?

Yo quiero llevarle
leche y mantequillas,
e para empañarle
algunas mantillas,
por ir con amor
a ver al Redemptor.

Con aquel cabrito
de la cabra mocha
darle algún quesito
e una miga cocha,
que terná sabor,
sabor al Redemptor.

Villancico

Ya cerradas son las puertas
de mi vida
y la llave es ya perdida.

Tiénelas tan bien cerradas
el portero del Amor;
no tiene ningún temor
que de mí sean quebradas.
Son las puertas ya cerradas
de mi vida,
y la llave es ya perdida.

Las puertas son mis servicios,
la cerradura es olvido,
la llave que s' ha perdido
es perder los beneficios.
Así que fuera de quicios
va mi vida,
y la llave es ya perdida.

Puse la vida en poder
d' aquella que siempre amo;
ahora triste, aunque llamo,
no me quiere responder.
Cerróme con su poder
la salida,
y la llave es ya perdida.

FIN

Servíla con tanta fe,
con cuanta nadie sirvió;
el galardón que me dió
fué peor que nunca fué.
Cerróme no sé por qué
la salida
y la llave es ya perdida.

Villancico

No te tardes que me muero,
carcelero,
no te tardes que me muero.

Apresura tu venida
porque no pierda la vida,
que la fe no está perdida.
Carcelero,
no te tardes que me muero.

Bien sabes que la tardanza
trae gran desconfianza;
ven y cumple mi esperanza.
Carcelero,
no te tardes que me muero.

Sácame desta cadena,
que recibo muy gran pena,
pues tu tardar me condena.
Carcelero,
no te tardes que me muero.

La primera vez que me viste
sin te vencer me venciste;
suéltame pues me prendiste.
Carcelero,
no te tardes que me muero. . . .

Canción

¡Ay triste, que vengo
vencido d' amor,
maguera pastor!

Más sano me fuera
no ir al mercado
que no que viniera
tan aquerenciado
que vengo cuitado,
vencido d'amor,
maguera pastor . . .

Con vista halaguera
miréla y miróme.
Yo no sé quién era,
mas ella agradóme,
y fuése y dejóme
vencido d' amor,
maguera pastor . . .

FIN

Sin dar yo tras ella
no cuido ser vivo,
pues que por querella
de mi soy esquivo,
y estoy muy cativo,
vencido d' amor,
maguera pastor.

GARCÍA DE RESENDE

(? † 1536)

Villancico

Mira gentil dama,
el tu servidor
cómo está triste
con tanto dolor.

Mira que merezco
no ser desamado
ni tan olvidado
pues tanto padezco.
Y pues con dolor
mi vida te llama,
mira, gentil dama,
el tu servidor.

Pues tu hermosura
causó mi dolor,
mira mi tristura
y tu disfavor.
No trates peor
el que más te ama,
mira, gentil dama,
el tu servidor.

GIL VICENTE

(1470–1536)

Canciones

I

¡ Sañosa está la niña !
¡ Ay, Dios !, ¿ quién le hablaría ?

En la sierra anda la niña
su ganado a repastar,
hermosa como las flores,
sañosa como la mar.
Sañosa como la mar
está la niña.
¡ Ay, Dios !, ¿ quién le hablaría ?

II

Muy graciosa es la doncella,
¡ cómo es bella y hermosa !

Digas tú, el marinero
que en las naves vivías,
si la nave o la vela o la estrella
es tan bella.

Digas tú, el caballero
que las armas vestías,
si el caballo o las armas o la guerra
es tan bella.

Digas tú, el pastorcico
que el ganadico guardas,
si el ganado o los valles o la sierra
es tan bella.

III

En la huerta nace la rosa:
quiérome ir allá
por mirar al ruiseñor
cómo cantaba.

Por las riberas del río
limones coge la virgo:
quiérome ir allá
por mirar al ruiseñor
cómo cantaba.

Limones cogía la virgo
para dar al su amigo:
quiérome ir allá
para ver al ruiseñor
cómo cantaba.

Para dar al su amigo
en un sombrero de sirgo:
quiérome ir allá
para ver al ruiseñor
cómo cantaba.

IV

Consuelo, vete con Dios.
Pues ves la vida que sigo,
¡no pierdas tiempo comigo!

Consuelo mal empleado,
no consueles mi tristura:
¡vete a quien tiene ventura,
y deja el desventurado!
No quiero ser consolado,
antes me pesa contigo,
¡no pierdas tiempo comigo!

LUCAS FERNÁNDEZ

(*c.* 1474–1542)

Villancico

En esta montaña
de gran hermosura
tomemos holgura.

Haremos cabaña
de rosas y flores
en esta montaña
cercada de amores,
y nuestros dolores
y nuestra tristura
tornarse ha en holgura.

Gran gozo y placer
aquí tomaremos
y amor y querer
aquí nos ternemos;
y aquí viviremos
en grande frescura
en esta verdura.

ANÓNIMO

Seguidillas de los siglos XVI y XVII

I

Al espejo se toca
el sol de mi vida
dando luz a la luna
donde se mira.

II

Negra la cara, negro
el corazón,
que como amores fuego
volvióm' en carbón.

III

Río de Sivilla
quien te pasase,
sin que la mi servilla
se me mojase.

IV

Río de Sivilla,
arenas de oro,
desa banda tienes
el bien que adoro.

CANCIONERO ANÓNIMO

Canciones cortas

I

Luna que reluces,
toda la noche alumbres.

Ay, luna que reluces
blanca y plateada,
toda la noche alumbres
a mi linda enamorada.
Amada que reluces,
toda la noche alumbres.

II

A Salamanca, el escolarillo,
a Salamanca irás.

Irás a do no te vean
ni te escuchen ni te crean,
pues a las que te desean
tan ingrato pago das.
A Salamanca, el escolarillo,
a Salamanca irás.

III

Que no cogeré yo verbena
la mañana de San Juan,
pues mis amores se van.

Que no cogeré yo claveles,
madreselva ni mirabeles,
sino penas tan crueles
cual jamás se cogerán,
pues mis amores se van.

IV

En Ávila, mis ojos,
dentro en Ávila.

En Ávila del Río
mataron a mi amigo
dentro en Ávila.

V

¡ Ay que non era,
mas ay, que non hay
quien de mi pena se duela !

Madre, la mi madre
el mi lindo amigo
moricos de allende
lo llevan cativo ;
cadenas de oro,
candado morisco.

¡ Ay que non era
mas ay, que non hay
quien de mi pena se duela !

VI

Mi vida nunca reposa,
¡Triste yo!
porque en veros se perdió.

En miraros tan esquiva
me sentí el corazón
tan lleno de passión,
que me da mortal fatiga.
Ya de mí no sé que diga.
¡Triste yo!
pues la vida se perdió.

VII

Entra Mayo y sale Abril
tan garridico le vi venir.

Entra Mayo con sus flores
sale Abril con sus amores,
y los dulces amadores
comienzan a bien servir.

VIII

A los baños del amor
sola m' iré
y en ellos me bañaré.

Porque sane deste mal
que me causa desventura
qu' es un dolor tan mortal
que destruye mi figura.
A los baños de tristura
sola m' iré
y en ellos me bañaré.

IX

Si lo dicen, digan
   alma mía,
si lo dicen, digan.

   Dicen que vos quiero
y que por vos me muero
dicho es verdadero,
   alma mía
si lo dicen, digan.

Canción de la mal casada

   Miraba la mar
la mal casada,
que miraba la mar
cómo es ancha y larga.

   Descuidos ajenos
y propios gemidos
tienen sus sentidos
de pesares llenos.
Con ojos serenos
la mal casada,
que miraba la mar
cómo es ancha y larga.

   Muy ancho es el mar
que miran sus ojos,
aunque a sus enojos
bien puede igualar.
Mas por se alegrar
la mal casada,
que miraba la mar
cómo es ancha y larga.

Canción de amigo

Al alba venid, buen amigo,
al alba venid.

Amigo, el que yo más quería,
venid al alba del día.

Amigo, el que yo más amaba,
venid a la luz del alba.

Venid a la luz del día,
no traigáis compañía.

Venid a la luz del alba,
no traigáis gran compaña.

Canción de romería

So ell encina, encina,
so ell encina.

Yo me iba, mi madre,
a la romería ;
por ir más devota
fuí sin compañía :
so ell encina. . . .

Por ir más devota
fuí sin compañía ;
tomé otro camino,
dejé el que tenía ;
so ell encina.

Halléme perdida
en una montiña,
echéme a dormir
al pie dell encina :
so ell encina.

A la media noche
recordé, mezquina;
halléme en los brazos
del que más quería:
so ell encina.

Pesóme, cuitada,
de que amanecía,
porque yo gozaba
del que más quería:
so ell encina.

Muy bendita sía
la tal romería,
so ell encina.

Canción de las tres morillas

Tres morillas me enamoran
en Jaén:
Axa y Fátima y Marién.

Tres morillas tan garridas
iban a coger olivas,
y hallábanlas cogidas
en Jaén:
Axa y Fátima y Marién.

Y hallábanlas cogidas,
y tornaban desmaídas
y las colores perdidas
en Jaén:
Axa y Fátima y Marién.

Tres moricas tan lozanas,
tres moricas tan lozanas

iban a coger manzanas
a Jaén:
Axa y Fátima y Marién.

Canción

Que no quiero amores
en Ingalaterra,
pues otros mejores
tengo yo en mi tierra.

No quiero ni estimo
ser favorecido;
de amores me eximo,
qu' es tiempo perdido
seguir a Cupido
en Ingalaterra,
pues otros mejores
tengo yo en mi tierra.

¿Qué favores puede
darme la fortuna,
por mucho que ruede
el sol ni la luna,
ni mujer alguna
en Ingalaterra,
pues otros mejores
tengo yo en mi tierra?

Que cuando allá vaya,
a fe yo lo fío,
buen galardón haya
del servicio mío;
que son desvarío
los de Ingalaterra,
pues otros mejores
tengo yo en mi tierra.

CRISTÓBAL DE CASTILLEJO

(*c.* 1490–1550)

Soneto

Garcilaso y Boscán, siendo llegados
al lugar donde están los trovadores
que en esta nuestra lengua y sus primores
fueron en este siglo señalados,
los unos a los otros alterados
se miran, demudadas las colores,
temiéndose que fuesen corredores
o espías o enemigos desmandados;
y juzgando primero por el traje,
pareciéronles ser, como debía,
gentiles españoles caballeros;
y oyéndoles hablar nuevo lenguaje
mezclado de extranjera poesía,
con ojos los miraban de extranjeros.

Décimas

Mas ellos, caso que estaban
sin favor y tan a solas,
contra todos se mostraban
y claramente burlaban
de las coplas españolas,
canciones y villancicos,
romances y cosa tal
arte mayor y real,
y pies quebrados y chicos
y todo nuestro caudal.

Y en lugar de estas maneras
de vocablos ya sabidos
en nuestras trovas caseras,
cantan otras forasteras,
nuevas a nuestros oídos;
sonetos de grande estima,

madrigales y canciones
de diferentes renglones,
de tercia y octava rima,
y otras lindas invenciones . . .

Canción de una aldeana

Aquí no hay
sino ver y desear
aquí no veo
sino morir con deseo.

Madre, un caballero
qu'estaba en este corro
a cada vuelta
hacíame del ojo.
Yo como era bonica
teníaselo en poco.

Madre, un escudero
qu'estaba en esta baila
a cada vuelta
asíame de la manga.
Yo, como era bonica
teníaselo en poco.

Canción

Aquel caballero, madre
como a mí le quiero yo
y remedio no le dó.

Él me quiere más que a sí,
yo le mato de cruel;
mas en serlo contra él
también lo soy contra mí.
De verle penar así
muy penada vivo yo,
y remedio no le dó.

JUAN BOSCNÁ
(c. 1493–1542)

Soneto

En alta mar rompido está el navío
con tempestad y temoroso viento;
pero la luz que ya amanecer siento,
y aun el cielo, me hacen que confío.
La estrella con la cual mi noche guío,
a vueltas de mi triste lasamiento,
alzo los ojos por miralla atento,
y dice que si alargo, el puerto es mío.
Da luego un viento que nos da por popa;
a manera de nubes vemos tierra,
y ha rato ya que dicen que la vimos.
Ya comenzamos a enjugar la ropa,
y a encarecer del mar la brava guerra,
y a recontar los votos que hicimos.

Soneto

Como, después del tempestoso día,
la tarde clara suele ser sabrosa,
y después de la noche tenebrosa,
el resplandor del sol placer envía;
así en su padecer el alma mía
con la tarde del bien es tan gozosa,
que se entrega, en un hora que reposa,
de todos los trabajos que tenía.
Mas este bien no suele ser barato;
mucho cuesta tan fuerte medicina,
y es lo peor que presto ha de pagarse.
Es reposar de un hombre que camina,
que a la sombra descansa un breve rato,
para luego volver a más cansarse.

Canción

Claros y frescos ríos
que mansamente vais
siguiendo vuestro natural camino;
desiertos montes míos,
que en un estado estáis
de soledad muy triste de contino;
aves, en quien hay tino
de descansar cantando;
árboles que vivís,
y en fin también morís,
y estáis perdiendo a tiempos y ganando;
oídme juntamente
mi voz amarga, ronca y tan doliente.
Pues quiso mi ventura
que hubiese de apartarme
de quien jamás osé pensar partirme;
en tanta desventura
conviene consolarme,
que no es agora tiempo de morirme.
El alma ha de estar firme:
que en un tan bajo estado
vergonzosa es la muerte;
si acabo en mal tan fuerte,
todos dirán que voy desesperado;
y quien tan bien amó
no es bien que digan que tan mal murió. . . .

Las horas estoy viendo
en ella, y los momentos:
y cada cosa pongo en su razón.
Conmigo acá la entiendo:
pienso sus pensamientos:
por mí saco los suyos cuáles son.
Díceme el corazón,
y pienso yo que acierta;
" Ya está alegre, ya triste;

ya sale, ya se viste;
agora duerme, agora está despierta."
El sesó y el amor
andan por quién la pintara mejor. . . .

El vano imaginar
en yéndoseme, cayo
en cómo para vella no hay remedio.
Allí empiezo a pensar,
y en el pensar desmayo,
de ver cuántos lugares dejo en medio.
Si entonces me remedio,
rasgo más la herida.
Viénenseme a los ojos
los presentes enojos,
y los gozos de la pasada vida.
Cada palmo de tierra
para mí triste es ora una gran sierra.
Tengo en el alma puesto
su gesto tan hermoso,
y aquel saber estar adonde quiera;
el recoger honesto,
el alegre reposo,
el no sé qué de no sé qué manera;
y con llaneza entera
el saber descansado,
el dulce trato hablando,
el acudir callando,
y aquel grave mirar disimulado.
Todo esto está ausente,
y otro tiempo lo tuve muy presente.
Contando estoy los días
que paso no sé como;
con los pasados no oso entrar en cuenta.
Acuden fantasías;
allí a llorar me tomo,
de ver tanta flaqueza en tanta afrenta.
Allí se me presenta

la llaga del penar.
Hácenseme mil años
las horas de mis daños;
por otra parte, el siempre imaginar
me hace parecer
que cuanto he pasado fué ayer. . . .

Canción: bien sé donde volver querrías,
y la que ver deseas;
pero no quiero que sin mí la veas.

Villancico

Si no os hubiera mirado,
no penara:
pero tampoco os mirara.
Veros harto mal ha sido,
mas no veros peor fuera;
no quedara tan perdido,
pero mucho más perdiera.
¿Qué viera aquel que no os viera?
¿Cuál quedara,
señora, si no os mirara?

GARCILASO DE LA VEGA

(1503–36)

Canción

Nadie puede ser dichoso,
señora, ni desdichado,
sino que os haya mirado.
Porque la gloria de veros
en ese punto se quita
que se piensa mereceros.
Así que, sin conoceros,

nadie puede ser dichoso,
señora, ni desdichado,
sino que os haya mirado.

‘ *Saliendo de las ondas encendido . . .* ’

[The shepherds’ colloquy.]

. . . Saliendo de las ondas encendido
rayaba de los montes el altura
el sol, cuando Salicio, recostado
al pie de una alta haya, en la verdura,
por donde una agua clara con sonido
atravesaba el fresco y verde prado,
él, con canto acordado
al rumor que sonaba
del agua que pasaba,
se quejaba tan dulce y blandamente
como si no estuviera de allí ausente
la que de su dolor culpa tenía:
y así como presente,
razonando con ella le decía.

SALICIO

¡ Oh más dura que mármol a mis quejas,
y al encendido fuego en que me quemo
más helada que nieve, Galatea!
Estoy muriendo, y aun la vida temo,
témola con razón, pues tú me dejas;
que no hay, sin ti, el vivir para qué sea.
Vergüenza he que me vea
ninguno en tal estado,
de ti desamparado,
y de mí mismo yo me corro agora.
¿ De un alma te desdeñas ser señora
donde siempre moraste, no pudiendo
della salir un hora?
Salid sin duelo, lágrimas, corriendo.

El sol tiende los rayos de su lumbre
por montes y por valles, despertando
las aves y animales y la gente:
cuál por el aire claro va volando,
cuál por el verde valle o alta cumbre
paciendo va segura y libremente:
cuál, con el sol presente,
va de nuevo al oficio
y al usado ejercicio
do su natura o menester le inclina;
siempre está en llanto esta ánima mezquina,
cuando la sombra el mundo va cubriendo,
o la luz se avecina.
Salid sin duelo, lágrimas, corriendo. . . .

Por ti el silencio de la selva umbrosa,
por ti la esquividad y apartamiento
del solitario monte me agradaba:
por ti la verde yerba, el fresco viento,
el blanco lirio y colorada rosa
y dulce primavera deseaba.
¡ Ay, cuánto me engañaba!
¡ Ay, cuán diferente era,
y cuán de otra manera
lo que en tu falso pecho se escondía!
Bien claro con su voz me lo decía
la siniestra corneja repitiendo
la desventura mía.
Salid sin duelo, lágrimas, corriendo. . . .

Tu dulce habla, ¿en cúya oreja suena?
Tus claros ojos, ¿a quién los volviste?
¿Por quién tan sin respeto me trocaste?
Tu quebrantada fe, ¿dó la pusiste?
¿Cuál es el cuello que, como en cadena,
de tus hermosos brazos anudaste?
No hay corazón que baste,

aunque fuese de piedra,
viendo mi amada yedra
de mí arrancada, en otro muro asida,
y mi parra en otro olmo entretejida,
que no se esté con llanto deshaciendo
hasta acabar la vida.
Salid sin duelo, lágrimas corriendo. . . .

¿Cómo te vine en tanto menosprecio?
¿Cómo te fuí tan presto aborrecible?
¿Cómo te faltó en mí el conocimiento?
Si no tuvieras condición terrible,
siempre fuera tenido de ti en precio,
y no viera de ti este apartamiento.
¿No sabes que sin cuento
buscan en el estío
mis ovejas el frío
de la sierra de Cuenca, y el gobierno
del abrigado Estremo en el invierno?
Mas ¿qué vale el tener, si derritiendo
me estoy en llanto eterno?
Salid sin duelo, lágrimas, corriendo. . . .

Mas ya que a socorrerme aquí no vienes,
no dejes el lugar que tanto amaste;
que bien podrás venir de mí segura;
y dejaré el lugar do me dejaste;
ven si por sólo esto te detienes.
Ves aquí un prado lleno de verdura,
ves aquí una espesura,
ves aquí una agua clara,
en otro tiempo cara,
a quien de ti con lágrimas me quejo.
Quizá aquí hallarás, pues yo me alejo,
al que todo mi bien quitarme puede;
que pues el bien le dejo,
no es mucho que al lugar también le quede.

Aquí dió fin a su cantar Salicio,
y suspirando en el postrero acento,
soltó de llanto una profunda vena.
Queriendo el monte al grave sentimiento
de aquel dolor en algo ser propicio,
con la pesada voz retumba y suena.
La blanda Filomena,
casi como dolida
y a compasión movida,
dulcemente responde al son lloroso.
Lo que cantó tras esto Nemoroso
decidlo vos, Piérides; que tanto
no puedo yo ni oso,
que siento enflaquecer mi débil canto.

NEMOROSO

Corrientes aguas, puras, cristalinas;
árboles que os estáis mirando en ellas,
verde prado de fresca sombra lleno,
aves que aquí sembráis vuestras querellas,
yedra que por los árboles caminas,
torciendo el paso por su verde seno;
yo me vi tan ajeno
del grave mal que siento,
que de puro contento
con vuestra soledad me recreaba,
donde con dulce sueño reposaba,
o con el pensamiento discurría
por donde no hallaba
sino memorias llenas de alegría;

y en este mismo valle donde agora
me entristezco y me canso, en el reposo
estuve ya contento y descansado.
¡Oh bien caduco, vano y presuroso!
Acuérdate durmiendo aquí algún hora,
que despertando, a Elisa vi a mi lado.

¡Oh miserable hado!
¡Oh tela delicada,
antes de tiempo dada
a los agudos filos de la muerte!
Más convenible fuera aquesta suerte
a los cansados años de mi vida,
que es más que el hierro fuerte,
pues no la ha quebrantado tu partida. . . .

¿Quién me dijera, Elisa, vida mía,
cuando en aqueste valle al fresco viento
andábamos cogiendo tiernas flores,
que había de ver con largo apartamiento
venir el triste y solitario día
que diese amargo fin a mis amores?
El cielo en mis dolores
cargó la mano tanto,
que a sempiterno llanto
y a triste soledad me ha condenado:
y lo que siento más es verme atado
a la pesada vida y enojosa,
solo, desamparado,
ciego sin lumbre en cárcel tenebrosa. . . .

Como al partir del sol la sombra crece,
y en cayendo su rayo se levanta
la negra escuridad que el mundo cubre,
de do viene el temor que nos espanta,
y la medrosa forma en que se ofrece
aquello que la noche nos encubre,
hasta que el sol descubre
su luz pura y hermosa,
tal es la tenebrosa
noche de tu partir, en que he quedado
de sombra y de temor atormentado,
hasta que muerte el tiempo determine
que a ver el deseado
sol de tu clara vista me encamine.

Cual suele el ruiseñor con triste canto
quejarse, entre las hojas escondido,
del duro labrador, que cautamente
le despojó su caro y dulce nido
de los tiernos hijuelos, entre tanto
que del amado ramo estaba ausente,
y aquel dolor que siente,
con diferencia tanta
por la dulce garganta
despide, y a su canto el aire suena,
y la callada noche no refrena
su lamentable oficio y sus querellas,
trayendo de su pena
al cielo por testigo y las estrellas;

desta manera suelto yo la rienda
a mi dolor, y así me quejo en vano
de la dureza de la muerte airada.
Ella en mi corazón metió la mano,
y de allí me llevó mi dulce prenda,
que aquél era su nido y su morada.
¡Ay muerte arrebatada!
Por ti me estoy quejando
al cielo, y enojando
con importuno llanto al mundo todo.
Tan desigual dolor no sufre modo.
No me podrán quitar el dolorido
sentir, si ya del todo
primero no me quitan el sentido. . . .

Divina Elisa, pues agora el cielo
con inmortales pies pisas y mides,
y su mudanza ves, estando queda,
¿por qué de mí te olvidas, y no pides
que se apresure el tiempo en que este velo
rompa del cuerpo, y verme libre pueda,
y en la tercera rueda

contigo mano a mano
busquemos otro llano,
busquemos otros montes y otros ríos,
otros valles floridos y sombríos,
donde descanse y siempre pueda verte
ante los ojos míos,
sin miedo y sobresalto de perderte?

Nunca pusieran fin al triste lloro
los pastores, ni fueran acabadas
las canciones que sólo el monte oía,
si mirando las nubes coloradas,
al trasmontar del sol bordadas de oro,
no vieran que era ya pasado el día.
La sombra se veía
venir corriendo apriesa
ya por la falda espesa
del altísimo monte, y recordando
ambos como de sueño, y acabando
el fugitivo sol, de luz escaso,
su ganado llevando,
se fueron recogiendo paso a paso.

Égloga I

Sonetos

I

Cuando me paro a contemplar mi estado,
y a ver los pasos por do me ha traído,
hallo, según por do anduve perdido,
que a mayor mal pudiera haber llegado.
Mas cuando del camino estoy olvidado,
a tanto mal no sé por do he venido;
sé que me acabo, y más he yo sentido
ver acabar conmigo mi cuidado.
Yo acabaré, que me entregué sin arte
a quien sabrá perderme y acabarme,

si ella quisiere, y aun sabrá querello
que pues mi voluntad puede matarme,
la suya, que no es tanto de mi parte,
pudiendo, ¿qué hará sino hacello?

VI

Por ásperos caminos he llegado
a parte que de miedo no me muevo;
y si a mudarme o dar un paso pruebo,
allí por los cabellos soy tornado.
Mas tal estoy que con la muerte al lado
busco de mi vivir consejo nuevo;
conozco lo mejor, lo peor apruebo,
o por costumbre mala, o por mi hado.
Por otra parte el breve tiempo mío,
y el errado proceso de mis años
en su primer principio y en su medio,
mi inclinación, con quien yo no porfío,
la cierta muerte, fin de tantos daños,
me hacen descuidar de mi remedio.

XXIII

En tanto que de rosa y azucena
se muestra la color en vuestro gesto,
y que vuestro mirar ardiente, honesto,
enciende el corazón y lo refrena,
y en tanto que el cabello, que en la vena
del oro se encogió, con vuelo presto
por el hermoso cuello blanco, enhiesto,
el viento mueve, esparce y desordena;
coged de vuestra alegre primavera
el dulce fruto, antes que al tiempo airado
cubra de nieve la hermosa cumbre.
Marchitará la rosa el viento helado;
todo lo mudará la edad ligera,
por no hacer mudanza en su costumbre.

XXVII

Amor, amor, un habito vestí
el cual de vuestro paño fué cortado;
al vestir ancho fué, mas apretado
y estrecho cuando estuvo sobre mí.
Después acá de lo que consentí
tal arrepentimiento me ha tornado,
que pruebo alguna vez de congojado
a romper esto en que yo me metí.
Mas ¿quién podrá deste hábito librarse,
teniendo tan contraria su natura,
que con él ha venido a conformarse?
Si alguna parte queda por ventura
de mi razón, por mí no osa mostrarse;
que en tal contradición no está segura.

Epístola a Boscán

Señor Boscán, quien tanto gusto tiene
de daros cuenta de los pensamientos,
hasta en las cosas que no tienen nombre,
no le podrá faltar en vos materia,
ni será menester buscar estilo
presto, distinto, de ornamento puro,
tal cual a culta epístola conviene.
Entre muy grandes bienes que consigo
el amistad perfecta nos concede,
es aqueste descuido suelto y puro,
lejos de la curiosa pesadumbre;
y así de aquesta libertad gozando,
digo que vine, cuanto a lo primero,
tan sano como aquel que en doce días
lo que sólo veréis ha caminado
cuando el fin de la carta os lo mostrare.
Alargo y suelto a su placer la rienda,
mucho más que al caballo, al pensamiento,
y llévame a las veces por camino

tan dulce y agradable que me hace
olvidar el trabajo del pasado.
Otras me lleva por tan duros pasos,
que con la fuerza del afán presente
también de los pasados se me olvida.
A veces sigo un agradable medio
honesto y reposado, en que el discurso
del gusto y del ingenio se ejercita.
Iba pensando y discurriendo un día
a cuántos bienes alargó la mano
el que de la amistad mostró el camino;
y luego vos de la amistad ejemplo
os me ofrecéis en estos pensamientos.
Y con vos a lo menos me acontece
una gran cosa al parecer estraña,
y porque la sepáis en pocos versos,
es que considerando los provechos,
las honras y los gustos que me vienen
desta vuestra amistad, que en tanto tengo,
ninguna cosa en mayor precio estimo,
ni me hace gozar del dulce estado
tanto como el amor de parte mía.
Éste conmigo tiene tanta fuerza,
que sabiendo muy bien las otras partes
de la amistad, de la estrecheza nuestra,
con sólo aquéste el alma se enternece;
y yo sé que otramente me aprovecha,
que el deleite, que suele ser pospuesto
a las útiles cosas y a las graves.
Llévame a escudriñar la causa desto
ver contino tan recio en mí el efeto;
y hallo que el provecho, el ornamento,
el gusto y el placer que se me sigue
del vínculo de amor que nuestro genio
enredó sobre nuestros corazones,
son cosas que de mí no salen fuera,
y en mí el provecho sólo se convierte.
Mas el amor (de donde por ventura

nacen todas las cosas, si hay algunas
que a vuestra utilidad y gusto miren)
es razón grande que en mayor estima
tenido sea de mí, que todo el resto,
cuanto más generosa y alta parte
es el hacer el bien, que el recebillo.
así que amando me deleito, y hallo
que no es locura este deleite mío.
¡Oh cuán corrido estoy, y arrepentido
de haberos alabado el tratamiento
del camino de Francia y las posadas!
corrido de que ya por mentiroso
con razón me tendréis, arrepentido
de haber perdido tiempo en alabaros
cosa tan digna ya de vituperio;
donde no hallaréis sino mentiras,
vinos acedos, camareras feas,
varletes codiciosos, malas postas,
gran paga, poco argén, largo camino;
llegar al fin a Nápoles, no habiendo
dejado allá enterrado algún tesoro,
salvo sino decís que es enterrado
lo que nunca se halla ni se tiene.
A mi señor Dural estrechamente
abrazad de mi parte, si pudierdes.
Doce del mes de octubre, de la tierra
do nació el claro fuego del Petrarca,
y donde están del fuego las cenizas.[1]

[1] Written in 1534, probably from Avignon, where Petrarch first saw Laura and where he is buried.

DIEGO HURTADO DE MENDOZA

(1503–75)

Soneto

Tu gracia, tu valor, tu hermosura,
muestra de todo el cielo, retratada,

como cosa que está sobre natura,
ni pudiera ser vista ni pintada.
  Pero ya que en el alma tu figura
tengo, en humana forma abreviada,
tal hice retratarte de pintura,
que el amor te dejó en ella estampada.
  No por ambición vana o por memoria
tuya, o ya por manifestar mis males;
mas por verte más veces que te veo,
  y por sólo gozar de tanta gloria,
señora, con los ojos corporales,
como con los del alma y del deseo.

SANTA TERESA DE JESÚS

(1515–82)

Versos nacidos del fuego del amor de Dios

Vivo sin vivir en mí,
y tan alta vida espero,
que muero porque no muero.

Aquesta divina unión,
del amor con que yo vivo,
haze a Dios ser mi cativo,
y libre mi corazón:
mas causa en mi tal pasión
ver a Dios mi prisionero,
que muero porque no muero.

¡Ay! qué larga es esta vida,
qué duros estos destierros,
esta cárcel, y estos hierros,
en que el alma está metida!
Sólo esperar la salida
me causa un dolor tan fiero,
que muero porque no muero.

¡ Ay ! qué vida tan amarga
do no se goza el Señor !
y si es dulce el amor,
no lo es la esperanza larga ;
quíteme Dios esta carga,
más pesada que de acero,
que muero porque no muero.

Sólo con la confianza
vivo dé que he de morir ;
porque muriendo el vivir
me asegura mi esperanza :
muerte do el vivir se alcanza,
no te tardes que te espero,
que muero porque no muero.

Mira que el amor es fuerte ;
vida, no seas molesta ;
mira que sólo te resta,
para ganarte, perderte ;
venga ya la dulce muerte,
venga el morir muy ligero,
que muero porque no muero.

Aquella vida de arriba
es la vida verdadera :
hasta que esta vida muera,
no se goza estando viva :
muerte no seas esquiva ;
vivo muriendo primero,
que muero porque no muero.

Vida, ¿ qué puedo yo darle
a mi Dios, que vive en mí
si no es perderte a ti,
para mejor a Él gozarle ?
Quiero muriendo alcanzarle,
pues a Él solo es el que quiero,
que muero porque no muero.

Estando ausente de ti,
¿ qué vida puedo tener,
sino muerte padecer
la mayor que nunca vi ?
Lástima tengo de mí,
por ser mi mal tan entero,
que muero porque no muero . . .

FRANCISCO DE LA TORRE

(*c.* 1534–94)

Oda

Tirsis, ¡ ah Tirsis ! vuelve y endereza
tu navecilla contratada y frágil
a la seguridad del puerto ; mira
que se te cierra el cielo.

El frío Boreas, y el ardiente Noto,
apoderados de la mar insana,
anegaron agora en este piélago
una dichosa nave.

Clamó la gente mísera, y el cielo
escondió los clamores y gemidos
entre los rayos y espantosos truenos
de su turbada cara.

¡ Ay ! que me dice tu animoso pecho
que tus atrevimientos mal regidos
te ordenan algún caso desastrado
al romper de tu Oriente.

No ves cuitado, que el hinchado Noto
trae en sus remolinos polvorosos
las imitadas mal seguras alas
de un atrevido mozo.

No ves que la tormenta rigurosa
viene del abrasado monte, donde
yace muriendo vivo el temerario
Enzelado y Tipheo.

Conoce, desdichado, tu fortuna,
y prevén a tu mal: que la desdicha
prevenida con tiempo, no penetra
tanto como la súbita.

¡ Ay ! que te pierdes; vuelve, Tirsis, vuelve,
tierra, tierra que brama tu navío,
hecho prisión, y cueva sonorosa
de los hinchados vientos.

Allá se avenga el mar, allá se avengan
los mal regidos súbditos del fiero
Eolo, con soberbios navegantes
que su furor desprecian.

Miremos la tormenta rigurosa
dende la playa, que el airado cielo
menos se encruelece de contino
con quien se anima menos.

HERNANDO DE ACUÑA

(*c.* 1520–*c.* 1585)

Al rey nuestro señor

Ya se acerca, señor, o es ya llegada
la edad gloriosa en que promete el cielo
una grey, y un pastor solo en el suelo,
por suerte a vuestros tiempos reservada;
ya tan alto principio en tal jornada
os muestra el fin de vuestro santo celo,
y anuncia al mundo para más consuelo
un monarca, un imperio y una espada:

Ya el orbe de la tierra siente en parte
y espera en todo vuestra monarquía
conquistada por vos en justa guerra,
que a quien ha dado Cristo su estandarte,
dará el segundo más dichoso día
en que vencido el mar, venza la tierra.

ANÓNIMO

(sixteenth century)

A Cristo crucificado

No me mueve, mi Dios, para quererte,
el cielo que me tienes prometido,
ni me mueve el infierno tan temido
para dejar por eso de ofenderte.
Tú me mueves, Señor; muéveme el verte
clavado en esa cruz, y escarnecido;
muéveme el ver tu cuerpo tan herido;
muévenme tus afrentas, y tu muerte.
Muéveme, al fin, tu amor, y en tal manera,
que aunque no hubiera cielo, yo te amara,
y aunque no hubiera infierno te temiera.
No me tienes que dar porque te quiera;
pues aunque lo que espero no esperara,
lo mismo que te quiero te quisiera.

GUTIERRE DE CETINA

(1526–60)

Madrigales

I

Ojos claros, serenos,
si de un dulce mirar sois alabados,
¿por qué, si me miráis, miráis airados?
Si cuanto más piadosos

más bellos parecéis a aquel que os mira.
no me miráis con ira,
porque no parezcáis menos hermosos.
¡ Ay, tormentos rabiosos !
Ojos claros, serenos,
ya que así me miráis, miradme al menos.

II

Cubrir los bellos ojos
con la mano que ya me tiene muerto
cautela fué por cierto ;
que ansí doblar pensastes mis enojos,
pero de tal cautela
harto mayor ha sido el bien que el daño ;
que el resplandor extraño
del sol se puede ver mientra se cela.
Así que, aunque pensastes
cubrir vuestra beldad, única, inmensa
yo os perdono la ofensa,
pues cubiertos, mejor verlos dejastes.

FRAY LUIS DE LEÓN

(1529–91)

Vida retirada

¡ Qué descansada vida
la del que huye el mundanal ruido
y sigue la escondida
senda por donde han ido
los pocos sabios que en el mundo han sido !

Que no le enturbia el pecho
de los soberbios grandes el estado,
ni del dorado techo
se admira, fabricado
del sabio moro, en jaspes sustentado.

No cura si la fama
canta con voz su nombre pregonera,
ni cura si encarama
la lengua lisonjera
lo que condena la verdad sincera.

¿ Qué presta a mi contento,
si soy del vano dedo señalado,
si en busca de este viento
ando desalentado
con ansias vivas, con mortal cuidado ?

¡ Oh monte, oh fuente, oh río !
¡ Oh secreto seguro, deleitoso !
Roto casi el navío
a vuestro almo reposo,
huyo de aqueste mar tempestuoso.

Un no rompido sueño,
un día puro, alegre, libre quiero ;
no quiero ver el ceño
vanamente severo
de quien la sangre ensalza o el dinero.

Despiértenme las aves
con su cantar sabroso no aprendido,
no los cuidados graves
de que es siempre seguido
el que al ajeno arbitrio está atenido.

Vivir quiero conmigo,
gozar quiero del bien que debo al cielo
a solas, sin testigo,
libre de amor, de celo,
de odio, de esperanzas, de recelo.

Del monte en la ladera
por mi mano plantado tengo un huerto,

que con la primavera,.
de bella flor cubierto,
ya muestra en esperanza el fruto cierto.

Y como codiciosa
por ver y acrecentar su hermosura,
desde la cumbre airosa
una fontana pura
hasta llegar corriendo se apresura.

Y luego sosegada,
el paso entre los árboles torciendo,
el suelo de pasada
de verdura vistiendo,
y con diversas flores va esparciendo.

El aire el huerto orea
y ofrece mil olores al sentido,
los árboles menea
con un manso rüido
que del oro y del cetro pone olvido.

Ténganse su tesoro
los que de un falso leño se confían:
no es mío ver el lloro
de los que desconfían
cuando el cierzo y el ábrego porfían.

La combatida antena
cruje, y en ciega noche el claro día
se torna, al cielo suena
confusa vocería,
y la mar enriquecen a porfía.

A mí una pobrecilla
mesa de amable paz bien abastada
me basta, y la vajilla
de fino oro labrada
sea de quien la mar no teme airada.

Y mientras miserable-
mente se están los otros abrasando
con sed insacïable
del no durable mando,
tendido yo a la sombra esté cantando

A la sombra tendido,
de hiedra y lauro eterno coronado,
puesto el atento oído
al son dulce, acordado,
del plectro sabiamente meneado.

En la Ascensión

¿Y dejas, Pastor santo,
tu grey en este valle hondo, escuro,
con soledad y llanto,
y tú rompiendo el puro
aire, te vas al inmortal seguro?

Los antes bienhadados,
y los agora tristes y afligidos,
a tus pechos criados,
de ti desposeídos,
¿a dó convertirán ya sus sentidos?

¿Qué mirarán los ojos
que vieron de tu rostro la hermosura,
que no les sea enojos?
Quien oyó tu dulzura,
¿qué no tendrá por sordo y desventura?

Aqueste mar turbado,
¿Quién le pondrá ya freno? ¿Quién concierto
al viento fiero airado?
Estando tú encubierto,
¿qué norte guiará la nave al puerto?

¡ Ay !, nube invidiosa
aun de este breve gozo, ¿ qué te aquejas ?
¿ Dó vuelas presurosa ?
¡ Cuán rica tú te alejas !
¡ Cuán pobres y cuán ciegos, ¡ ay, nos dejas !

Décima

Al salir de la cárcel :

Aquí la envidia y mentira
me tuvieron encerrado.
¡ Dichoso el humilde estado
del sabio que se retira
de este mundo malvado !
y con pobre mesa y casa
en el campo deleitoso,
con solo Dios se compasa,
a solas su vida pasa ;
ni envidiado ni envidioso.

A Francisco Salinas

El aire se serena
y viste de hermosura y luz no usada,
Salinas, cuando suena
la música extremada
por vuestra sabia mano gobernada.

A cuyo son divino
mi alma, que en olvido está sumida,
torna a cobrar el tino
y memoria perdida
de su origen primera esclarecida.

Y como se conoce,
en suerte y pensamientos se mejora;
el oro desconoce
que el vulgo ciego adora,
la belleza caduca engañadora.

Traspasa el aire todo
hasta llegar a la más alta esfera,
y oye allí otro modo
de no perecedera
música, que es de todas la primera.

Ve cómo el gran maestro
a aquesta inmensa cítara aplicado,
con movimiento diestro
produce el son sagrado
con que este eterno templo es sustentado.

Y como está compuesta
de números concordes, luego envía
consonante respuesta,
y entrambas a profía
mezclan una dulcísima armonía.

Aquí la alma navega
por un mar de dulzura, y finalmente
en él así se anega,
que ningún accidente
extraño o peregrino oye o siente.

¡Oh desmayo dichoso!
¡Oh muerte que das vida! ¡Oh dulce olvido!
¡Durase en tu reposo
sin ser restituído
jamás a aqueste bajo y vil sentido!

A este bien os llamo,
gloria del apolíneo sacro coro,

amigos, a quien amo
sobre todo tesoro;
que todo lo demás es triste lloro.

¡Oh! Suene de contino,
Salinas, vuestro son en mis oídos,
por quien al bien divino
despiertan los sentidos,
quedando a lo demás amortecidos.

A Felipe Ruiz

¿Cuándo será que pueda
libre de esta prisión volar al cielo,
Felipe, y en la rueda
que huye más del suelo
contemplar la verdad pura sin duelo?

Allí, a mi vida junto,
en luz resplandeciente convertido,
veré distinto y junto
lo que es y lo que ha sido,
y su principio propio y escondido.

Entonces veré cómo
la soberana mano echó el cimiento
tan a nivel y plomo,
do estable y firme asiento
posee el pesadísimo elemento.

Veré las inmortales
columnas do la tierra está fundada,
las lindes y señales
con que a la mar hinchada
la Providencia tiene aprisionada;

por qué tiembla la tierra,
por qué las hondas mares se embravecen,
dó sale a mover guerra
el cierzo, y por qué crecen
las aguas del océano y decrecen;

de dó manan las fuentes,
quién ceba y quién bastece de los ríos
las perpetuas corrientes;
de los helados fríos
veré las causas, y de los estíos;

las soberanas aguas,
del aire en la región, quién las sostiene;
de los rayos las fraguas;
dó los tesoros tiene
de nieve Dios, y el trueno dónde viene.

¿No ves cuando acontece
turbarse el aire todo en el verano,
el día se ennegrece,
sopla el gallego insano,
y sube hasta el cielo el polvo vano?

Y entre las nubes mueve
su carro Dios, ligero y reluciente,
horrible son conmueve,
relumbra fuego ardiente,
treme la tierra, humíllase la gente.

La lluvia baña el techo,
envían largos ríos los collados;
su trabajo deshecho,
los campos anegados,
miran los labradores espantados.

Y de allí levantado,
veré los movimientos celestiales,

así el arrebatado
como los naturales;
la causa de los hados, las señales.

Quién rige las estrellas
veré, y quién las enciende con hermosas
y eficaces centellas;
por qué están las dos Osas
de bañarse en el mar siempre medrosas.

Veré este fuego eterno,
fuente de vida y luz, dó se mantiene;
y por qué en el invierno
tan presuroso viene;
quién en las noches largas le detiene.

Veré sin movimiento
en la más alta esfera las moradas
del gozo y del contento,
de oro y luz labradas,
de espíritus dichosos habitadas.

Soneto

Cuando me paro a contemplar mi vida
y echo los ojos con mi pensamiento
a ver los lasos miembros sin aliento
y la robusta edad enflaquecida,
y aquella juventud rica y florida,
cual llama de candela en presto viento,
batida con tan recio movimiento
que a pique estuvo ya de ser perdida,
condeno de mi vida la tibieza
y el grande desconcierto en que he andado,
que a tal peligro puesto me tuvieron;
y con velocidad y ligereza
determino de huir de aqueste estado
do mis continuas culpas me pusieron.

BALTASAR DEL ALCÁZAR

(1530–1606)

Redondillas

Tres cosas me tienen preso
de amores el corazón:
la bella Inés, el jamón
y berengenas con queso.
Esta Inés, amantes, es
quien tuvo en mí tal poder,
que me hizo aborrecer
todo lo que no era Inés.
Trájome un año sin seso,
hasta que en una ocasión
me dió a merendar jamón
y berengenas con queso.
Fué de Inés la primer palma,
pero ya júzguese mal
entre todos ellos cuál
tiene más parte en mi alma.
En gusto, medida y peso
no le hallo distinción;
ya quiero Inés, ya jamón,
ya berengenas con queso.
Alega Inés su beldad,
el jamón que es de Aracena,
el queso y la berengena
la española antigüedad.
Y está tan en fiel el peso,
que juzgado sin pasión,
todo es uno: Inés, jamón
y berengenas con queso.
A lo menos este trato
destos mis nuevos amores
hará que Inés sus favores
me los venda más barata,
Pues tendrá por contrapeso,

si no hiciere la razón,
una lonja de jamón
y berengenas con queso.

Madrigal

Dejó la venda, el arco y el aljaba
el lascivo rapaz, ¡ donosa cosa !
por coger una bella mariposa
que por el aire andaba.
Magdalena, la ninfa, que miraba
su descuido, hurtóle
las armas y dejóle
en el hermoso prado,
como a muchacho bobo y descuidado.
Ya de hoy más no da Amor gloria ni pena ;
que el verdadero amor es Magdalena.

FERNANDO DE HERRERA

(*c.* 1534–94)

Canción por la pérdida del rey don Sebastián

Voz de dolor, y canto de gemido
y espíritu de miedo, envuelto en ira,
hagan principio acerbo a la memoria
de aquel día fatal, aborrecido,
que Lusitania mísera suspira,
desnuda de valor, falta de gloria ;
y la llorosa historia
asombre con horror funesto y triste
desde el áfrico Atlante y seno ardiente
hasta do el mar de otro color se viste,
y do el límite rojo de Oriente
y todas sus vencidas gentes fieras
ven tremolar de Cristo las banderas.

¡ Ay de los que pasaron, confiados
en sus caballos, y en la muchedumbre
de sus carros, en ti, Libia desierta,
y en su vigor y fuerzas engañados,
no alzaron su esperanza a aquella cumbre
de eterna luz ; mas con soberbia cierta
se ofrecieron la incierta
vitoria, y sin volver a Dios sus ojos,
con yerto cuello y corazón ufano
sólo atendieron siempre a los despojos !
Y el Santo de Israel abrió su mano.
y los dejó y cayó en despeñadero
el carro y el caballo y caballero.

Vino el día cruel, el día lleno
de indinación, de ira y furor, que puso
en soledad y en profundo llanto,
de gente y de placer el reino ajeno.
El cielo no alumbró, quedó confuso
el nuevo sol, presagio de mal tanto,
y con terrible espanto
el Señor visitó sobre sus males.
para humillar los fuertes arrogantes,
y levantó los bárbaros no iguales,
que con osados pechos y constantes
no busquen oro, mas con hierro airado
la ofensa venguen y el error culpado.

Los impios y robustos, indinados,
las ardientes espadas desnudaron
sobre la claridad y hermosura
de tu gloria y valor, y no cansados
en tu muerte, tu honor todo afearon,
mezquina Lusitania sin ventura ;
y con frente segura
rompieron sin temor con fiero estrago
tus armadas escuadras y braveza.
La arena se tornó sangriento lago,

la llanura con muertos, aspereza;
cayó en unos vigor, cayó denuedo;
mas en otros desmayo y torpe miedo.

¿Son éstos por ventura los famosos,
los fuertes, los belígeros varones
que conturbaron con furor la tierra,
que sacudieron reinos poderosos,
que domaron las hórridas naciones,
que pusieron desierto en cruda guerra
cuanto el mar Indo encierra,
y soberbias ciudades destruyeron?
¿Dó el corazón seguro y la osadía?
¿Cómo así se acabaron, y perdieron
tanto heroico valor en solo un día;
y lejos de su patria derribados,
no fueron justamente sepultados?

Tales ya fueron éstos cual hermoso
cedro del alto Líbano, vestido
de ramos, hojas, con excelsa alteza;
las aguas lo criaron poderoso
sobre empinados árboles crecido,
y se multiplicaron en grandeza
sus ramos con belleza;
y extendiendo su sombra, se anidaron
las aves que sustenta el grande cielo,
y en sus hojas las fieras engendraron,
y hizo a mucha gente umbroso velo;
no igualó en celsitud y en hermosura
jamás árbol alguno a su figura.

Pero elevóse con su verde cima,
y sublimó la presunción su pecho,
desvaneciendo todo y confiado,
haciendo de su alteza sólo estima.
Por eso Dios lo derribó deshecho,
a los impios y ajenos entregado,
por la raíz cortado;

que opreso de los montes arrojados,
sin ramos y sin hojas y desnudo,
huyeron dél los hombres, espantados,
que su sombra tuvieron por escudo;
en su rüina y ramos cuantas fueron
las aves y las fieras se pusieron.

Tú, infanda Libia, en cuya seca arena
murió el vencido reino lusitano,
y se acabó su generosa gloria,
no estés alegre y de ufanía llena;
porque tu temerosa y flaca mano
hubo sin esperanza tal vitoria,
indina de memoria;
que si el justo dolor mueve a venganza
alguna vez el español coraje,
despedazada con aguda lanza,
compensarás muriendo el hecho ultraje;
y Luco amedrentado, al mar inmenso
pagará de africana sangre el censo.

Soneto

(*Por la victoria de Lepanto*)

Hondo Ponto, que bramas atronado
con tumulto y terror, del turbio seno
saca el rostro, de torpe miedo lleno;
mira tu campo arder ensangrentado;
y junto en este cerco y encontrado
todo el cristiano esfuerzo y sarraceno,
y cubierto de humo y fuego y trueno,
huir temblando el impio quebrantado.
Con profundo murmurio la victoria
mayor celebra que jamás vió el cielo,
y más dudosa y singular hazaña;
y de que sólo mereció la gloria
que tanto nombre da a tu sacro suelo
el joven de Austria y el valor de España.

Soneto

Rojo sol, que con hacha luminosa
coloras él purpúreo y alto cielo,
¿ hallaste tal belleza en todo el suelo
que iguale a mi serena luz dichosa ?
Aura suave, blanda y amorosa
que nos halagas con tu fresco vuelo,
cuando el oro descubre y rico velo
mi luz, ¿ trenza tocaste más hermosa ?
Luna, honor de la noche, ilustre coro
de los errantes astros y fijados,
¿ consideraste tales dos estrellas ?
Sol puro, aura, luna, luces de oro,
¿ oístes mis dolores nunca usados ?
¿ Vistes luz más ingrata a mis querellas ?

Soneto

El color bello en el humor de Tiro
ardió, y la nieve vuestra en llama pura,
cuando, Estrella, volvistes con dulzura
los ojos, por quien mísero suspiro.
Vivo color de lúcido safiro,
dorado cielo, eterna hermosura,
pues merecí alcanzar esta ventura
acoged blandamente mi suspiro.
Con él mi alma, en el celeste fuego
vuestro abrasada, viene, y se trasforma
en la belleza vuestra soberana.
Y en tanto gozo, en su mayor sosiego
su bien, en cuantas almas halla, informa ;
que en el comunicar más gloria gana.

Soneto

Por un camino, solo, al Sol abierto,
de espinas y de abrojos mal sembrado,
el tardo passo muevo, y voy cansado
a do cierra la vuelta el mar incierto.

Silencio triste habita este desierto:
y el mal que ahí conviene ser callado;
cuando pienso acaballo, acrecentado
veo el camino, y mi trabajo cierto.
A un lado levantan su grandeza
los riscos juntos, con el cielo iguales,
al otro cae un gran despeñadero.
No sé de quién me valga en mi estrecheza,
que me libre de Amor y destos males,
pues remedio sin vos, mi Luz, no espero.

Soneto

Al rey Felipe segundo

Ya que el sujeto reino lusitano
inclina al yugo la cerviz paciente,
y todo el grande esfuerzo de occidente
tenéis, sacro señor, en vuestra mano,
volved contra el suelo hórrido africano
el firme pecho y vuestra osada gente;
que su poder, su corazón valiente,
que tanto fué, será ante el vuestro en vano.
Cristo os da la pujanza deste imperio,
para que la fe nuestra se adelante,
por do su santo nombre es ofendido.
¿Quién contra vos, quién contra el reino hesperio
bastará alzar la frente, que al instante
no se derribe a vuestros pies rendido?

Elegía

No bañes en el mar sagrado y cano,
callada Noche, tu corona oscura,
antes de oír este amador ufano.
Y tú, alza de la húmida hondura
las verdes hebras de la bella frente,
de Náyades lozana hermosura.
Aquí, do el grande Betis ve presente

la armada vencedora, que el Egeo
manchó con sangre de la turca gente,
quiero decir la gloria en que me veo;
pero no cause invidia este bien mío
a quien aun no merece mi deseo.
Sosiega el curso, tú, profundo río,
oye mi gloria, pues también oíste
mis quejas en tu puro asiento frío.
Tú amaste, y como yo también supiste
del mal dolerte, y celebrar la gloria
de los pequeños bienes que tuviste.
Breve será la venturosa historia
de mi favor; que breve es la alegría
que tiene algún lugar en mi memoria.
Cuando del claro cielo se desvía
del Sol ardiente el alto carro apena,
y casi igual espacio muestra el día,
con blanda voz, que entre las perlas suena,
teñido el rostro de color de rosa,
de honesto miedo, y de amor tierno llena,
me dijo así la bella desdeñosa
que un tiempo me negara la esperanza,
sorda a mi llanto y ansia congojosa:
"Si por firmeza y dulce amar se alcanza
premio de amor, yo [ya] tener bien debo,
de los males que sufro más holganza.
Mil veces, por no ser ingrata, pruebo
vencer tu amor, pero al fin no puedo;
que es mi pecho a sentillo rudo y nuevo.
Si en sufrir más me vences, yo te excedo
en pura fe y afectos de terneza:
vive de hoy más ya confiado y ledo."
No sé si oí, si fuí de su belleza
arrebatado, si perdí el sentido;
sé que allí se perdió mi fortaleza.
Turbado dije al fin: "Por no haber sido
este tan grande bien de mí esperado,
pienso que debe ser, (si es bien), fingido.

Señora, bien sabéis que mi cuidado
todo se ocupa en vos; que yo no siento,
ni pienso, sino en verme más penado.
Mayor es que el humano mi tormento,
y al mayor mal igual esfuerzo tengo,
igual con el trabajo el sentimiento.
Las penas que por sola vos sostengo
me dan valor, y mi firmeza crece
cuanto más en mis males me entretengo.
No quiero concederos que merece
mi afán tal bien, que vos sintáis el daño;
más ama quien más sufre y más padece.
No es mi pecho tan rudo, o tan extraño,
que no conozca en el dolor primero
si en esto que dijistes cabe engaño.
Un corazón de impenetrable acero
tengo para sufrir, y está más fuerte,
cuanto más el asalto es bravo y fiero.
Dióme el cielo en destino aquesta suerte,
y yo la procuré, y hallé el camino
para poder honrarme con mi muerte."
Lo demás que entre nos pasó no es dino,
Noche, de oír el Austro presuroso,
ni el viento de tus lechos más vecino.
Mete en el ancho piélago espumoso
tus negras trenzas y húmido semblante;
que en tanto que tú yaces en reposo
podrá Amor darme gloria semejante.

SAN JUAN DE LA CRUZ

(1542–91)

Canción a lo divino de Cristo y el alma

Un pastorcico solo está penado,
ajeno de placer y de contento,
y en su pastora puesto el pensamiento,
y el pecho del amor muy lastimado.

No llora por haberle amor llagado
que no le pena verse así afligido,
aunque en el corazón está herido;
mas llora por pensar que está olvidado.

Que sólo de pensar que está olvidado
de su bella pastora, con gran pena
se deja maltratar en tierra ajena,
el pecho del amor muy lastimado.

Y dice el pastorcico: " ¡ Ay, desdichado
de aquel que de mi amor ha hecho ausencia,
y no quiere gozar la mi presencia,
y el pecho por su amor muy lastimado! "

Y a cabo de un gran rato se ha encumbrado
sobre un árbol do abrió sus brazos bellos,
y muerto se ha quedado, asido de ellos.
el pecho del amor muy lastimado.

Noche oscura

En una noche oscura,
çon ansias en amores inflamada,
¡ oh dichosa ventura!
salí sin ser notada,
estando ya mi casa sosegada.

A oscuras, y segura,
por la secreta escala disfrazada,
¡ oh dichosa ventura!
a oscuras, y en celada,
estando ya mi casa sosegada.

En la noche dichosa,
en secreto, que nadie me veía,
ni yo miraba cosa,
sin otra luz ni guía,
sino la que en el corazón ardía.

Aquésta me guiaba
más cierto que la luz de mediodía,
a donde me esperaba
quien yo bien me sabía,
en parte donde nadie parecía.

¡ Oh noche, que guiaste,
oh noche amable más que el alborada :
oh noche, que juntaste
Amado con amada,
amada en el Amado transformada !

En mi pecho florido,
que entero para él solo se guardaba,
allí quedó dormido,
y yo le regalaba,
y el ventalle de cedros aire daba.

El aire de la almena,
cuando ya sus cabellos esparcía,
con su mano serena
en mi cuello hería,
y todos mis sentidos suspendía.

Quedéme, y olvidéme,
el rostro recliné sobre el Amado.
Cesó todo, y dejéme,
dejando mi cuidado
entre las azucenas olvidado.

Llama de amor viva

¡ Oh llama de amor viva,
que tiernamente hieres
de mi alma en el más profundo centro !
Pues ya no eres esquiva,
acaba ya si quieres,
rompe la tela deste dulce encuentro.

¡ Oh cauterio suave !
¡ Oh regalada llaga !
¡ Oh mano blanda ! ¡ Oh toque delicado,
que a vida eterna sabe,
y toda deuda paga !
Matando, muerte en vida la has trocado.

¡ Oh lámparas de fuego,
en cuyos resplandores
las profundas cavernas del sentido,
que estaba oscuro y ciego,
con extraños primores
calor y luz dan junto a su querido !

¡ Cuán manso y amoroso
recuerdas en mi seno,
donde secretamente solo moras !
y en tu aspirar sabroso
de bien y gloria lleno
¡ cuán delicadamente me enamoras !

MIGUEL DE CERVANTES SAAVEDRA

(1547–1616)

Copla real a la muerte de Isabel de Valois

Cuando dejaba la guerra
libre nuestro hispano suelo,
con un repentino vuelo,
la mejor flor de la tierra
fué trasplantada en el cielo.
Y, al cortarla de su rama,
el mortífero accidente
fué tan oculto a la gente,
como el que no ve la llama
hasta que quemar se siente.

Soneto al Marqués de Santa Cruz

No ha menester el que tus hechos canta,
¡o gran marqués!, el artificio humano,
que a la más sutil pluma y docta mano
ellos le ofrecen al que al orbe espanta.
Y éste que sobre el cielo se levanta,
llevado de tu nombre soberano,
a par del griego y escritor toscano,
sus sienes ciñe con la verde planta.
Y fué muy justa prevención del cielo,
que a un tiempo ejercitases tú la espada
y él su prudente y verdadera pluma,
porque, rompiendo de la invidia el velo,
tu fama, en sus escritos dilatada,
ni olvido, o tiempo, o muerte la consuma.

Seguidilla glosada

Pisaré yo el polvico
atán menudico;
pisaré yo el polvó
atán menudó.

Pisaré yo la tierra
por más que esté dura,
puesto que me abra en ella
amor sepultura,
pues ya mi buena ventura
amor la pisó
atán menudó.

Pisaré yo lozana
el más duro suelo,
si en él acaso pisas
el mal que recelo;
mi bien se ha pasado en vuelo
y el polvo dejó
atán menudó.

VICENTE ESPINEL

(1550–1624)

Letrilla

Contentamientos pasados,
¿ qué queréis ?
Dejadme, no me canséis.
Contentos, cuya memoria
a cruel muerte condena,
idos de mí en horabuena,
y pues que no me dais gloria
no vengáis a darme pena.
Ya están los tiempos trocados,
mi bien llevóselo el viento,
no me deis ya más cuidados,
que son para más tormento
contentamientos pasados.
No me mostréis lisonjeros,
que no habéis de ser creídos,
ni me amenacéis con fieros,
porque el temor de perderos
le perdí en siendo perdidos,
y si acaso pretendéis
cumplir vuestra voluntad
con mi muerte, bien podréis
matarme ; y si no, mirad,
¿ qué queréis ?
Si dar disgusto y desdén
es vuestro propio caudal,
sabed que he quedado tal
que aun no me ha dejado el bien
de suerte que sienta el mal :
mas con todo, pues me habéis
dejado y estoy sin vos,
¡ paso ! ; ¡ no me atormentéis !
Contentos, idos con Dios,
dejadme, no me canséis.

Décima

No hay bien que del mal me guarde;
temeroso y encogido,
de sin razón ofendido:
y de ofendido cobarde;
y aunque mi queja ya es tarde,
y razón me la defiende,
más en mi daño se enciende;
que voy contra quien me agravia,
como el perro que con rabia
a su mismo dueño ofende.

LUPERCIO LEONARDO DE ARGENSOLA

(1559–1613)

Décimas

Bien pensará quien me oyere,
viendo que he llorado tanto,
que me alegro agora y canto
como el cisne cuando muere.
Créalo quien mal me quiere;
mas sepa quien se lastima
de que el duro Amor me oprima
que con este mismo son
puede romper la prisión
y disimular la lima. . . .

En dulce correspondencia
crece el amor cada día;
mas en la descortesía
mengua toda su potencia.
Ya se acabó mi paciencia,
ya el tiempo me desengaña,
y la razón me acompaña;
que no siempre un hombre debe
contemplar un corcho leve,
como pescador de caña. . . .

Ya de la memoria borro
todas las obligaciones,
porque vuestras sinrazones
me han dado carta de horro;
y tal estoy que me corro
de que tengáis prendas mías;
mas por no mover porfías,
en vuestras manos las dejo,
cual la culebra el pellejo
para renovar sus días.

Soneto

Cuitada navecilla, ¿quién creyera
que osaran estas olas ofenderte,
viéndolas otro tiempo obedecerte,
como si tuyo el mar soberbio fuera?
Tus bienes les he dado, y persevera
su saña: no sé como valerte;
el arte dejo en manos de la suerte,
para que ella te arroje adonde quiera.
Bien sé que se aplacaran al momento
si, como les he dado la esperanza,
entregara también el pensamiento;
pero avéngase allá con su bonanza;
que más quiero morir en mi tormento
que morir con infamia en su mudanza.

Soneto

Vuelve del campo el labrador cansado
y mientras se restaura en fácil cena,
para nuevo trabajo se condena,
que al venidero sol quedó obligado.
Cuando descansa en el rincón su arado,
con hoz la vid sin pámpanos cercena;

siega la mes y la vendimia ordena,
y luego al yugo vuelve ya olvidado.
  Es el trabajo propio a los mortales,
en el cual los alivia la esperanza
con premio que al trabajo nuevo llama.
  Así pasan los bienes por los males,
así sustenta al mundo la mudanza,
y así es tirano en él quien la desama.

BARTOLOMÉ LEONARDO DE ARGENSOLA

(1562–1631)

Romance

  No debe a mayo las flores,
Ebro, esta vez tu ribera,
sino a la luz que despiden
los ojos de Silvia y Celia.
  Salieron de la ciudad
por vestir de honor las huertas
que tus márgenes adornan,
y en tu corriente se espejan.
  Las almas, que el esplendor
de su hermosura contemplan,
reciben de su virtud
otra interior primavera.
  Volviendo al campo los ojos,
le convierten en floresta;
súbitas nacen las rosas,
los claveles, las violetas.
  Mas cuando al árbol gentil
lasciva abraza la hiedra,
lo confunden con jazmines
entre tejidos apriesa.
  La honestidad los produce,
que en las dos ninfas severas
no permite que un ejemplo

de posesión se parezca,
porque a ningún trofeo
aspiran la esperanza ni el deseo.

Soneto

Ni opinión, Carlos, ni esperanza fundo
en los aplausos que el favor derrama;
¿quién los aprueba o sus lisonjas ama,
por más que en bronce las escriba el mundo?
Si, rotas por el tiempo vagabundo,
muere el hombre otra vez cuando su fama,
¿son más que esfuerzos de una débil llama
que turbia cesa en el morir segundo?
Y si el no conocerse es el abismo
de todo error y cunde sin mudanza
una vez en los ánimos impreso,
¿buscaré mi verdad en mi alabanza?
¿Cuándo has visto volver con buen suceso
a quien se busca fuera de sí mismo?

Soneto

¿Estás libre, Damón,? pues no blasones;
que la jactancia, ni en seguro es buena;
y si te queda un átomo de pena,
te traerá a las primeras ocasiones.
No se juzga por libre de prisiones
el can, por más que rompa la cadena,
mientras que asida a la cerviz le suena
alguna parte de los eslabones.
Paz suelen ser de amor breves enojos,
y todos los nublados de tu ira
los volverá en tranquilidad tu diosa,

si se humana a poner, cuando te mira,
de aquella risa todopoderosa
un süave relámpago en sus ojos.

JOSÉ DE VALDIVIELSO

(*c.* 1560–1638)

Seguidilla con glosa

Libre ser solía,
vendido muero;
nadie fíe, Madre,
de ingratos pechos.
Con fingido trato,
Madre, un falso amigo,
que cenó conmigo
en mi mismo plato
me vendió el ingrato
como un cordero;
nadie fíe, Madre,
de ingratos pechos.
Dábale mi lado,
el plato le hacía,
con él repartía
el mejor bocado;
mas en buen mercado
vendió al Hijo vuestro;
nadie fíe, Madre,
de ingratos pechos.
Sus plantas desnudas
lavé con mi llanto,
con ser Jueves Santo,
fué conmigo un Judas;
con entrañas crudas
me dió traidor beso;
nadie fíe, Madre,
de ingratos pechos.

LUIS DE GÓNGORA Y ARGOTE

(1561–1627)

Letrilla

Aprended, flores, de mí
lo que va de ayer a hoy,
que ayer maravilla fuí,
y hoy sombra mía aun no soy.

La aurora ayer me dió cuna,
la noche ataúd me dió,
sin luz muriera, si no
me la prestara la luna,
pues de vosotras ninguna
deja de morir así.

Aprended, flores, de mí
lo que va de ayer a hoy,
que ayer maravilla fuí,
y hoy sombra mía aun no soy.

Consuelo dulce el clavel
es a la brevedad mía,
pues quien me concedió un día,
dos apenas le dió a él;
efímeras del vergel,
yo cárdena, él carmesí.

Aprended, flores, de mí
lo que va de ayer hoy,
que ayer maravilla fuí,
y hoy sombra mía aun no soy.

Flor es el jazmín y bella,
no de las más vividoras,
pues vive pocas más horas
que rayos tiene de estrella;
si el ámbar florece, es ella
la flor que contiene en sí.

Aprended, flores de mí
lo que va de ayer a hoy,
que ayer maravilla fuí,
y hoy sombra mía aun no soy.

El alhelí, aunque grosero
en fragancia y en olor,
más días ve que otra flor,
que ve los de mayo entero;
morir maravilla quiero,
y no vivir alhelí.

Aprended, flores de mí
lo que va de ayer a hoy,
que ayer maravilla fuí,
y hoy sombra mía aun no soy.

A ninguna flor mayores
términos concede el sol
que al sublime girasol,
matusalén de las flores;
ojos son aduladores
cuantas en él hojas vi.

Aprended, flores de mí
lo que va de ayer a hoy,
que ayer maravilla fuí,
y hoy sombra mía aun no soy.

Romance

Las flores del romero,
niña Isabel,
hoy son flores azules,
mañana serán miel.

Celosa estás, la niña,
celosa estás de aquel
dichoso, pues le buscas,
ciego, pues no te ve,
ingrato, pues te enoja
y confiado, pues
no se disculpa hoy
de lo que hizo ayer.
Enjuguen esperanzas
lo que lloras por él;
que celos entre aquellos
que se han querido bien
hoy son flores azules
mañana serán miel.

Aurora de ti misma,
que cuando a amanecer
a tu placer empiezas,
te eclipsa tu placer.
Serénense tus ojos,
y más perlas no des,
porque al sol le está mal
lo que a la aurora bien.
Desata como nieblas
todo lo que no ves;
que sospechas de amantes
y querellas después
hoy son flores azules,
mañana serán miel.

Romance

¡Que se nos va la Pascua, mozas,
que se nos va la Pascua!

Mozuelas, las de mi barrio,
loquillas y confiadas,

mirad no os engañe el tiempo,
la edad y la confianza.
No os dejéis lisonjear
de la juventud lozana,
porque de caducas flores
teje el tiempo sus guirnaldas.

¡Que se nos va la Pascua, mozas,
que se nos va la Pascua!

Vuelan los ligeros años,
y con presurosas alas
nos roban, como harpías,
nuestras sabrosas viandas.
La flor de la maravilla
esta verdad nos declara,
porque le hurta la tarde
lo que le dió la mañana.

¡Que se nos va la Pascua, mozas,
que se nos va la Pascua!

Mirad que cuando pensáis
que hacen la señal del alba
las campanas de la vida,
es la queda, y os desarma
de vuestro color y lustre,
de vuestro donaire y gracia,
y quedáis todas perdidas
por mayores de la marca.

¡Que se nos va la Pascua, mozas,
que se nos va la Pascua!

Villancico

Caído se le ha un clavel
hoy a la Aurora del seno;
¡qué glorioso que está el heno,
porque ha caído sobre él!

Cuando el silencio tenía
todas las cosas del suelo,
y coronada de hielo,
reinaba la noche fría,
en medio la monarquía
de tiniebla tan cruel,
caído se le ha un clavel.

De un solo clavel ceñida
la Virgen, aurora bella,
al mundo se le dió, y ella
quedó cual antes florida.
A la púrpura caída
solo fué el heno fiel;
caído se le ha un clavel.

El heno pues que fué dino,
a pesar de tantas nieves,
de ver en sus brazos leves
este rosicler divino,
para su lecho fué lino,
oro para su dosel;
caído se le ha un clavel.

Letrilla

No son todos ruiseñores
los que cantan entre flores,
sino campanitas de plata,
que tocan al alba;

sino trompeticas de oro,
que hacen la salva
a los soles que adoro.

No todas las voces ledas
son de sirenas con plumas,
cuyas humildes espumas
son las verdes alamedas,
si suspendido te quedas
a los süaves clamores.

No son todos ruiseñores
los que cantan entre flores,
sino campanitas de plata,
que tocan al alba;
sino trompeticas de oro,
que hacen la salva
a los soles que adoro.

Lo artificioso, que admira,
y lo dulce, que consuela,
no es de aquel violín que vuela
ni desotra inquieta lira;
otro instrumento es quien tira
de los sentidos mejores.

Sonetos

A un arroyo

¡Oh claro honor del líquido elemento,
dulce arroyuelo de luciente plata,
cuya agua entre la yerba se dilata
con regalado son y paso lento;
pues la por quien helar y arder me siento,
mientras en ti se mira, Amor retrata
de su rostro la nieve y escarlata
en tu tranquilo y blando movimiento.

Vete como te vas; no dejes floja
la undosa rienda al cristalino freno
con que gobiernas tu veloz corriente;
que no es bien que confusamente acoja
tanta belleza en su profundo seno
el gran señor del húmido tridente.

A una rosa

Ayer naciste, y morirás mañana.
Para tan breve ser ¿ quién te dió vida?
¡ Para vivir tan poco estás lucida,
y para no ser nada estás lozana!
Si te engañó tu hermosura vana,
bien presto la verás desvanecida,
porque en esa hermosura está escondida
la ocasión de morir muerte temprana.
Cuando te corte la robusta mano,
ley de la agricultura permitida,
grosero aliento acabará tu suerte.
No salgas, que te aguarda algún tirano;
dilata tu nacer para tu vida;
que anticipas tu ser para tu muerte.

Silva

Sobre trastes de guijas
cuerdas mueve de plata
Pisuerga, hecho cítara doliente;
y en robustas clavijas
de álamos, las ata
hasta Simancas, que le da su puente:
al son deste instrumento
partía un pastor sus quejas con el viento.

" ¡ Oh, río!—le decía—
que al tronco menos verde
le guarnecen de perlas tus espumas,

si la enemiga mía
pasos por aquí pierde
calzado el fugitivo pie de plumas,
porque no vuele tanto,
deténgala tu música, o mi llanto."

" Si tú haces que oya
debajo desta yedra
mis lágrimas, que siguen tu armonía,
octavo muro a Troya
renacer piedra a piedra
hará tu son de su ceniza fría:
que es más posible caso
convocar piedras que enfrenalle el paso."

Coro himeneo

Ven, Himeneo, ven donde te espera
con ojos y sin alas un Cupido,
cuyo cabello intonso dulcemente
niega el vello que el vulto ha colorido:
el vello, flores de su primavera,
y rayos el cabello de su frente.
Niño amó la que adora adolescente,
villana Psique, ninfa labradora
de la tostada Ceres. Ésta, ahora,
en los inciertos de su edad segunda
crepúsculos, vincule tu coyunda
a tu ardiente deseo.
Ven, Himeneo, ven; ven Himeneo.

Ven, Himeneo, donde entre arreboles
de honesto rosicler, previene el día
—aurora de sus ojos soberanos—
virgen tan bella, que hacer podría
tórrida la Noruega con dos soles,

y blanca la Etiopía con dos manos.
Claveles de abril, rubíes tempranos,
cuantos engasta el oro de el cabello,
cuantas—de el uno y del otro cuello,
cadenas—la concordia engarza rosas,
de sus mejillas, siempre vergonzosas,
purpúreo son trofeo.
Ven, Himeneo, ven; ven, Himeneo. . . .

Ven, Himeneo, y nuestra agricultura
de copia tal a estrellas deba amigas
progenie tan robusta, que su mano
toros dome, y de un rubio mar de espigas
inunde liberal la tierra dura;
y al verde, joven, floreciente llano
blancas ovejas suyas hagan cano,
en breves horas caducar la hierba;
oro le expriman líquido a Minerva,
y—los olmos casando con las vides—
mientras coronan pámpanos a Alcides
clava empuñe Lieo.
Ven, Himeneo, ven; ven, Himeneo.

Ven, Himeneo, y tantas le dé a Pales
cuantas a Palas dulces prendas ésta
apenas hija hoy, madre mañana.
De errantes lilios unas la floresta
cubran; corderos mil, que los cristales
vistan del río en breve undosa lana;
de Aracnes otras la arrogancia vana
modestas acusando en blancas telas,
no los hurtos de amor, no las cautelas
de Jupiter compulsen; que, aun en lino,
ni a la pluvia luciente de oro fino,
ni al blanco cisne creo.
Ven, Himeneo, ven; ven, Himeneo.

Soledad primera (*Las soledades*)

LOPE DE VEGA CARPIO

(1562–1635)

Canción a la muerte de Carlos Felix

Este de mis entrañas dulce fruto,
con vuestra bendición, ¡ oh Rey eterno !,
ofrezco humildemente a vuestras aras,
que si es de todos el mejor tributo
un puro corazón humilde y tierno,
y el más precioso de las prendas caras,
no las aromas raras
entre olores fenicios
y licores sabeos,
os rinden mis deseos,
por menos olorosos sacrificios,
sino mi corazón, que Carlos era,
que en el que me quedó menos os diera.
Diréis, Señor, que en daros lo que es vuestro
ninguna cosa os doy, y que querría
hacer virtud necesidad tan fuerte,
y que no es lo que siento lo que muestro,
pues anima su cuerpo el alma mía
y se divide entre los dos la muerte.
Confieso que de suerte
vive a la suya asida,
que cuanto a la vil tierra
que el ser mortal encierra,
tuviera más contento de su vida;
mas cuanto al alma, ¿ qué mayor consuelo
que lo que pierdo yo me gane el cielo ? . . .

Y vos, dichoso niño, que en siete años
que tuvistes de vida, no tuvistes
con vuestro padre inobediencia alguna,
corred con vuestro ejemplo mis engaños,
serenad mis paternos ojos tristes,
pues ya sois sol donde pisáis la luna.

De la primera cuna
a la postrera cama
no distes sola un hora
de disgusto, y agora
parece que le dais, si así se llama
lo que es pena y dolor de parte nuestra,
pues no es la culpa, aunque es la causa vuestra. . . .

  Yo para vos los pajarillos nuevos,
diversos en el canto y las colores,
encerraba, gozoso de alegraros;
yo plantaba los fértiles renuevos
de los árboles verdes, yo las flores
en quien mejor pudiera contemplaros,
pues a los aires claros
del alba hermosa apenas
salistes, Carlos mío,
bañado de rocío,
cuando, marchitas las doradas venas,
el blanco lirio convertido en hielo
cayó en la tierra, aunque traspuesto al cielo.
  ¡ Oh qué divinos pájaros agora,
Carlos, gozáis, que con pintadas alas
discurren por los campos celestiales
en el jardín eterno, que atesora
por cuadros ricos de doradas salas
más hermosos jacintos orientales,
adonde a los mortales
ojos la luz excede!
¡ Dichoso yo que os veo
donde está mi deseo
y donde no tocó pesar ni puede,
que sólo con el bien de tal memoria
toda la pena me trocáis en gloria! . . .

  Yo os di la mejor patria que yo pude
para nacer, y agora en vuestra muerte
entre santos dichosa sepultura;

resta que vos roguéis a Dios que mude
mi sentimiento en gozo, de tal suerte,
que, a pesar de la sangre que procura
cubrir de noche escura
la luz desta memoria,
viváis vos en la mía,
que espero que algún día
la que me da dolor me dará gloria,
viendo al partir de aquesta tierra ajena,
que no quedáis adonde todo es pena.

Rimas sacras

Soneto

Cuando me paro a contemplar mi estado
y a ver los pasos por donde he venido,
me espanto de que un hombre tan perdido
a conocer su error haya llegado.
Cuando miro los años que he pasado
la divina razón puesta en olvido,
conozco que piedad del cielo ha sido
no haberme en tanto mal precipitado.
Entré por laberinto tan extraño
fiando al débil hilo de la vida
el tarde conocido desengaño,
mas de tu luz mi oscuridad vencida,
el monstruo muerto de mi ciego engaño
vuelve a la patria, la razón perdida.

Rimas sacras

Soneto

¿Qué tengo yo que mi amistad procuras?
¿Qué interés se te sigue, Jesús mío,
que a mi puerta, cubierto de rocío
pasas las noches del invierno oscuras?

¡ Oh, cuánto fueron mis entrañas duras
pues no te abrí ! ¡ Qué extraño desvarío
si de mi ingratitud el yelo frío
secó las llagas de tus plantas puras !
¡ Cuántas veces el ángel me decía :
Alma, asómate agora a la ventana,
verás con cuánto amor llamar porfía !
¡ Y cuántas, hermosura soberana :
Mañana le abriremos—respondía—,
para lo mismo responder mañana !

Rimas sacras

Soneto

Suelta mi manso, mayoral extraño,
pues otro tienes de tu igual decoro
deja la prenda que en el alma adoro,
perdida por tu bien y por mi daño.
Ponle su esquila de labrado estaño
y no le engañen tus collares de oro ;
toma en albricias este blanco toro
que a las primeras yerbas cumple un año.
Si pides señas, tiene el vellocino
pardo, encrespado, y los ojuelos tiene
como durmiendo en regalado sueño.
Si piensas que no soy su dueño, Alcino,
suelta y verásle si a mi choza viene,
que aun tienen sal las manos de su dueño.

Rimas humanas

Romance a Filis

Por las riberas famosas
de las aguas del Jarama,
junto del mismo lugar
que Tajo las acompaña,

alegre sale Belardo
a recibir justa paga
de tantos años de amor,
celos, temor y mudanza.
¡ Dichoso el pastor que alcanza
tan regalado fin de su esperanza !
Vase a casar a su aldea
con Filis su enamorada,
que se la entrega su padre
después de tantas desgracias.
Contento lleva el villano,
por los ojos muestra el alma,
que al fin de tanta fortuna
promete el cielo bonanza.
¡ Dichoso el pastor que alcanza
tan regalado fin de su esperanza !
Va mostrando en el vestido
las esperanzas del alma,
tan cerca ya de cumplirlas
como tardías y largas.
Guardadas lleva en el seno
de Filis todas las cartas,
que si son obligaciones
quiere pagar y borrarlas.
¡ Dichoso el pastor qne alcanza
tan regalado fin de su esperanza !
Llegó Belardo a la villa
y de su suegro a la casa,
sale a tener el estribo
mientras de la yegua baja
Filis, abiertos los brazos,
marido y señor le llama,
él señora y dulce esposa ;
besóla y ella le abraza.
¡ Dichoso el pastor que alcanza
tan regalado fin de su esperanza !

Romance morisco

Mira, Zaide, que te aviso
que no pases por mi calle
ni hables con mis mujeres,
ni con mis cautivos trates,
ni preguntes en qué entiendo
ni quién viene a visitarme,
qué fiestas me dan contento
o qué colores me aplacen;
basta que son por tu causa
las que en el rostro me salen,
corrida de haber mirado
moro que tan poco sabe.
Confieso que eres valiente,
que hiendes, rajas y partes
que has muerto más cristianos
que tienes gotas de sangre;
que eres gallardo jinete,
que danzas, cantas y tañes,
gentil hombre, bien criado
cuanto puede imaginarse;
blanco, rubio por extremo,
señalado por linaje,
el gallo de las bravatas,
la nata de los donaires,
y pierdo mucho en perderte
y gano mucho en amarte,
y que si nacieras mudo
fuera posible adorarte;
y por este inconveniente
determino de dejarte,
que eres pródigo de lengua
y amargan tus libertades
y habrá menester ponerte
quien quisiere sustentarte
un alcázar en el pecho
y en los labios un alcaide. . . .

De mala gana me río;
¡qué donoso disparate!
No guardas tú tu secreto
¿y quieres que otro le guarde?
No quiero admitir disculpa;
otra vez vuelvo a avisarte
que ésta será la postrera
que me hables y te hable.—
Dijo la discreta Zaida
a un altivo bencerraje
y al despedirle repite:
" Quien tal hace, que tal pague."

Letra para cantar

Naranjitas me tira la niña
en Valencia por Navidad,
pues a fe que si se las tiro
que se le han de volver azâr.

A una máscara salí
y paréme a su ventana,
amaneció su mañana
y el sol en sus ojos vi.
Naranjitas desde allí
me tirò para furor;
como no sabe de amor
piensa que todo es burlar,
pues a fe que si se las tiro
que se la han de volver azâr.

Naranjitas me tira la niña
en Valencia por Navidad,
pues a fe que si las tiro
que se le han de volver azâr.

El bobo del colegio

Trébole

¡Trébole, ay Jesús, cómo huele!
¡Trébole, ay Jesús, qué olor!

Trébole de la casada
que a su esposo quiere bien;
de la doncella también
entre paredes guardada,
que fácilmente engañada
sigue su primer amor.
¡Trébole, ay Jesús, cómo huele!
¡Trébole, ay Jesús, qué olor!

Trébole de la soltera
que tantos amores muda,
trébole de la vïuda
que otra vez casarse espera,
tocas blancas por defuera
y faldellín de color.
¡Trébole, ay Jesús, cómo huele!
¡Trébole, ay Jesús, qué olor!

Peribáñez y el comendador de Ocaña

Canción de vela

—" Velador que el castillo velas,
vélale bien y mira por ti,
que velando en él me perdí."

—" Mira las campañas llenas
de tanto enemigo armado."
——" Ya estoy, amor, desvelado
de velar en las almenas.
Ya que las campanas suenas,
toma ejemplo y mira en mí
que velando en él me perdí."

Las almenas de Toro

Canción de siega

Esta sí que es siega de vida;
esta sí que es siega de flor.

Hoy segadores de España,
vení a ver a la Moraña
trigo blanco y sin argaña,
que de verlo es benedición.
Esta sí que es siega de vida;
esta sí que es siega de flor.

Labradores de Castilla,
vení a ver a maravilla
trigo blanco y sin neguilla,
que de verlo es benedición.
Esta sí que es siega de vida;
esta sí que es siega de flor.

El vaquero de Moraña

Canción a la Virgen

I

Nace el alba María
y el sol con ella,
desterrando la noche
de nuestras penas.

Nace el alba clara,
la noche pisa;
del cielo la risa
su paz declara;
el tiempo se para
por sólo vella
desterrando la noche
de nuestras penas.

Para ser señora
del cielo, levanta
esta niña santa
su luz como aurora;
él canta, ella llora
divinas perlas,
desterrando la noche
de nuestras penas.

Aquella luz pura
del sol procede,
porque cuanto puede
le da hermosura.
El alba asegura
que viene cerca,
desterrando la noche
de nuestras penas.

II

¿Dónde vais, zagala,
sola en el monte?
Mas quien lleva el sol
no teme la noche.

¿Dónde vais, María,
divina esposa,
madre gloriosa
de quien os cría?
¿Qué haréis, si el día
se va al ocaso
y en el monte acaso
la noche os coge?
Mas quien lleva el sol
no teme la noche.

El ver las estrellas
me causa enojos,
pero vuestros ojos

más lucen que ellas.
Ya sale con ellas
la noche oscura,
a vuestra hermosura
la luz se esconde.
Mas quien lleva el sol
no teme la noche.

Los pastores de Belén

Cantarcillo de la Virgen

Pues andáis en las palmas,
ángeles santos,
que se duerme mi niño,
tened los ramos.

Palmas de Belén
que mueven airados
los furiosos vientos
que suenan tanto:
no le hagáis ruido,
corred más paso.
que se duerme mi niño,
tened los ramos.

El niño divino
que está cansado
de llorar en la tierra,
por su descanso
sosegar quiere un poco
del tierno llanto.
Que se duerme mi niño,
tened los ramos.

Rigurosos yelos
le están cercando;
ya veis que no tengo
con qué guardarlo.

Ángeles divinos
que vais volando,
que se duerme mi niño,
tened los ramos.

Los pastores de Belén

ANÓNIMO

(seventeenth century)

Romance de don Álvaro de Luna

—Hagan bien para hacer bien
por el alma deste hombre.
Al son de las campanillas
van diciendo en altas voces.
—Den para enterrar el cuerpo
del rico ayer y hoy tan pobre,
que si no le dan mortaja,
no la tiene, ni hay de donde;
mueva a compasión su muerte;
socorredle, pretensores,
pues que tanto dió y dar pudo
a tantos de los que le oyen.
El que daba dignidades
haciendo duques y condes,
grandes, marqueses, prelados,
maestres, comendadores;
el que con la voluntad
pudo hacer y hizo hombres,
como delincuente muere:
dadle limosna, señores.
Ayer el mundo mandó;
hoy de un bochín sucio y torpe
se sujeta al proceder,
y humilde a sus pies se pone.
Por estas calles que hoy pasa,

entre confusos pregones
le vimos acompañado
del mismo rey y su corte,
¡ y dichoso el que alcanzaba
su lado, a ponerse adonde
con su vista le alcanzase,
ya que no con sus razones!
Hoy a este mismo acompañan
mil populares montones
de gente ociosa, perdida,
vagamundos, malhechores.
El que pudo lo que quiso
con los dados por tutores,
como delincuente hoy muere;
dadle limosna, señores.
—¡ Oh mundo vano, caduco,
cómo pagas a quien pone
sus esperanzas en ti!
¡ Y cuán pocos te conocen!
  Esto un cofrade decía
de la caridad a voces,
cuando por la costanilla
un tropel de gente rompe;
la guardia del rey don Juan
se divide en escuadrones,
para que de su justicia
la ejecución no se estorbe.
Gran cantidad de alguaciles,
dos alcaldes de su corte,
tres capitanes con gente
por las calles y cantones:
—Plaza, aparte, aparte, claman
diciendo los muñidores.
—Hagan bien para hacer bien
por el alma deste hombre.
  En medio viene el de Luna
rompiendo los corazones,
en una mula enlutada,

capuz hasta los talones,
una caperuza negra,
agravado con prisiones,
a los lados uno y otro
un par de predicadores.
Todos se conmueven de él,
no hay quien de vello no llore,
y al preguntar por qué muere,
todos los hombros encogen:
los pregoneros lo dicen,
unos a otros responden.
Llegaron a un cadahalso,
encima del cual le ponen,
teatro de su tragedia,
donde lo que dicen oye.
—Hagan bien por hacer bien
por el alma deste pobre.

PEDRO DE ESPINOSA

(1578–1650)

Soneto

Estas purpúreas rosas que a la Aurora
se le cayeron hoy del blanco seno,
y un vaso de pintadas flores lleno,
¡ O dulces auras os ofrezco agora,
si defendéis de la divina Flora
con vuestras alas el color moreno
del Sol, que ardiente y de piedad ageno
su rostro ofende, porque el campo dora.
¡ O hijas de la tierra peregrinas,
mirad si tiene Mayo en sus guirnaldas
más frescas rosas, más bizarras flores!
Llorando les dió el Alba perlas finas,
el Sol colores, mi afición la falda
de mi hermosa Flora, y ella olores.

Estancia

En una red prendiste tu cabello,
por salteador de triunfos y despojos,
y siendo el delincuente,
lo sueltas, y me hazes dél cadena.
No fíes dél, o lumbre de mis ojos,
que es lazo, y mucho se te llega al cuello,
llégalo al mío, y pagaré la pena,
porque diga el amor, siendo testigo,
que mi premio nació de su castigo.

Octava real

Pobre viste, perdiendo tu decoro,
arroyuelo gentil con noble pena,
lecho y margen sin oro ni verbena,
agua sin lustre, arena sin tesoro.
Mas ya miras riquezas al trasfloro,
después que el nombre de mi Laura suena,
en lecho, en agua, en margen, en arena,
de perlas, de cristal, de flores, de oro.

FRANCISCO DE QUEVEDO Y VILLEGAS

(1580–1645)

Epístola al conde-duque de Olivares

No he de callar, por más que con el dedo,
ya tocando la boca, o ya la frente,
silencio avises o amenaces miedo.
¿No ha de haber un espíritu valiente?
¿Siempre se ha de sentir lo que se dice?
¿Nunca se ha de decir lo que se siente?
Hoy sin miedo que libre escandalice

puede hablar el ingenio, asegurado
de que mayor poder le atemorice.
   En otros siglos pudo ser pecado
severo estudio y la verdad desnuda,
y romper el silencio el bien hablado.
   Pues sepa quien lo niega y quien lo duda
que es lengua la verdad de Dios severo
y la lengua de Dios nunca fué muda.
   Son la verdad y Dios, Dios verdadero:
ni eternidad divina los separa,
ni de los dos alguno fué primero.
   Si Dios a la verdad se adelantara,
siendo verdad, implicación hubiera
en ser y en que verdad de ser dejara.
   La justicia de Dios es verdadera
y la misericordia, y todo cuanto
es Dios todo ha de ser verdad entera.
   Señor Excelentísimo, mi llanto
ya no consiente márgenes ni orillas:
inundación será la de mi canto.
   Ya sumergirse miro mis mejillas,
la vista por dos urnas derramada
sobre las aras de las dos Castillas.
   Yace aquella virtud desaliñada,
que fué, si rica menos, más temida,
en vanidad y en sueño sepultada.
   Y aquella libertad esclarecida,
que en donde supo hallar honrada muerte
nunca quiso tener más larga vida.
   Y, pródiga del alma, nación fuerte
contaba por afrenta de los años
envejecer en brazos de la suerte. . . .
   Que la cortés estrella que os inclina
a privar sin intento y sin venganza,
milagro que a la invidia desatina,
   tiene por sola bienaventuranza
el reconocimiento temeroso
no presumida y ciega confianza.

Y si os dió el ascendiente generoso
escudos de armas y blasones llenos,
y por timbre el martirio glorioso,
mejores sean por vos los que eran buenos
Guzmanes, y la cumbre desdeñosa
os muestre a su pesar campos serenos.
Lograd, señor, edad tan venturosa;
y cuando nuestras fuerzas examina
persecución unida y belicosa,
la militar valiente disciplina
tenga más platicantes que la plaza:
descansen tela falsa y tela fina. . . .
Mandadlo así, que aseguraros puedo
que habéis de restaurar más que Pelayo,
pues valdrá por ejércitos el miedo
y os verá el cielo administrar su rayo.

Soneto

Los cabellos de Lisi

En crespa tempestad del oro undoso
nada en golfos de luz ardiente y pura
mi corazón, sediento de hermosura,
si el cabello deslazas generoso.
Leandro en mar de fuego proceloso
su amor ostenta, su vivir apura;
Ícaro en senda de oro mal segura
arde sus alas por morir glorioso.
Con pretensión de fénix, encendidas
sus esperanzas, que difuntas lloro,
intenta que su muerte engendre vidas.
Avaro y rico, y pobre en el tesoro,
el castigo y la hambre imita a Midas,
Tántalo en fugitiva fuente de oro.

Soneto

La vida fugitiva

Todo tras sí lo lleva el año breve
de la vida mortal, burlando el brío
al acero valiente, al mármol frío
que contra el tiempo su dureza atreve.
Antes que sepa andar el pie, se mueve
camino de la muerte, donde envío
mi vida oscura: pobre y turbio río,
que negro mar con altas ondas bebe.
Todo corto momento es paso largo
que doy, a mi pesar, en tal jornada,
pues, parado y durmiendo, siempre aguijo.
Breve suspiro, y último, y amargo,
es la muerte, forzosa y heredada;
mas si es ley y no pena, ¿qué me aflijo?

Letrilla

Rosal, menos presunción,
donde están las clavellinas,
pues serán mañana espinas,
las que agora rosas son.

¿De qué sirve presumir,
rosal, de buen parecer,
si aun no acabas de nacer
cuando empiezas a morir?
Hace llorar y reír,
vivo y muerto tu arrebol,
en un día o en un sol;
desde el oriente al ocaso
va tu hermosura en un paso,
y en menos tu perfección.

Rosal, menos presunción,
donde están las clavellinas,
pues serán mañana espinas,
las que agora rosas son.

No es muy grande la ventaja
que tu calidad mejora:
si es tus mantillas la aurora,
es la noche tu mortaja:
no hay florecilla tan baja
que no te alcance de días,
y de tus caballerías,
por descendiente del alba,
se está riyendo la malva,
caballera de un terrón.

Rosal, menos presunción,
donde están las clavellinas,
pues serán mañana espinas,
las que agora rosas son.

Punta en boca

Las cuerdas de mi instrumento
ya son en mis soledades,
locas en dezir verdades,
con vozes de mi tormento:
su lazo a mi cuello siento,
que me aflige y me importuna
con los trastes de fortuna,
mas pues su puente si canto
la hago puente de llanto,
que vierte mi pasión loca,
punto en boca.

Hemos venido a llegar
a tiempo, que en damas claras

son de solimán las caras,
las almas de rejalgar.
Piensan ya remozar,
y volver al color nuevo,
haciendo Jordán un huevo,
que les renueve los años.
Quiero callar desengaños,
y pues a todas les toca,
punto en boca.

Dase al diablo por no dar
el avaro al pobre bajo,
y hasta los días de trabajo
los hace días de guardar,
cautivo por ahorrar.
Pobre para sí en dinero,
rico para su heredero,
pues de miedo del ladrón,
a sí se hurta el bolsón,
y cuando muere le invoca,
punto en boca. . . .

EL CONDE DE VILLAMEDIANA

(1582–1622)

Quintillas

¿Cómo se puede dudar
de quien hizo mi elección,
que en el alma y corazón
os haya dado el lugar
que se os debe por razón?

Porque el hombre que de un sueño
despierta, y comienza a ver,
cobra vida y nuevo ser,
entregado a mejor dueño,
y el alma en vuestro poder.

La resistencia es en vano,
buscar remedio es locura;
que donde el mal es ventura,
heridas de vuestra mano,
la misma mano las cura.

Y aunque es sobresalto esquivo
no llegar a tomar puerto,
quedaré con un bien cierto,
o para serviros vivo,
o por vuestra mano muerto.

Epigrama

Cuando el marqués de Malpica,
caballero de la llave,
con su silencio replica,
dice todo cuanto sabe.

FRANCISCO DE RIOJA

(1583–1659)

A la rosa amarilla

¿Cuál suprema piedad, rosa divina,
de alta belleza transformó colores
en tu flor peregrina,
teñida del color de los amores?
Cuando en ti floreció el aliento humano,
sin duda fué soberbio, amante y necio
cuidado tuyo y llama,
y tu descuido suyo y su desprecio;
diste voces al aire, fiel en vano.
¡Oh triste, y cuántas veces
y cuántas, ay, tu lengua enmudecieron
lágrimas que copiosas la ciñeron!

Mas tal hubo deidad que conmovida
(fuese al rigor del amoroso fuego
o al pío afecto del humilde ruego),
borró tus luces bellas
y apagó de tu encendio las centellas,
desvaneció la púrpura y la nieve
de tu belleza pura
en corteza y en hojas y astil breve.
El oro solamente
que en crespos lazos coronó tu frente,
en igual copia dura,
sombra de la belleza,
que pródiga te dió naturaleza
para que seas, oh flor resplandeciente,
ejemplo eterno y solo de amadores,
sola eterna amarilla entre las flores.

ESTEBAN MANUEL DE VILLEGAS

(1589–1660)

Oda sáfica

Dulce vecino de la verde selva,
huésped eterno del abril florido,
vital aliento de la madre Venus,
céfiro blando;

si de mis ansias el amor supiste,
tú, que las quejas de mi voz llevaste,
oye, no temas, y a mi ninfa dile,
dile que muero.

Filis un tiempo mi dolor sabía;
Filis un tiempo mi dolor lloraba;
quísome un tiempo; mas agora temo,
temo sus iras.

Así los dioses con amor paterno,
así los cielos con amor benigno,
nieguen al tiempo que feliz volares
nieve a la tierra.

Jamás el peso de la nube parda
cuando amanece en la elevada cumbre,
toque tus hombros ni su mal granizo
hiera tus alas.

PEDRO CALDERÓN DE LA BARCA

(1600–81)

'*Sueña el rey . . .*'

Sueña el rey que es rey, y vive
con este engaño mandando,
disponiendo y gobernando;
y este aplauso, que recibe
prestado, en el viento escribe;
y en cenizas le convierte
la muerte (¡ desdicha fuerte !)
¿ Que hay quien intente reinar,
viendo que ha de despertar
en el sueño de la muerte?
Sueña el rico en su riqueza,
que más cuidados le ofrece;
sueña el pobre que padece
su miseria y su pobreza;
sueña el que a medrar empieza,
sueña el que afana y pretende,
sueña el que agravia y ofende,
y en el mundo, en conclusión,
todos sueñan lo que son,
aunque ninguno lo entiende.
Yo sueño que estoy aquí
destas prisiones cargado,

y soñé que en otro estado
más lisonjero me vi.
¿ Qué es la vida ? Un frenesí.
¿ Qué es la vida ? Una ilusión,
una sombra, una ficción,
y el mayor bien es pequeño ;
que toda la vida es sueño,
y los sueños sueños son.

La vida es sueño

Sonetos

Éstas que fueron pompa y alegría
despertando al albor de la mañana,
a la tarde serán lástima vana
durmiendo en brazos de la noche fría.
Este matiz que al cielo desafía,
iris listado de oro, nieve y grana,
será escarmiento de la vida humana :
¡ tanto se emprende en término de un día !
A florecer las rosas madrugaron
y para envejecerse florecieron :
cuna y sepulcro en un botón hallaron.
Tales los hombres sus fortunas vieron :
en un día nacieron y expiraron ;
que pasados los siglos, horas fueron.

Esos rasgos de luz, esas centellas
que cobran con amagos superiores
alimentos del sol en resplandores,
aquello viven que se duele dellas.
Flores nocturnas son ; aunque tan bellas,
efímeras padecen sus ardores ;
pues si un día es el siglo de las flores,
una noche es la edad de las estrellas.
De esa, pues, primavera fugitiva
ya nuestro mal, ya nuestro bien se infiere :
registro es nuestro, o muera el sol o viva.

¿ Qué duración habrá que el hombre espere,
o qué mudanza habrá, que no reciba
de astro, que cada noche nace y muere ?

El príncipe constante

Cantarcillo

Ruiseñor que volando vas,
cantando finezas, cantando favores,
¡ oh cuánta pena y envidia me das !
Pero no, que si hoy cantas amores,
tú tendrás celos y tú llorarás.

¡ Qué alegre y desvanecido
cantas, dulce ruiseñor,
las venturas de tu amor
olvidado de tu olvido !
En ti, de ti entretenido
al ver cuán ufano estás,
¡ oh cuánta pena me das
publicando tus favores !
Pero no, que si hoy cantas amores,
tú tendrás celos y tú llorarás.

Los dos amantes del cielo

La tentación de Justina

UNA VOZ. *¿ Cuál es la gloria mayor*
desta vida ?
CORO. *Amor, amor.*
UNA VOZ. *No hay sujeto en que no imprima*
el fuego de amor su llama,
pues vive más donde ama
el hombre, que donde anima.

Amor solamente estima
cuanto tener vida sabe,
el tronco, la flor y el ave:
luego es la gloria mayor
de esta vida. . . .

CORO. *Amor, amor.*

JUSTINA (*asombrada y inquieta*).

Pesada imaginación,
al parecer lisonjera,
¿Cuándo te he dado ocasión
para que desta manera
aflijas mi corazón?
¿Cuál es la causa, en rigor,
deste fuego, deste ardor,
que en mí por instantes creces?
¿Qué dolor el que padece
mi sentido?

CORO (*dentro*). *Amor, amor.*

JUSTINA (*sosegándose*).

Aquel ruiseñor amante
es quien respuesta me da,
enamorando constante
a su consorte, que está
un ramo más adelante.
Calla, ruiseñor; no aquí
imaginar me hagas ya,
por las quejas que te oí,
cómo un hombre sentirá,
si siente un pájaro así.
Mas no: una vid fué lasciva,
que buscando fugitiva
va al tronco donde se enlace,
siendo el verdor con que abrace
el peso con que derriba.
No así con verdes abrazos
me hagas pensar en quien amas,
vid; que dudaré en tus lazos,
si así abrazan unas ramas,

cómo enraman unos brazos.
Y si no es la vid, será
aquel girasol, que está
viendo cara a cara al sol,
tras cuyo hermoso arrebol
siempre moviéndose va.
No sigas, no, tus enojos,
flor, con marchitos despojos,
que pensarán mis congojas,
si así lloran unas hojas,
cómo lloran unos ojos.
Cesa, amante ruiseñor;
desúnete, vid frondosa;
párate, inconstante flor,
o decid, ¿qué venenosa
fuerza usáis?

CORO (*dentro*). *Amor, amor.*

El mágico pr

Disputa entre los cuatro elementos

AGUA

¡Mía ha de ser la corona!

AIRE

¡El laurel ha de ser mío!

TIERRA

¡No hará mientras yo no muero!

FUEGO

¡No será mientras yo vivo!

AGUA

Este lazo de los cuatro,
nunca hasta aquí dividido,
no ha de romperse si yo
no reino.

TIERRA

Quc en el principio
Dios hizo el cielo y la tierra
se dirá; luego debido
me es el vasallaje, siendo
la que a los tres me anticipo;
pues será de fe que a mí
a par del cielo me hizo.

AIRE

Tierra que árida y vacía
estás, que así ha de decirlo
la misma letra, si soy
el Aire a cuyos alivios
has de beber los alientos,
¿Por qué compites conmigo?

AGUA

El espíritu de Dios,
inspirado de sí mismo,
sobre las aguas fluctúa,
que son la faz del abismo.
Luego si sobre las aguas
el espíritu divino
de Dios es llevado, al Agua
debéis los demás rendiros.

FUEGO

Un globo y masa confusa
que poéticos estilos
llamarán *caos* y *nada*
los profetas, compusimos
los cuatro; pues ¿por qué, siendo
hija hermosa de mis visos
la luz, la primer criatura
con que a todos ilumino,
queréis que el Fuego no sea
de los cuatro el preferido?

La vida es sueño. Auto sacramental

SOR JUANA INÉS DE LA CRUZ
(1651–95)

Redondillas

Hombres necios, que acusáis
a la mujer sin razón,
sin ver que sois la ocasión
de lo mismo que culpáis;
si con ansia sin igual
solicitáis su desdén,
¿por qué queréis que obren bien
si las incitáis al mal?
Combatís su resistencia,
y luego con gravedad
decís que fué liviandad
lo que hizo la diligencia.
Parecer quiere el denuedo
de vuestro parecer loco
al niño que pone el coco
y luego le tiene miedo.
Queréis con presunción necia
hallar a la que buscáis,
para pretendida, Tais,
y en la posesión, Lucrecia.
¿Qué humor puede ser más raro
que el que, falto de consejo,
el mismo empaña el espejo
y siente que no esté claro?
Con el favor y el desdén
tenéis condición igual,
quejándoos, si os tratan mal,
burlándoos, si os quieren bien.
Opinión ninguna gana,
pues la que más se recata,
si no os admite, es ingrata,
y si os admite, es liviana. . . .
Pues ¿cómo ha de estar templada
la que vuestro amor pretende,

si la que es ingrata ofende
y la que es fácil enfada?
  Mas entre el enfado y pena
que vuestro gusto refiere,
bien haya la que no os quiere
y quejaos enhorabuena. . . .
  ¿Cuál mayor culpa ha tenido
en una pasión errada;
la que cae de rogada
o el que ruega de caído?
  O ¿cuál es más de culpar
aunque cualquiera mal haga:
la que peca por la paga
o el que paga por pecar?
  Pues ¿para qué os espantáis
de la culpa que tenéis?
Queredlas cual las hacéis
o hacedlas cual las buscáis.
  Dejad de solicitar,
y después, con más razón,
acusaréis la afición
de la que os fuere a rogar.
  Bien con muchas armas fundo
que lidia vuestra arrogancia,
pues en promesa e instancia
juntáis diablo, carne y mundo.

DIEGO DE TORRES Y VILLARROEL
(1693–1770)

Seguidillas

  Dicen que la fortuna
es varia y loca;
es mentira, que es cuerda
que aprieta y afloja;
cuidado alerta,
que a muchos ahoga
si los aprieta. . . .

En el mundo que corre
todo está vario;
no llega a ser comedia,
todo es ensayo;
y en esto encuentro
que el galán es el oro,
gracioso el tiempo.

En el mundo que siempre
fué una baraja,
una vez juega el oro
y otra la espada;
y de esta suerte,
lo que un día se gana
otro se pierde.

Danzando en la maroma
de sus trofeos,
un volatín del mundo
cae en el suelo;
y es tal el golpe,
que hasta en lo más remoto
los ecos se oyen.

FRAY DIEGO GONZÁLEZ

(1733–94)

Pintura deseada

Si la efigie verdadera
de Mirta se ha de formar
debe el cielo aparejar
todo el lienzo de su esfera.
Es preciso que le diera
sus rayos para pinceles,

color sus virtudes fieles
en grande prudencia el tiento,
digna idea su talento,
la mano el supremo Apeles.

NICOLÁS FERNÁNDEZ DE MORATÍN

(1737–80)

Madrid antigua y moderna

Los soberbios palacios
con que ¡ oh Madrid altiva ! te engrandeces,
ocupan los espacios
anchos que en tus niñeces
los arados rompieron tantas veces.

Viñedos y aranzadas
del suelo que ocupaste has apartado,
y hay torres levantadas
donde en tiempo pasado
creció el olivo a Palas consagrado.

Por donde con el trillo
circularon las yuntas de bueyes
sobre el haz amarillo,
van dando al orbe leyes
en carro ebúrneo príncipes y reyes.

Fuiste ignorada aldea,
y eres cabeza ya de entrambos mundos :
no aparta la febea
luz sus rayos fecundos
de sus tierras y piélagos profundos.

Mas no de la grandeza
presente fíes : todo es vanidades,
y acaba cuanto empieza,
pues ya en nuestras edades
ni Troya, ni Palmira son ciudades.

La Atlántica famosa
se hundió en el mar: voraz el tiempo altera
el globo, no reposa,
no es hoy lo que antes era;
ni ya Tule tampoco es la postrera.

JOSÉ CADALSO

(1741–82)

Soneto

Todo lo muda el tiempo, Filis mía;
todo cede al rigor de sus guadañas:
ya transforma los valles en montañas,
ya pone campo donde mar había.
Él muda en noche opaca el claro día,
en fábulas pueriles las hazañas,
alcázares soberbios en cabañas,
y el juvenil ardor en vejez fría.
Doma el tiempo al caballo desbocado,
detiene el mar y viento enfurecido,
postra al león y rinde al bravo toro.
Sola una cosa al tiempo denodado
ni cederá, ni cede, ni ha cedido,
y es el constante amor con que te adoro.

GASPAR MELCHOR DE JOVELLANOS

(1744–1811)

Epístola de Fabio a Anfriso

Escrita desde El Paular en la Sierra Guadarrama

Credibile est illi numen inesse loco.
OVIDIO

Desde el oculto y venerable asilo,
do la virtud austera y penitente
vive ignorada, y del liviano mundo

huída, en santa soledad se esconde,
el triste Fabio al venturoso Anfriso,
salud en versos flébiles envía;
salud le envía a Anfriso, al que inspirado
de las mantuanas musas, tal vez suele
al grave son de su celeste canto
precipitar del viejo Manzanares
el curso perezoso, tal süave
suele ablandar con amorosa lira
la altiva condición de sus zagalas.
¡ Pluguiera a Dios, oh Anfriso, que el cuitado,
a quien no dió la suerte tal ventura,
pudiese huir del mundo y sus peligros!
¡ Pluguiera a Dios, pues ya con su barquilla
logró arribar a puerto tan seguro,
que esconderla supiera en este abrigo,
a tanta luz y ejemplos enseñado!
Huyera así la furia tempestuosa
de los contrarios vientos, los escollos
y las fieras borrascas, tantas veces
entre sustos y lágrimas corridas.
Así también del mundanal tumulto
lejos, y en estos montes guarecido,
alguna vez gozara del reposo,
que hoy desterrado de su pecho vive.
  Mas ¡ ay de aquel que hasta en el santo asilo
de la virtud arrastra la cadena,
la pesada cadena, con que el mundo
oprime a sus esclavos! ¡ Ay del triste
en cuyo oído suena con espanto,
por esta oculta soledad rompiendo,
de su señor el imperioso grito!
  Busco en estas moradas silenciosas
el reposo y la paz, que aquí se esconden,
y sólo encuentro la inquietud funesta,
que mis sentidos y razón conturba.
  Busco paz y reposo, pero en vano
los busco, oh caro Anfriso; que estos dones,

herencia santa, que al partir del mundo
dejó Bruno en sus hijos vinculada,
nunca en profano corazón entraron
ni a los parciales del placer se dieron.
Conozco bien que, fuera de este asilo,
sólo me guarda el mundo sinrazones,
vanos deseos, duros desengaños,
susto y dolor; empero todavía
a entrar en él no puedo resolverme.
No puedo resolverme, y despechado
sigo el impulso del fatal destino
que a muy más dura esclavitud me guía.
Sigo su fiero impulso, y llevo siempre
por todas partes los pesados grillos
que de la ansiada libertad me privan.
De afán y angustia el pecho traspasado,
pido a la muda soledad consuelo
y con dolientes quejas la importuno.
Salgo al ameno valle, subo al monte,
sigo del claro río las corrientes,
busco la fresca y deleitosa sombra,
corro por todas partes, y no encuentro
en parte alguna la quietud perdida. . . .

¡Ah, dichoso el mortal de cuyos ojos
un pronto desengaño corrió el velo
de la ciega ilusión! ¡Una y mil veces
dichoso el solitario penitente,
que, triunfando del mundo y de sí mismo,
vive en la soledad libre y contento!
Unido a Dios por medio de la santa
contemplación, le goza ya en la tierra;
y, retirado en su tranquilo albergue,
observa reflexivo los milagros
de la naturaleza, sin que nunca
turben el susto ni el dolor su pecho.
Regálanle las aves con su canto,
mientras la aurora sale refulgente

a cubrir de alegría y luz el mundo.
Nácele siempre el sol claro y brillante,
y nunca a él levanta conturbados
sus ojos, ora en el oriente raye,
ora, del cielo a la mitad subiendo,
en pompa guíe el reluciente carro,
ora con tibia luz, más perezoso,
su faz esconda en los vecinos montes.
Cuando en las claras noches cuidadoso
vuelve desde los santos ejercicios,
la plateada luna en lo más alto
del cielo mueve la luciente rueda
con augusto silencio; y recreando
con blando resplendor su humilde vista,
eleva su razón, y la dispone
a contemplar la alteza y la inefable
gloria del Padre y Criador del mundo. . . .

FELIX MARÍA SAMANIEGO

(1745–1801)

Fábula

El león vencido por el hombre

Cierto artífice pintó
una lucha, en que valiente
un hombre tan solamente
a un horrible león venció.
Otro león que el cuadro vió,
sin preguntar por su autor,
en tono despreciador
dijo: " Bien se deja ver
que es pintar como querer,
y no fué león el pintor."

Fábula

El hombre y la culebra

A una culebra que, de frío yerta,
en el suelo yacía medio muerta
un labrador cogió ; mas fué tan bueno,
que incautamente la abrigó en su seno.
Apenas revivió, cuando la ingrata
a su gran bienhechor traidora mata.

Fábula

El gran Zapirón

Desde el gran Zapirón, el blanco y rubio,
que después de las aguas del diluvio
fué padre universal de todo gato,
ha sido Miauragato
quien más sangrientamente
persiguió a la infeliz ratona gente.
Lo cierto es que, obligada
de su persecución la desdichada,
en Ratópolis tuvo su congreso.
Propuso el elocuente Roequeso
echarle un cascabel, y de esa suerte
al ruido escaparían de la muerte.
El proyecto aprobaron uno a uno ;
¿ Quién lo ha de ejecutar ?—eso ninguno.
" Yo soy corto de vista.—Yo muy viejo.—
Yo gotoso." decían. El concejo
se acabó como muchos en el mundo.
Proponen un proyecto sin segundo :
lo aprueban : hacen otro. ¡ Qué portento !
Pero, ¿ la ejecución ? Ahí está el cuento.

JOSÉ IGLESIAS DE LA CASA

(1748–91)

Letrilla

El mi pastorcillo
bien sé yo que suele
por mí preguntaros,
si estoy de él ausente.
Y que, aunque lo calla,
llora muchas veces
porque a verle venga
y su mal consuele.
Por otra zagala
no temo me deje,
aun cuando enojado
de sí me deseche;
pues sé que a la hora
su amiga han de hacerme
de miel una orzuela,
y un cuerno de leche.
Y si esto no le basta,
con que le deje
jugar cierto juego
no podrá él valerse.

TOMÁS DE IRIARTE

(1750–91)

Fábula

La lechuza

Cobardes son y traidores
ciertos críticos, que esperan,
para impugnar, a que mueran
los infelices autores,
porque vivos respondieran.

Un breve caso a este intento
contaba una abuela mía.
Diz que un día en un convento
entró una lechuza . . . miento,
que no debió ser un día;

fué sin duda estando el sol
ya muy lejos del ocaso . . .
ella, en fin, encontró al paso
una lámpara o farol
(que es lo mismo para el caso).

Y volviendo la trasera,
exclamó de esta manera:
"Lámpara, ¡con qué deleite
te chupara yo el aceite,
si tu luz no me ofendiera!

Mas ya que ahora no puedo,
porque estás bien atizada,
si otra vez te hallo apagada,
sabré perdiéndote el miedo,
darme una buena panzada."

(Atreverse a los autores muertos, y no a los vivos, no sólo es cobardía sino traición.)

Fábula

La ardilla y el caballo

Mirando estaba una ardilla
a un generoso alazán,
que dócil a espuela y rienda,
se adiestraba en galopar.
Viéndole hacer movimientos
tan veloces y a compás,

de aquesta suerte le dijo
con muy poca cortedad:
"Señor mío,
de ese brío,
ligereza
y destreza
no me espanto,
que otro tanto
suelo hacer, y acaso más.
Yo soy viva,
soy activa,
me meneo,
me paseo,
yo trabajo,
subo y bajo,
no me estoy quieta jamás."

El paso detiene entonces
el buen potro, y muy formal
en los términos siguientes
respuesta a la ardilla da:
"Tantas idas
y venidas,
tantas vueltas
(quiero, amiga,
que me diga),
son de alguna utilidad?
Yo me afano,
mas no en vano.
Sé mi oficio,
y en servicio
de mi dueño
tengo empeño
de lucir mi habilidad."
Con que algunos escritores
ardillas también serán
si en obras frívolas gastan
todo el calor natural.

Fábula

El fabricante de galones y la encajera

Cerca de una encajera
vivía un fabricante de galones.
" Vecina, ¡ quién creyera
(le dijo) que valiesen más doblones
de tu encaje tres varas
que diez de un galón de oro de dos caras!

" De que a tu mercancía
(esto es lo que ella respondió al vecino)
tanto exceda la mía,
aunque en oro trabajas y yo en lino,
no debes admirarte,
pues más que la materia vale el arte."

Quien desprecie el estilo,
y diga que a las cosas sólo atiende,
advierta que si el hilo
más que el noble metal caro se vende,
también da la elegancia
su principal valor a la substancia.

JUAN MELÉNDEZ VALDÉS

(1754–1817)

Romance

La mañana de San Juan

Madrugada de San Juan
por el prado de la aldea
a celebrar se salen
pastores y zagalejas.
Bailándolas ellos vienen
con mil mudanzas y vueltas,
y cantando mil tonadas
del dulce amor vienen ellas . . .

No hay corazón que esté triste,
ni voluntad que esté exenta;
todo es amores el valle,
los zagales todo fiesta.
Cuál saltando se adelanta,
cuál burlando atrás se queda,
y cuál en medio de todas
repica la pandereta.
El crótalo y el tamborino
con la alegre flauta alternan,
y el regocijo y los vivas
suben hasta las estrellas.
Unos de trébol y flores
y misteriosa verbena
sus cándidas sienes ciñen,
matizan sus rubias trenzas.
Otros por detrás sus ojos
con un lienzo, arteros, vendan,
y del juego alegres ríen
si con el engaño aciertan;
y otros de menuda juncia
tejiendo blandas cadenas,
hacen como que las prenden,
y en sus lazos más se enredan.
Cuáles, alzando los ramos,
en triunfo de amor los llevan,
y cuáles, porque los pisen,
de ellos el camino siembran.
Así llegan a la fuente
que el gran álamo hermosea
con su pomposo ramaje,
do en alegre paz se asientan.
El gusto y el júbilo crecen,
la risa y el placer vuelan
de boca en boca, y más vivos
canto y danzas se renuevan.
La aurora, de su albo seno
rosas derramando y perlas,

cede el cielo al sol, que asoma
y se para y las contempla;
  y en medio su trono de oro,
por las lucientes esferas
ostentando de sus llamas
la inagotable riqueza;
  este día más hermoso
parece que da a la tierra
más rica luz y a las flores
alegría y vida nueva.
  Con la fiesta y el bullicio
las avecillas despiertan,
pueblan y animan los aires,
y la nueva luz celebran. . . .
  Libre en tanto el amor vaga
nadie sus tiros recela;
el campo, el día, la hora,
todo la ilusión aumenta.
  Todo encanta los sentidos;
por una llanada inmensa
vaga la vista, las aves
con sus trinos embelesan.
  Entre el grato cefirillo
el labio aromas alienta,
el tacto en delicias nada,
y el pecho inflamado anhela;
  gratamente así corriendo
por las agitadas venas,
del placer la suave llama,
que a todos arrastra y ciega.
  La ocasión brinda al deseo,
las miradas son más tiernas,
los requiebros más ardientes,
más traviesa la agudeza.
  Nadie desairado llora
ni enojar amando tiembla;
el baile mismo autoriza
mil cariñosas licencias.

Quién rendido se declara,
quién tierno la mano premia
de sú amada, y quién la roba
un beso al dar una vuelta;
beso de que no se ofende
la zagala más severa,
pues fueran culpa ese día
el rigor o la tibieza.
Todos arden y suspiran,
todo se aplaude y festeja;
la timidez es osada,
menos cauta la modestia.
Y entre tantos regocijos,
un pastor a quien las nuevas
de su dulce bien faltaban,
cantó, angustiado, esta letra:

" Ya no hay, zagales, amor,
que lo acabara el olvido;
nada de Fili he sabido,
y tiemblo su disfavor;
ausente estoy, fuí querido;
¡ Ved si es justo mi dolor!

" También yo un tiempo dichoso
cual ora os gozáis, me vi,
y en mi embeleso amoroso
alegre canté y reí
a par de mi dueño hermoso.

" Después que dejé su lado
perdí la dicha y el gusto;
y hoy con más grave cuidado,
al ver su silencio injusto,
sólo exclamo desolado:

" Ya no hay, zagales, amor,
que lo acabara el olvido;
nada de Fili he sabido,

y tiemblo su disfavor;
ausente estoy, fuí querido;
¡Ved si es justo mi dolor!"

Soneto

El despecho

Los ojos tristes, de llorar cansados,
alzando al cielo su clemencia imploro;
mas vuelven luego al encendido lloro,
que el grave peso no los sufre alzados;
mil dolorosos ayes desdeñados
son ¡ay! trasunto de la luz que adoro;
y ni me alivia el día, ni mejoro
con la callada noche mis cuidados.
Huyo a la soledad, y va conmigo
oculto el mal, y nada me recrea;
en la ciudad en lágrimas me anego;
aborrezco mi ser; y aunque maldigo
la vida, temo que la muerte aun sea
remedio débil para tanto fuego.

Soneto

La paloma

Suelta mi palomita pequeñuela,
y déjamela libre, ladrón fiero;
suéltamela, pues ves cuánto la quiero,
y mi dolor con ella se consuela.
Tú allá me la entretienes con cautela;
dos noches no ha venido, aunque la espero.
¡Ay! si ésta se detiene, cierto muero;
suéltala, ¡oh crudo! y tú verás cuál vuela.
Si señas quieres, el color de nieve,
manchadas las alitas, amorosa
la vista, y el arrullo soberano,
lumbroso el cuello, y el piquito breve—
mas suéltala y verásla bulliciosa
cuál viene y pica de mi palma el grano.

Mi vuelta al campo

Ya vuelvo a ti, pacífico retiro;
altas colinas, valle silencioso,
término de mis deseos,
faustos me recibid; dadme el reposo
por que en vano suspiro
entre el tumulto y tristes devaneos
de la corte engañosa.
Con vuestra sombra amiga
mi inocencia cubrid, y en paz dichosa
dadme esperar el golpe doloroso
de la Parca enemiga,
que lento alcance a mi vejez cansada,
cual de otoño templado
en deleitosa tarde, desmayada
huye su luz del cárdeno occidente
el rubio sol con paso sosegado.
¡ Oh cómo, vegas plácidas, ya siente
vuestro influjo feliz el alma mía!
Os tengo, os gozaré; con libre planta
discurriré por vos; veré la aurora,
bañada en perlas que riendo llora,
purpúrea abrir la puerta al nuevo día,
su dudoso esplendor vago esmaltando
del monte, que a las nubes se adelanta,
la opuesta negra cumbre;
del sol naciente la benigna lumbre
veré alentar, vivificar el suelo,
que en nublosos vapores
adormeciera de la noche el hielo;
del aura matinal el soplo blando
de vida henchido, y olorosas flores,
aspiraré gozoso;
el himno de alborada bullicioso
oiré a las sueltas aves,
estático en sus cánticos süaves;
y mi vista encantada,

libre vagando en inquietud curiosa
por la inmensa llanada,
aquí verá los fértiles sembrados
ceder en ondas fáciles al viento,
de sus plácidas alas regalados;
sobre la esteva honrada
allí cantar al arador contento
en la esperanza de la mies futura;
alegre en su inocencia y su ventura,
más allá un pastorcillo
lento guiar sus cándidas corderas
a las frescas praderas,
tañendo el concertado caramillo;
y el río ondisonante,
entre copados árboles torciendo,
engañar en su fuga circulante
los ojos que sus pasos van siguiendo,
lento aquí sobre un lecho de verdura,
allí celando su corriente pura;
cerrando el horizonte
el bosque impenetrable y arduo monte. . . .
¡Afortunado el que en humilde choza
mora en los campos, en seguir se goza
los rústicos trabajos, compañeros
de virtud e inocencia,
y salvar logra con feliz prudencia
del mar su barca y huracanes fieros!

EL CONDE DE NOROÑA

(1760–1815)

Oda a Belisa

Belisa, ¡cuán hermoso
es ver de rubias mieses coronado
un terreno espacioso
de arbustos rodeado
y flores olorosas esmaltado!

¡ Cuán dulce el arroyuelo,
que con curso apacible retorcido
riega el ameno suelo,
y halagando el oído
convida al sueño con su lento ruido !

¡ Cuán gracioso parece
el pájaro en el árbol ir saltando,
que en la rama se mece,
y que está requebrando
a su amada, canciones entonando !

¡ Cuán grato es ver hinchadas
las velas de un convoy muy numeroso,
y que las aceradas
proas al mar furioso
dividen con su surco prodigioso !

Pero más lisonjero
que el campo, que el arroyo, más que el ave
más que el convoy ligero
y a mi alma más süave
es gozar de tu pecho, que amar sabe.

Y en tus brazos preciosos
hallar todos los gustos reunidos ;
esos gustos sabrosos,
y tan apetecidos,
que adormecen al punto los sentidos.

NICASIO ÁLVAREZ DE CIENFUEGOS

(1764–1809)

Canción guerrera

La guerra tronó : los ecos,
a su voz, " Abenhamet ",

mil veces claman, y lejos
" ¡ Ay, ay ! responde Jaén,
mis fuertes torres
van a caer."

El clarín sonó : guerreros,
marchad blandiendo las lanzas
sobre el relinchante bruto
que el freno espumando tasca.
Allí donde el fiero Marte
acerada muerte os guarda ;
allí con sangre regado,
nace el laurel de la fama.

La guerra tronó : los ecos, etc.

¿ Qué vale que cien provincias
mueva contra vos España,
si ocho siglos de heroísmo
se encierran sólo en Granada ?
Doquier os cercan gloriosos
las paternales hazañas ;
cien triunfos moriscos yacen
doquier posáreis las plantas.

La guerra tronó : los ecos, etc.

¡ Ay, que las tumbas se abren !
¿ Oís que de ellas os claman
" Vencer o morir " ? ¡ Perezca
quien viva para la infamia !
Jurado está : el que a la muerte
vuelva cobarde la espalda,
amor será su enemigo
y su verdugo la patria.

La guerra tronó : los ecos, etc.

Si os desalientan los rayos
de las diestras castellanas,
volved un punto la vista
a las torres de Granada.
Allí del Genil las bellas
os miran, y enamoradas,
seguras de la victoria,
os tejen ya las guirnaldas.

La guerra tronó : los ecos, etc.

¿ Será que en baldón vencidos
dejéis marchitar las palmas
que en loor de vuestra gloria
su amor ardiente prepara ?
Lejos el temor. Doncellas,
tejed sin cesar guirnaldas ;
que Abenhamet es caudillo
y ordena triunfar Zoraida.

La guerra tronó : los ecos, etc.

Canción

Rosal, rosal, do está el tiempo
que me oyó tu sombra amiga
jurar un amor eterno
al que el suyo me ofrecía ?
Cuando en ti fijaba
la risueña vista,
¡ Con qué amor tus rosas
su prisión cerrada abrían !
¿ Ahora sin amparo,
qué harán ? Afligidas,
del pajizo trono
para siempre caen marchitas.

¡ Cuántas veces ¡ ay ! tu tronco
nos vió en amantes caricias
darle en cristalinas aguas
su frescor y hermosa vida !
   Árbol infelice,
mi recreo un día,
ya tu solo riego
serán las lágrimas mías.
   Muerte son tus galas :
pluguiese a mi dicha
que al caer, tus hojas
cubriesen mi tumba fría !

MANUEL JOSÉ QUINTANA

(1772–1857)

Ariadna

(Se supone a Ariadna sentada en una actitud profundamente triste sobre una peña a la orilla del mar : a un lado una tienda, a otro un gran peñasco que se encorva sobre las aguas.)

¡ Nadie me escucha ! . . . ¡ Nadie ! . . . El eco sólo,
eterno compañero
de este silencio lóbrego, responde
a mi agudo clamor, y mudamente
mi mal aumenta y mi dolor presente.

¿ Y es aquesto verdad ? ¿ Pudo Teseo
sin mí partir, y pudo
desampararme así ? . . . ¡ Pecho de bronce,
de todo amor y de piedad desnudo !
¿ Qué te hice yo para tan vil huída ?
Le vi, le amé ; mi corazón, mi vida,
toda yo suya fuí, toda . . . El ingrato,
¿ qué no me debe ? . . . Encadenado llega
a la cretense playa,
destinado a morir : su sangre odiosa
al monstruo horrible apacentar debía,

que en la prisión del laberinto erraba.
¿Qué hubiera él sido sin la industria mía?
Entra, combate, vence, y coronado
de nueva gloria se presenta al mundo.
Esto era poco: enfurecida y ciega,
frenética después, mi hogar, mi padre,
todo lo olvido a un tiempo, y me confío
al amable impostor, enajenado
con su halago y su amor mi tierno pecho.
¡Falso amor, falso halago! ¿Qué se han hecho
pasión tan viva y perdición tan loca?
Yo lloro aquí desesperada en tanto
que el pérfido se ríe
de mi amor lamentable y de mi llanto.

Pero no; ¿cómo es posible
que tan deliciosos lazos
así los haga pedazos
una horrenda ingratitud?

(Levántase exaltada hacia la tienda.)

¡Ah! no es posible. ¡Oh lecho! tú que has sido
testigo de mi gloria y mi contento,
vuélveme al punto el bien que en ti he perdido.
¡Así mientras sus labios me halagaban,
y en tanto que sus brazos me ceñían,
ya allá en su pecho las traiciones viles
este lazo fatal me preparaban!
¡Oh unión inconcebible
de perfidia y placer! ¡con que, engañoso
puede ser el halago, y la ternura
lleva tras sí maldad y alevosía!
Yo triste, envuelta en la inocencia mía,
al delirio de amor me abandonaba.
Tú sabes cuál mi seno palpitaba,
tú viste cuál mi sangre se encendía,
y cómo de su boca engañadora
deleite, amor y perdición bebía.

Dos ayer éramos,
y hoy sola y mísera
me ves llorando
a par de tí.
Mira estas lágrimas,
mírame trémula,
donde gozando
me estremecí.
¿Qué se hizo el pérfido?
Mi angustia muévate,
y haz que volando
torne hacia mí.

Vuelve, adorado fugitivo, vuelve,
yo te perdono. El ardoroso llanto
que ora inunda mi rostro y me le abrasa,
enjugarás; reclinaré en tu pecho
mi atormentada frente, y aplicando
tu mano al corazón, verás cuál bate
de anhelo palpitante y de alegría.
Mas ¡mísero y ciego devaneo!
mientras imploro al execrable amigo,
lleva el viento consigo
mi gritar, mi esperanza y mi deseo.
¡Y esto, oh dioses, sufrís! ¡Y va seguro
y contento el perjuro
por medio de la mar, que le consiente
sin abrirse y tragarle! . . . ¡Oh tú, divino
astro del claro día, sol luciente,
sagrado autor de la familia mía!
Mira el trance terrible a que he venido;
mírame junto al mar volver llorando
la vista a todas partes, y en ninguna
asilo hallar a mi fatal fortuna;
mírame perecer sin un amigo
que dé a mi suerte lamentable lloro.
¿Dónde, dónde volverme? ¿A quién imploro?

“ Muerte, no hay medio, muerte ; ” éste es el grito
que por do quiera escucho ; ésta la senda
que encuentro abierta a mi infelice suerte.
Brama el mar, silba el viento, y dicen : “ Muerte.”

Y muerte hallaré yo . . . Las ondas fieras
que senda amiga al seductor abrieron,
me la darán . . . ¡ Qué horror ! Un sudor frío
baña mi triste frente, y el cabello
se eriza . . . Sí . . . las veo ;
las furias del averno me arrebatan
tras de sí a fenecer . . . Voy desgraciada
víctima del amor. . . . ¡ Ah ! ¡ Si el ingrato
presente ahora a mi dolor se hallara,
quizá al verme llorar también llorara !
¡ Mas no, mísera ! muere ; el mar te espera,
el universo te olvidó, los dioses
airados te miraron,
y sobre ti, cuitada, en un momento
el peso de su cólera lanzaron.

¡ Oh qué triunfo tan bárbaro y fiero !
Avergüénzate, cielo tirano,
avergüénzate, o dobla inhumano
mi tormento y tu odioso rencor.
¿ Dudo ? ¿ Temo ? ¿ A qué atiendo ? ¿ Qué espero ?
Dame ¡ oh mar ! en tu seno un abrigo,
y las ondas escondan conmigo
mi infortunio, mi oprobio y mi amor.

(Arrójase al mar.)

ALBERTO LISTA Y ARAGÓN

(1775–1848)

A Elisa

Cuando a los campos sales, bella Elisa,
se reverdece el prado;
brota la selva amor y el cielo risa,
y ledo trisca el juguetón ganado.

Las márgenes del río a tu hermosura
tributan amorosas,
sobre lechos de plácida verdura,
cándidos lirios y encendidas rosas.

El ave te saluda dulcemente,
cuando en la selva amiga
contra el sol en los fresnos de la fuente,
cual bajo manto maternal, se abriga;

y cuando a ocaso entre celajes de oro
decline el rayo estivo,
tejerán los zagales dulce coro
al son del arroyuelo fugitivo.

Y allí tu nombre el amoroso canto
y tu desdén gracioso
celebrará, y la risa y el encanto,
que enajena al pastor más desdeñoso,

y luego en los alisos de la cumbre
lo grabarán risueños;
y cuando siga a la vencida lumbre
la noche oscura derramando sueños,

con frescas y apacibles enramadas
ornarán tus umbrales,
y para ti de pomas sazonadas
esquilmarán los fértiles frutales.

Luego vendrá la sonrosada aurora
y en tu serena frente,
que la inocencia plácida colora,
nacerá un sol más bello y refulgente.

Así en gozoso círculo girando
tu juventud florida,
de la beldad los triunfos disfrutando,
en continuo solaz gozas tu vida.

Ama, Elisa gentil. Sereno el cielo
ora brilla y tranquilo;
de la edad teme el inminente vuelo,
y contra su furor busca un asilo.

La esperanza amorosa

No hay diosa que iguale
mi dulce adorada,
ni aurora rosada,
ni sol cuando sale.
Dale, Venus, dale
la poma de oro,
que es Filis el tesoro
más lindo de amor;
Filis bella es la gloria del Ebro,
y de la hermosura la gala y la flor.

El alma arrebata
su blando desvío;
hirió el pecho mío,
severa, no ingrata;
si tal vez maltrata
osados desvelos,
con dulces ojuelos
mitiga el dolor;
Filis bella es la gloria del Ebro,
y de la hermosura la gala y la flor.

Si el mirto y la rosa
los huertos florece,
guirnaldas le ofrece,
mi mano amorosa;
su frente graciosa
con ellas ciñendo,
mi amada riendo
aumenta mi ardor;
robo un beso a sus labios divinos,
y no se me enoja del Ebro la flor.

Mi afecto constante
su nieve ya enflama,
y dulce me llama
su amado y amante;
y cuando brillante
robare el estío
las ondas al río,
y al prado el color,
será mía la gloria del Ebro,
y de la hermosura la gala y la flor.

JUAN NICASIO GALLEGO

(1777–1853)

El dos de mayo

Noche, lóbrega noche, eterno asilo
del miserable que, esquivando el sueño,
en tu silencio pavoroso gime,
no desdeñes mi voz; letal beleño
presta a mis sienes, y en tu horror sublime
empapada la ardiente fantasía,
da a mi pincel fatídicos colores
con que el tremendo día
trace al fulgor de vengadora tea,
y el odio irrite de la patria mía,
y escándalo y terror al orbe sea.

¡Día de execración! La destructora
mano del tiempo le arrojó al averno;
mas ¿quién el sempiterno
clamor con que los ecos importuna
la madre España en enlutado arreo
podrá atajar? Junto al sepulcro frío,
al pálido lucir de opaca luna,
entre cipreses fúnebres la veo:
trémula, yerta, desceñido el manto,
los ojos moribundos
al cielo vuelve, que le oculta el llanto;
roto y sin brillo el cetro de dos mundos
yace entre el polvo, y el león guerrero
lanza a sus pies rugido lastimero. . . .

¡Cuánta escena de muerte! ¡Cuánto estrago!
¡Cuántos ayes doquier! Despavorido
mirad ese infelice
quejarse al adalid empedernido
de otra cuadrillla atroz: "¡Ah! ¿qué te hice?"
exclama el triste, en lágrimas deshecho.

"Mi pan y mi mansión partí contigo
te abrí mis brazos, te cedí mi lecho,
templé tu sed, y me llamé tu amigo;
y ¿hora pagar podrás nuestro hospedaje
sincero, franco, sin doblez ni engaño,
con dura muerte y con indigno ultraje?"
¡Perdido suplicar! ¡Inútil ruego!
El monstruo infame a sus ministros mira,
y con tremenda voz gritando: "¡Fuego!"
tinto en su sangre el desgraciado espira.

Y en tanto ¿dó se esconden?
¿Dó están ¡oh cara patria! tus soldados,
que a tu clamor de muerte no responden?
Presos, encarcelados
por jefes sin honor, que, haciendo alarde

de su perfidia y dolo,
a merced de los vándalos te dejan,
como entre hierros el león, forcejan
con inútil afán. Vosotros sólo,
fuerte Daoiz, intrépido Velarde,
que osando resistir al gran torrente
dar supísteis en flor la dulce vida
con firme pecho y con serena frente;
si de mi libre musa
jamás el eco adormeció a tiranos,
ni vil lisonja emponzoñó su aliento,
allá del alto asiento
a que la acción magnánima os eleva,
el himno oíd que a vuestro nombre entona,
mientras la fama alígera le lleva
del mar de hielo a la abrasada zona.

Mas ¡ ay ! que en tanto sus funestas alas,
por la opresa metrópoli tendiendo,
la yerma asolación sus plazas cubre,
y al áspero silbar de ardientes balas,
y al ronco son de los preñados bronces,
nuevo fragor y estrépito sucede.
¿ Oís como rompiendo
de moradores tímidos las puertas,
caen estallando de los fuertes gonces?
¡ Con qué espantoso estruendo
los dueños buscan, que medrosos huyen !
Cuanto encuentran destruyen,
bramando, los atroces foragidos,
que el robo infame y la matanza ciegan.
¿ No veis cuál se despliegan,
penetrando en los hondos aposentos,
de sangre y oro y lágrimas sedientos?

Rompen, talan, destrozan
cuanto se ofrece a su sangrienta espada.
Aquí, matando al dueño, se alborozan,

hieren allí su esposa acongojada;
la familia asolada
yace espirando, y con feroz sonrisa
sorben voraces el fatal tesoro.
Suelta, a otro lado, la madeja de oro,
mustio el dulce carmín de su mejilla,
y en su frente marchita la azucena,
con voz turbada y anhelante lloro,
de su verdugo ante los pies se humilla
tímida virgen, de amargura llena;
mas con furor de hiena,
alzando el corvo alfanje damasquino,
hiende su cuello el bárbaro asesino.

¡Horrible atrocidad! . . . ¡Treguas, oh musa,
que ya la voz rehusa
embargada en suspiros mi garganta!
Y en ignominia tanta,
¿será que rinda el español bizarro
la indómita cerviz a la cadena?
No, que ya en torno suena
de Palas fiera el sanguinoso carro,
y el látigo estallante
los caballos flamígeros hostiga.
Ya el duro peto y el arnés brillante
visten los fuertes hijos de Pelayo.
Fuego arrojó su ruginoso acero:
"¡Venganza y guerra!" resonó en su tumba;
"¡Venganza y guerra!" repitió Moncayo;
y al grito heroico que en los aires zumba,
"¡Venganza y guerra!" claman Turia y Duero.
Guadalquivir guerrero
alza al bélico son la regia frente,
y del Patrón valiente
blandiendo altivo la nudosa lanza,
corre gritando al mar: "¡Guerra y venganza!" . . .

ÁNGEL SAAVEDRA, DUQUE DE RIVAS

(1791–1865)

El Fratricidio

De mosén Beltrán Claquín,
ante la tienda de pronto,
páranse dos caballeros
ocultos en los embozos.
El rey don Pedro era el uno,
Rodríguez Sanabria el otro,
que en la fe de un enemigo
piensan encontrar socorro.
Con gran prisa descabalgan,
y ya se encuentran en torno
rodeados de franceses
armados y silenciosos,
en cuyos cascos gascones,
y en cuyos azules ojos
refleja el farol, que alumbra
cual siniestro meteoro
Entran dentro de la tienda
ya vacilantes, pues todo
empiezan a verlo entonces
de aspecto siniestro y torvo.
Una lámpara de azófar
alumbra trémula y poco;
mas deja ver un bufete,
un sillón de roble tosco,
un lecho y una armadura,
y lo que fué más asombro,
cuatro hombres de armas inmobles,
de acero vivos escollos.

Don Pedro se desemboza,
y "Vamos ya", dice ronco,
y al instante uno de aquéllos,
con una mano de plomo,

que una manopla vestía
de dura malla, brioso
ase el regio brazo, y dice:
" Esperad, que será poco."
Al mismo tiempo a Sanabria
por detrás sujetan todos,
arráncanle de improviso
la espada, y cúbrenle el rostro.
" ¡ Traición, traición ! ", gritan ambos
luchando con noble arrojo;
cuando entre antorchas y lanzas
en la escena entran de pronto
Beltrán Claquín, desarmado,
y don Enrique, furioso,
cubierto de pie a cabeza
de un arnés de plata y oro,
y ardiendo limpia en su mano
la desnuda daga, como
arde el rayo de los cielos,
que va a trastornar el polo,
de don Pedro el brazo suelta
el forzudo armado, y todo
queda en profundo silencio,
silencio de horror y asombro.

Ni Enrique a Pedro conoce,
ni Pedro a Enrique; apartólos
el Cielo hace muchos años,
años de agravios y encono,
un mar de rugiente sangre,
de huesos un promontorio,
de crímenes un abismo,
poniendo entre el uno y otro.
Don Enrique fué el primero
que con satánico tono:
" ¿ Quién de estos dos es—prorrumpe—
el objeto de mis odios ? "
" Vil bastardo—responde

don Pedro, iracundo y torvo—
yo soy tu rey; tiembla, aleve;
hunde tu frente en el polvo."

Se embisten los dos hermanos;
y don Enrique, furioso,
como tigre embravecido,
hiere a don Pedro en el rostro.

Don Pedro cual león rugiente:
" ¡ Traidor ! ", grita; por los ojos
lanza infernal fuego, abraza
a su armado hermano, como

a la colmena ligera
feroz y forzudo el oso,
y traban lucha espantosa
que el mundo contempla absorto.

Caen al suelo, se revuelcan,
se hieren de un lado y otro;
la tierra inundan en sangre,
lidian cual canes rabiosos.

Se destrozan, se maldicen,
dagas, dientes, uñas, todo
es de aquellos dos hermanos
a saciar la furia poco.

Pedro a Enrique al cabo pone
debajo, y se apresta ansioso,
de su crueldad o justicia,
a dar nuevo testimonio;

cuando Claquín, ¡ oh desgracia !,
(en nuestros debates propios
siempre ha de haber extranjeros
que deciden a su antojo);

cuando Claquín, trastornando
la suerte llega de pronto,
sujeta a don Pedro, y pone
sobre él a Enrique, alevoso,

diciendo el aventurero
de tal maldad en abono:
" Sirvo en esto a mi señor:

ni rey quito ni rey pongo."
No duró más el combate;
de su rey en lo más hondo
del corazón, la corona
busca Enrique, hunde hasta el pomo
el acero fratricida,
y con él el puño todo
para asegurarse de ella,
para agarrarla furioso.
Y la sacó . . . ¡ goteando
sangre! . . . De funesto gozo
retumbó en el campo un " viva ",
y el infierno repitiólo.

Romance del rey don Pedro

Las cabezas de los siete infantes de Lara

. . . Quedando en pie Mudarra, hondo suspiro
arrojó Zaide, y con cansada lengua
anudó el hilo de la horrible historia,
y prosiguió en decir de esta manera;

" Sí, el noble Lara, el desdichado padre
vió de sus siete hijos las cabezas
encima del bufete, en una fila
y por orden de edad, ¡ ay triste! puestas.

" Aunque desfiguradas y espantables,
cual de lejos traídas, y entre yerbas,
espíritus y sales conservadas,
distinguió en cada cual las propias señas.

" En estatua de hielo convertido,
fijos los ojos, sin moverse, en ellas,
y los latidos del hinchado pecho
dando tan sólo en él de vida muestras,

" quedó Lara infeliz . . . ¡ Ah ! ¿ cómo puede
mi débil voz la situación horrenda
con palabras pintar ? . . . Padre es preciso,
padre es preciso ser para entenderla. . . .

" Sin habla Gustios, o mejor sin vida,
estuvo sin moverse una gran pieza :
luego un temblor ligero, imperceptible
apareció en sus miembros, y en violenta

" convulsión terminó ; pero tornando
a la inmovilidad, gira y pasea
los ojos, cual los ojos de un espectro,
por una y otra de las siete prendas.

" Sonrisa amarga agita un breve instante
sus labios sin color, y en tanto queman
sus mejillas dos lágrimas, y luego
los tiernos hijos a nombrar comienza,

" los ojos enclavando en el que nombra,
y esperando tal vez, ¡ ay ! su respuesta :
¡ Diego ! . . . ¡ Martín ! . . . ¡ Fernando ! . . . ¡ Suero ! . . . ¡ Enrico !
¡ Veremundo ! . . . ¡ Gonzalo ! . . . y cuando llega

" a este nombre, dos veces lo repite
y recobrando esfuerzo y vida nueva,
entrambas manos trémulas extiende,
agarra de Gonzalo la cabeza,

" y la alza ; pero al verla sin el cuerpo,
un grito arroja y súbito la suelta,
cual si hecha de encendido hierro fuese.
Empero torna a asirla, se la lleva

"a los labios, y un beso en la insensible
mejilla imprime. . . . La frialdad horrenda,
la ascosa fetidez sufrir no pudo,
y como cuerpo muerto cayó en tierra. . . ."

El moro expósito

JOSÉ MARÍA DE HEREDIA [1]

(1803–39)

Niágara

Dadme mi lira, dádmela: que siento
en mi alma estremecida y agitada
arder la inspiración. ¡Oh! ¡Cuánto tiempo
en tinieblas pasó, sin que mi frente
brillase con su luz! . . . Niágara undoso,
sola tu faz sublime ya podría
tornarme el don divino, que ensañada
me robó del dolor la mano impía.
Torrente prodigioso, calma, acalla
tu trueno aterrador: disipa un tanto
las tinieblas que en torno te circundan,
y déjame mirar tu faz serena,
y de entusiasmo ardiente mi alma llena.
Yo digno soy de contemplarte: siempre,
lo común y mezquino desdeñando,
ansié por lo terrífico y sublime.
Al despeñarse el huracán furioso,
al retumbar sobre mi frente el rayo,
palpitando gocé: vi al Océano
azotado del austro proceloso
combatir mi bajel, y ante mis plantas
sus abismos abrir, y amé el peligro,
y sus iras amé: mas su fiereza
en mi alma no dejara
la profunda impresión que tu grandeza.

[1] Cuban poet, related to the French poet of the same name.

Corres sereno y majestuoso, y luego
en ásperos peñascos quebrantado,
te abalanzas violento, arrebatado,
como el destino irresistible y ciego.
¿Qué voz humana describir podría
de la sirte rugiente
la aterradora faz? El alma mía
en vagos pensamientos se confunde,
al contemplar la férvida corriente,
que en vano quiere la turbada vista
en su vuelo seguir al borde oscuro
del precipicio altísimo: mil olas,
cual pensamiento rápidas pasando,
chocan y se enfurecen,
y otras mil y otras mil ya las alcanzan,
y entre espuma y fragor desaparecen.
Mas llegan . . . saltan . . . el abismo horrendo
devora los torrentes despeñados;
crúzanse en él mil iris, y asordados
vuelven los bosques el fragor tremendo.
Al golpe violentísimo en las peñas
rómpese el agua, y salta, y una nube
de revueltos vapores
cubre el abismo en remolinos, sube,
gira en torno, y al cielo
cual pirámide inmensa se levanta,
y por sobre los bosques que le cercan
al solitario cazador espanta.

Mas ¿qué en ti busca mi anhelante vista
con inquieto afanar? ¿Por qué no miro
alrededor de tu caverna inmensa
las palmas, ¡ay!, las palmas deliciosas,
que en las llanuras de mi ardiente patria [1]
nacen del sol a la sonrisa, y crecen,
y al soplo de la brisa del Océano
bajo un cielo purísimo se mecen?

[1] Cuba.

Este recuerdo a mi pesar me viene . . .
Nada ¡ oh Niágara ! falta a tu destino,
ni otra corona que el agreste pino
a tu terrible majestad conviene.
La palma y mirto, y delicada rosa,
muelle placer inspiren y ocio blando
en frívolo jardín : a ti la suerte
guarda más digno objeto y más sublime.
El alma libre, generosa y fuerte,
viene, te ve, se asombra,
menosprecia los frívolos deleites
y aun se siente elevar cuando te nombra. . . .

¡ Asombroso torrente !
¡ Cómo tu vista mi ánimo enajena
y de terror y admiración me llena !
¿ Dó tu origen está ? ¿ Quién fertiliza
por tantos siglos tu inexhausta fuente ?
¿ Qué poderosa mano
hace que al recibirte
no rebose en la tierra el Océano ?

Abrió el Señor su mano omnipotente,
cubrió tu faz de nubes agitadas
dió su voz a tus aguas despeñadas
y ornó con su arco tu terrible frente.

Miro tus aguas que incansables corren,
como el largo torrente de los siglos
rueda en la eternidad : así del hombre
pasan volando los floridos días
y despierta el dolor . . . ¡ Ay ! ya agotada
siento mi juventud, mi faz marchita,
y la profunda pena que me agita
ruga mi frente de dolor nublada. . . .

¡ Niágara poderoso !
Oye mi última voz : en pocos años
ya devorado habrá la tumba fría
a tu débil cantor. ¡ Duren mis versos
cual tu gloria inmortal ! Pueda, piadoso,
al contemplar tu faz algún viajero,
dar un suspiro a la memoria mía.
Y yo al hundirse el sol en Occidente,
vuele gozoso do el Criador me llama,
y al escuchar los ecos de mi fama
alce en las nubes la radiosa frente.

JOSÉ DE ESPRONCEDA

(1808–42)

Canción del pirata

Con diez cañones por banda,
viento en popa a toda vela
no corta el mar, sino vuela
un velero bergantín :
Bajel pirata que llaman
por su bravura el *Temido*,
en todo mar conocido
del uno al otro confín.

La luna en el mar riela,
en la lona gime el viento,
y alza en blando movimiento
olas de plata y azul ;
Y ve el capitán pirata,
cantando alegre en la popa,
Asia a un lado, al otro Europa
y allá a su frente Stambul.

" Navega, velero mío,
 sin temor,
que ni enemigo navío,
ni tormenta, ni bonanza
tu rumbo a torcer alcanza,
ni a sujetar tu valor.

" Veinte presas
hemos hecho
a despecho
del inglés
y han rendido
sus pendones
cien naciones
a mis pies.

" Que es mi barco mi tesoro,
que es mi dios la libertad,
mi ley la fuerza y el viento,
mi única patria la mar.

" Allá muevan feroz guerra
 ciegos reyes
por un palmo más de tierra:
que yo tengo aquí por mío
cuanto abarca el mar bravío
a quien nadie impuso leyes.

" Y no hay playa,
sea cualquiera,
ni bandera
de esplendor,
que no sienta
mi derecho,
y dé pecho
a mi valor.

" Que es mi barco mi tesoro, etc.

" A la voz de ' ¡ barco viene ! '
es de ver
cómo vira y se previene
a todo trapo a escapar :
que yo soy el rey del mar,
y mi furia es de temer.

" En las presas
yo divido
lo cogido
por igual :
sólo quiero
por riqueza
la belleza
sin rival.

" Que es mi barco mi tesoro, etc.

" ¡ Sentenciado estoy a muerte !
Yo me río :
no me abandone la suerte,
y al mismo que me condena,
colgaré de alguna antena,
quizá en su propio navío.

" Y si caigo,
¿ Qué es la vida ?
por perdida
ya la di,
cuando el yugo
del esclavo,
como un bravo,
sacudí.

" Que es mi barco mi tesoro, etc.

" Son mi música mejor
aquilones;
el estrépito y temblor
de los cables sacudidos,
del negro mar los bramidos
y el rugir de mis cañones.

" Y del trueno
al son violento,
y del viento
al rebramar,
yo me duermo
sosegado,
arrullado
por el mar.

" Que es mi barco mi tesoro,
que es mi dios la libertad,
mi ley la fuerza y el viento,
mi única patria la mar."

' *Una calle estrecha y alta . . .*'

. . . Una calle estrecha y alta,
la calle del Ataúd,
cual si de negro crespón
lóbrego eterno capuz
la vistiera, siempre oscura
y de noche sin más luz
que la lámpara que alumbra
una imagen de Jesús,
atraviesa el embozado
la espada en la mano aún,
que lanzó vivo reflejo
al pasar frente a la cruz. . . .

Segundo don Juan Tenorio,
alma fiera e insolente,
irreligioso y valiente,
altanero y reñidor:
siempre el insulto en los ojos,
en los labios la ironía,
nada teme y todo fía
de su espada y su valor.

Corazón gastado, mofa
de la mujer que corteja,
y, hoy despreciándola, deja
la que ayer se le rindió.
Ni el porvenir temió nunca,
ni recuerda en lo pasado
la mujer que ha abandonado,
ni el dinero que perdió.

Ni vió el fantasma entre sueños
del que mató en desafío,
ni turbó jamás su brío
recelosa previsión.
Siempre en lances y en amores,
siempre en báquicas orgías,
mezcla en palabras impías
un chiste a una maldición.

En Salamanca famoso
por su vida y buen talante,
al atrevido estudiante
le señalan entre mil;
fueros le da su osadía,
le disculpa su riqueza,
su generosa nobleza,
su hermosura varonil.

Que su arrogancia y sus vicios,
caballeresca apostura,
agilidad y bravura
ninguno alcanza a igualar:
que hasta en sus crímenes mismos,
en su impiedad y altiveza,
pone un sello de grandeza
don Félix de Montemar. . . .

Blanca nube de la aurora,
teñida de ópalo y grana,
naciente luz te colora
refulgente precursora
de la cándida mañana.

Mas ¡ ay ! que se disipó
tu pureza virginal,
tu encanto el aire llevó
cual la ventura ideal
que al amor te prometió.

Hojas del árbol caídas
juguetes del viento son:
las ilusiones perdidas
¡ ay ! son hojas desprendidas
del árbol del corazón !

¡ El corazón sin amor !
triste páramo cubierto
con la lava del dolor,
oscuro inmenso desierto
donde no nace una flor ! . . .

Mas ¡ ay ! dichosa tú, Elvira,
En tu misma desventura,
que aun deleites te procura,
cuando tu pecho suspira,
tu misteriosa locura . . .

Vedla, allí va que sueña en su locura
presente el bien que para siempre huyó.
Dulces palabras con amor murmura:
piensa que escucha al pérfido que amó. . . .

Y vedla cuidadosa escoger flores,
y las lleva mezcladas en la falda,
y, corona nupcial de sus amores,
se entretiene en tejer una guirnalda.

Y en medio de su dulce desvarío
triste recuerdo el alma le importuna
y al margen va del argentado río,
y allí las flores echa de una en una;

y las sigue su vista en la corriente,
unas tras otras rápidas pasar,
y confusos sus ojos y su mente
se siente con sus lágrimas ahogar:

y de amor canta, y en su tierna queja
entona melancólica canción,
canción que el alma desgarrada deja,
lamento ¡ ay! que llaga el corazón. . . .

Murió de amor la desdichada Elvira,
cándida rosa que agostó el dolor,
süave aroma que el viajero aspira
y en sus alas el aura arrebató. . . .

Y entonces la visión del blanco velo
al fiero Montemar tendió una mano,
y era su tacto de crispante hielo,
y resistirlo audaz intentó en vano:

galvánica, cruel, nerviosa y fría,
histérica y horrible sensación,
toda la sangre coagulada envía
agolpada y helada al corazón.

Y a su despecho y maldiciendo al cielo,
de ella apartó su mano Montemar,
y temerario alzándola al velo,
tirando de él la descubrió la faz.

¡ Es su esposo ! los ecos retumbaron,
¡ la esposa al fin que su consorte halló !
Los espectros con júbilo gritaron :
¡ Es el esposo de su eterno amor !

Y ella entonces gritó, ¡ Mi esposo ! Y era
(¡ Desengaño fatal ! ¡ triste verdad !)
una sórdida, horrible calavera,
¡ la blanca dama del gallardo andar !

Luego un caballero de espuela dorada,
airoso, aunque el rostro con mortal color,
traspasado el pecho de fiera estocada,
aun brotando sangre de su corazón,

se acerca y le dice, su diestra tendida,
que impávido estrecha también Montemar :
—" Al fin la palabra que dísteis cumplida,
doña Elvira, vedla, vuestra esposa es ya :

mi muerte os perdono."—" Por cierto, don Diego,"
repuso don Félix tranquilo a su vez,
" me alegro de veros con tanto sosiego,
que a fe no esperaba volveros a ver.

" En cuanto a ese espectro que decís mi esposa,
raro casamiento venísme a ofrecer:
su faz no es por cierto ni amable ni hermosa;
·mas no se os figure que os quiera ofender.

" Por mujer la tomo, porque es cosa cierta,
y espero no salga fallido mi plan,
que en caso tan raro y mi esposa muerta,
tanto como viva no me cansará.

" Mas antes decidme si Dios o el demonio
me trajo a este sitio, que quisiera ver
al uno u al otro, y en mi matrimonio
tener por padrino siquiera a Luzbel:

" cualquiera o entrambos con su corte toda,
estando estos nobles espectros aquí,
no perdiera mucho viniendo a mi boda,
hermano don Diego, ¿ no pensáis así ? "

Tal dijo don Félix con fruncido ceño,
en torno arrojando con fiero ademán
miradas audaces de altivo desdeño,
al Dios por quien jura capaz de arrostrar.

El carïado, lívido esqueleto,
los fríos, largos y asquerosos brazos,
le enreda en tanto en apretados lazos,
y ávido le acaricia en su ansiedad:
y con su boca cavernosa busca
la boca a Montemar, y a su mejilla
la árida, descarnada y amarilla
junta y refriega repugnante faz.

Y él, envuelto en sus secas coyunturas,
aun más sus nudos que se aprietan siente,
baña un mar de sudor su ardida frente
y crece en su impotencia su furor!

Pugna con ansia a desasirse en vano,
y cuanto más airado forcejea,
tanto más se le junta y le desea
el rudo espectro que le inspira horror.

Y en furioso, veloz remolino,
y en aérea fantástica danza,
que la mente del hombre no alcanza
en su rápido curso a seguir,
los espectros su ronda empezaron,
cual en círculos raudos el viento
remolinos de polvo violento
y hojas secas agita sin fin.

Y elevando sus áridas manos
resonando cual lúgubre eco,
levantóse en su cóncavo hueco
semejante a un aullido una voz
pavorosa, monótona, informe,
que pronuncia sin lengua su boca,
cual la voz que del áspera roca
en los senos el viento formó.

" Cantemos," dijeron sus gritos,
" la gloria, el amor de la esposa,
que enlaza en sus brazos dichosa,
por siempre al esposo que amó :
su boca a su boca se junte,
y selle su eterna delicia,
süave, amorosa caricia
y lánguido beso de amor.

" Y en mútuos abrazos unidos,
y en blando y eterno reposo,
la esposa enlazada al esposo
por siempre descansen en paz :
y en fúnebre luz ilumine
sus bodas fatídica tea,

les brinde deleites y sea
la tumba su lecho nupcial."

Mientras, la ronda frenética
que en raudo giro se agita,
más cada vez precipita
su vértigo sin ceder;
más cada vez se atropella,
más cada vez se arrebata,
y en círculos se desata
violentos más cada vez:

y escapa en rueda quimérica,
y negro punto parece
que en torno se desvanece
a la fantástica luz,
y sus lúgubres aullidos
que pavorosos se estienden,
los aires rápidos hienden
más prolongados aún.

Y a tan continuo vértigo,
a tan funesto encanto,
a tan horrible canto,
a tan tremenda lid;
entre los brazos lúbricos
que aprémianle sujeto,
del hórrido esqueleto,
entre caricias mil:

jamás vencido el ánimo,
su cuerpo ya rendido,
sintió desfallecido
faltarle, Montemar;
y a par que más su espíritu
desmiente su miseria
la flaca, vil materia
comienza a desmayar.

Y siente un confuso
loco devaneo,
languidez, mareo
y angustioso afán:
y sombras y luces,
la estancia que gira,
y espíritus mira
que vienen y van.

Y luego a lo lejos,
flébil en su oído,
eco dolorido
lánguido sonó,
cual la melodía
que el aura amorosa,
y el aura armoniosa
de noche formó:

Y siente luego
su pecho ahogado,
y desmayado,
turbios sus ojos,
sus graves párpados,
flojos caer:
la frente inclina
sobre su pecho,
y a su despecho,
siente sus brazos
lánguidos, débiles
desfallecer.

Y vió luego
una llama
que se inflama
y murió;
y perdido,
oyó el eco
de un gemido
que espiró.

Tal, dulce
suspira
la lira
que hirió
en blando
concento
del viento
la voz,

leve
breve
son.

En tanto en nubes de carmín y grana
su luz el alba arrebolada envía,
y alegre regocija y engalana
las altas torres el naciente día:
sereno el cielo, calma la mañana,
blanda la brisa, trasparente y fría,
vierte a la tierra el sol con su hermosura
rayos de paz y celestial ventura.

Y huyó la noche y con la noche huían
sus sombras y quiméricas mujeres,
y a su silencio y calma sucedían
el bullicio y rumor de los talleres:
y a su trabajo y a su afán volvían
los hombres y a sus frívolos placeres,
algunos hoy volviendo a su faena
de zozobra y temor el alma llena.

¡Que era pública voz, que llanto arranca
del pecho pecador y empedernido,
que en forma de mujer y en una blanca
túnica misteriosa revestido,
aquella noche el diablo a Salamanca
había en fin por Montemar venido!

Y si lector, dijerdes ser comento,
como me lo contaron, te lo cuento.

El estudiante de Salamanca

Soneto

A un ruiseñor

Canta en la noche, canta en la mañana,
ruiseñor, en el bosque tus amores;
canta, que llorará cuando tú llores
el alba perlas en la flor temprana.
Teñido el cielo de amaranto y grana,
la brisa de la tarde entre las flores
suspirará también a los rigores
de tu amor triste y tu esperanza vana.
Y en la noche serena, al puro rayo
de la callada luna, tus cantares
los ecos sonarán del bosque umbrío.
Y vertiendo dulcísimo desmayo,
cual bálsamo süave en mis pesares,
endulzará tu acento el labio mío.

GERTRUDIS GÓMEZ DE AVELLANEDA

(1814–73)

Soledad del alma

Huyeron veloces—cual nubes que el viento arrebata—
los breves momentos de dicha que el cielo le dió.
¿Por qué mi existencia, ya inútil, su curso dilata,
si el término ansiado a su espalda perdido dejó?

¿Qué resta ¡ay! qué resta de tanta ferviente esperanza?
¿Qué resta de tanto inefable continuo anhelar?
¡Recuerdo infecundo, cadáver que apenas alcanza
galvánica fuerza por sólo un minuto a agitar!

La flor delicada—que apenas existe una aurora—
tal vez largo tiempo al ambiente le deja su olor.
Mas ¡ ay ! que del alma las flores, que un día atesora,
muriendo marchitas no dejan perfume en redor.

La luz esplendente del astro fecundo del día,
se apaga, y sus huellas aun forman hermoso arrebol.
Mas ¡ ay ! cuando al alma le llega su noche sombría,
¿ qué guarda del fuego sagrado que ha sido su sol ? . . .

Sale la aurora risueña, de flores vestida,
dándole al cielo y al campo variado color ;
todo se anima sintiendo brotar nueva vida,
cantan las aves, y el aura suspira de amor.

Llega la tarde, de místico encanto colmada ;
triste acaricia los campos la luz al morir ;
busca el rebaño en silencio su dulce majada ;
tornan las aves, piando su nido a cubrir.

Luego la noche solemne su manto despliega ;
bordan estrellas lucientes la etérea región ;
todo hace pausa . . . la vida su impulso sosiega.
Reina en el mundo tranquilo feliz inacción.

Mas nada ; ni noche, ni aurora, ni tarde indecisa,
cambian del alma desierta la lúgubre faz.
A ella no llegan crepúsculo, aroma, ni brisa,
a ella no brindan las sombras ensueños de paz.

Vista los campos de flores gentil primavera,
doren las mieses los besos del cielo estival,
pámpanos ornen de otoño la faz placentera,
lance el invierno brumoso su aliento glacial.

Siempre perdidas—vagando en su estéril desierto—
siempre abrumadas del peso de vil nulidad,
gimen las almas do el fuego de amor está muerto.
¡ Nada hay que pueble o anime su gran soledad !

PABLO PIFERRER

(1817–48)

Canción de la primavera

Ya vuelve la primavera,
suene la gaita, ruede la danza:
tiende sobre la pradera
el verde manto de la esperanza.

Sopla caliente la brisa:
suene la gaita, ruede la danza:
las nubes pasan aprisa,
y el azur muestran de la esperanza.

La flor ríe en su capullo;
suene la gaita, ruede la danza:
canta el agua en su murmullo
el poder santo de la esperanza.

¿La oís que en los aires trina?
suene la gaita, ruede la danza:
"Abrid a la golondrina,
que vuelve en alas de la esperanza."

Niña, la niña modesta;
suene la gaita, ruede la danza:
el mayo trae tu fiesta
que el logro trae de tu esperanza.

Cubre la tierra el amor;
suene la gaita, ruede la danza:
el perfume engendrador
al seno sube de la esperanza.

Todo zumba y reverdece;
suene la gaita, ruede la danza:
cuanto el son y el verdor crece,
tanto más crece toda esperanza.

Sonido, aroma y color
(suene la gaita, ruede la danza)
únense en himnos de amor,
que engendra el himno de la esperanza.

Morirá la primavera;
suene la gaita, ruede la danza:
mas cada año en la pradera
tornará el manto de la esperanza.

La inocencia de la vida
(calle la gaita, pare la danza)
no torna una vez perdida.
¡Perdí la mía! ¡ay mi esperanza!

JOSÉ ZORRILLA

(1817–93)

A buen juez, mejor testigo

. . . Clara, apacible y serena
pasa la siguiente tarde,
y el sol tocando su ocaso
apaga su luz gigante:
se ve la imperial Toledo
dorada por los remates,
como una ciudad de grana
coronada de cristales.
El Tajo por entre rocas
sus anchos cimientos lame,
dibujando en las arenas
las ondas con que las bate.
Y la ciudad se retrata
en las ondas desiguales,
como en prendas de que el río
tan afanoso la bañe. . . .

Los labradores se acercan
al fuego de sus hogares,
cargados con sus aperos,
cansados de sus afanes.
Los ricos y sedentarios
se tornan con paso grave,
calado el ancho sombrero,
abrochados los gabanes;
y los clérigos y monjes
y los prelados y abades,
sacudiendo el leve polvo
de capelos y sayales.
Quédase sólo un mancebo
de impetuosos ademanes,
que se pasea ocultando
entre la capa el semblante.
Los que pasan le contemplan
con decisión de evitarle,
y él contempla a los que pasan
como si alguien aguardase. . . . .

Una mujer, también sola,
se viene el llano adelante,
la luz del rostro escondida
en tocas y tafetanes.
Mas en lo leve del paso,
y en lo flexible del talle,
puede a través de los velos
una hermosa adivinarse.
Vase derecha al que aguarda,
y él al encuentro le sale
diciendo . . . cuanto se dicen
en las citas los amantes.
Mas ella, galanterías
dejando severa aparte,
así al mancebo interrumpe
en voz decisiva y grave:
"Abreviemos de razones,

Diego Martínez; mi padre,
que un hombre ha entrado en su ausencia
dentro de mi aposento sabe,
y así quien mancha mi honra
con la suya me la lave;
o dadme mano de esposo,
o libre de vos dejadme."
Miróla Diego Martínez
atentamente un instante,
y echando a un lado el embozo,
repuso palabras tales:
"Dentro de un mes, Inés mía,
parto a la guerra de Flandes;
al año estaré de vuelta
y contigo en los altares.
Honra que yo te desluzca,
con honra mía se lave;
que por honra vuelven honra
hidalgos que en honra nacen."
—Júralo—exclamó la niña.
—Más que mi palabra vale
no te valdrá un juramento.
—Diego, la palabra es aire.
—¡Vive Dios que estás tenaz!
Dalo por jurado y baste.
—No me basta; que olvidar
puedes la palabra en Flandes.
—¡Voto a Dios! ¿qué más pretendes?
—Que a los pies de aquella imagen
lo jures como cristiano
del santo Cristo delante.
Vaciló un punto Martínez,
mas porfiando que jurase,
llevóle Inés hacia el templo
que en medio la vega yace.
Enclavado en un madero,
en duro y postrero trance,
ceñida la sien de espinas,

descolorido el semblante,
veíase allí un crucifijo
teñido de negra sangre,
a quien Toledo devota
acude hoy en sus azares.
Ante sus plantas divinas
llegaron ambos amantes,
y haciendo Inés que Martínez
los sagrados pies tocase,
preguntóle :—Diego, ¿juras
a tu vuelta desposarme?
Contestó el mozo :—¡ Sí juro!
Y ambos del templo se salen. . . .

Es una tarde serena,
cuya luz tornasolada
del purpurino horizonte
blandamente se derrama.
Plácido aroma las flores
sus hojas plegando exhalan,
y el céfiro entre perfumes
mece las trémulas alas.
Brillan abajo en el valle
con suave rumor las aguas,
y las aves en la orilla
despidiendo al día cantan.
Allá por el Miradero
por el Cambrón y Visagra
confuso tropel de gente
del Tajo a la vega baja. . . .

Llegado el gobernador
y gente que le acompaña,
entraron todos al claustro
que iglesia y patio separa.
Encendieron ante el Cristo
cuatro cirios y una lámpara,
y de hinojos un momento

le rezaron en voz baja.
Está el Cristo de la Vega
la cruz en tierra posada,
los pies alzados del suelo
poco menos de una vara;
hacia la severa imagen
un notario se adelanta,
de modo que con el rostro
al pecho santo llegaba.
A un lado tiene a Martínez
a otro lado a Inés de Vargas,
detrás al gobernador
con sus jueces y sus guardias.
Después de leer dos veces
la acusación entablada,
el notario a Jesucristo
así demandó en voz alta:
—Jesús, Hijo de María,
ante nos esta mañana
citado como testigo
por boca de Inés de Vargas,
¿juráis ser cierto que un día
a vuestras divinas plantas
juró a Inés Diego Martínez
por su mujer desposarla?
Asida a un brazo desnudo
una mano atarazada
vino a posar en los autos
la seca y hendida palma,
y allá en los aires—¡ Sí juro!
clamó una voz más que humana.
Alzó la turba medrosa
la vista a la imagen santa . . .
los labios tenía abiertos
y una mano desclavada.

La siesta

Son las tres de la tarde, julio, Castilla.
El sol alumbra, que arde; ciega, no brilla:
la luz es una llama que abrasa el cielo:
ni una brisa una rama mueve en el suelo.
Desde el hombre a la mosca todo se enerva;
la culebra se enrosca bajo la hierba;
la perdiz por la siembra suelta no corre,
y el cigüeño a la hembra deja en la torre.
Ni el topo, de galvana, se asoma a su hoyo,
ni el mosco pez se afana contra el arroyo
ni hoza la comadreja por la montaña
ni labra miel la abeja, ni hila la araña.
La agua el aire no arruga, la mies no ondea,
ni las flores la oruga torpe babea;
todo el fuego se agosta del seco estío:
duerme hasta la langosta sobre el plantío.
Sólo yo velo y gozo fresco y sereno;
sólo yo de alborozo me siento lleno:
porque mi Rosa,
reclinada en mi seno,
duerme y reposa.
Voraz la tierra tuesta el sol del estío;
mas el bosque nos presta su toldo umbrío.
Donde Rosa se acuesta brota el rocío,
susurra la floresta, murmura el río.
¡Duerme en calma tu siesta, dulce bien mío!
¡Duerme entretanto,
que yo te velo: duerme,
que yo te canto!

Como le canta y mece la madre al tierno niño
que duerme en su regazo, mi amor te arrullará;
como para él la madre mil frases de cariño
inventa, mil cantares mi amor te inventará.
Yo sé que siente, Rosa, tu corazón amante

los versos que te canto mientras dormida estás.
¿Qué quieres que te cuente? ¿Qué quieres que te cante?
¿Cuál de mis canciones es la que te gusta más?
¿Prefieres aquel cuento del silfo que tenía
en una red de tamo prisión en un rosal,
y al cual todas las noches a alimentar venía
la abeja que le amaba, con miel de su panal?
¿Prefieres una historia como la historia horrenda
de aquel que fué a su dama celoso a degollar,
cuya cabeza trunca guardó de amor en prenda
y la cabeza le iba de noche un beso a dar?
Di cómo hablarte debo cuando tu sueño arrullo;
porque mi voz anhelo que te parezca tal,
como la miel que daba, posada en un capullo,
la abeja de mis cuentos al silfo del rosal.
Mas duerme, vida mía, mientras te arrullo
yo de mi poesía con el murmullo.
Mientras la aura en tus rizos juega y te orea,
en contar tus hechizos mi alma se emplea.
Duerme, que te adormece fiel mi cariño,
como le canta y mece la madre al niño.
Duerme, que yo a millares pondré mi empeño
en inventar cantares para tu sueño.
La enramada nos presta su toldo umbrío,
susurra la floresta, murmura el río:
todo invita a la siesta; duerme, bien mío;
duerme entretanto
que yo te velo: duerme,
que yo te canto! . . .

Cantos del trovador

El culpado

¡Ay triste del viajero que pierde su camino
por el espeso bosque donde extraviado fué!
¡Ay, triste del que el cielo de su feliz destino
con negros nubarrones encapotarse ve!

¡ Ay, triste del que siente que airado torbellino
la lámpara le apaga de su dudosa fe !
Y ¡ ay, triste del que sufre, cual sufre Juan Guarino,
tribulaciones tales de la montaña al pie !

El día, entretanto, pasando declina,
cercano al dudoso crepúsculo ya ;
con rayos postreros el sol ilumina
la faz de Guarino, que inmóvil está.

Cualquiera que de lejos le mirara
tan inmóvil yacer sobre el peñón,
por efigie sin vida le tomara,
por sueño vano o ideal visión.

Él sus ojos sombríos, errantes,
fijos los tiene en ocaso, sin ver
los destellos del sol fulgurantes,
que se va el horizonte a sorber.

Y la pena de su alma
embrutece su razón,
y en siniestra y fría calma
paraliza el corazón.

Cual suele, tras sombrío
espeso nubarrón,
brotar en el estío
mefítico vapor,
que deja nuestro espíritu
sin fuerza ni vigor ;
cual pesadilla odiosa
que en sueños nos acosa,
girando en fatigosa
perpetua confusión,
sin que podamos, débiles,
calmar su agitación,
tal su ánimo, al peso

de crimen secreto,
prensado y sujeto
con miedo se ve,
y a impulso de asombro
que infúndele pánico,
el soplo satánico
ni espera ni cree. . . .

Nube errante
pasajera,
vagorosa,
do contempla
Juan Guarino
el destino
que le espera;
que expirante,
congojosa
e indecisa,
a su labio
la sonrisa
postrimera
le arrancó;
y el agravio
a su Dios hecho,
en el fondo de su pecho
con su luz iluminó. . . .

Y en tanto
que acude
al llanto
quizá
cuanto
existe,
niebla
triste
puebla
ya.

Y la tierra
toda inunda
la profunda
lobreguez,
montes, valles
y collados
sepultados
a su vez.

Espesas nubes
que apiña el viento
al firmamento
robando van
su luna pálida;
las luces bellas
de sus estrellas
muertas están.

Y en vez de los ojos
sirviendo el oído
ya sólo es el ruido
quien guía los pies,
al alma infundiendo
sus vagos rumores
extraños temores
de un mundo que no es.

Y se oye por las peñas
sonar en las montañas
de fieras y alimañas
los pasos o la voz,
mostrando en sus sonidos,
sus cóncavos gruñidos,
sus ásperos graznidos,
las fieras y las aves
su natural feroz.

Y a cada tenue lamento
a cada salvaje son
de ave o de fiera, de agua o viento,
se estremece el corazón.
¿ Y quién podrá en tal momento
dar del desierto razón ? . . .

¡ Lenta, amarga, terrible es la agonía
que su remordimiento al hombre da !
Quizá a Guarino, al despuntar el día,
sentado en el peñón le encontrará
de sí mismo espantado todavía,
muerto al impulso del dolor quizá.

La noche entretanto se pasa. Sumido
monte, llano, río, desierto, y ciudad
en lóbrega noche, doquiera dormido
cobijan al mundo el silencio y la paz.

Ni de hombre ni de fiera, gemido ni lamento
resuena por los senos de las montañas ya.
Y sólo tal vez se oye el susurrar del viento
o el ruido del arroyo que murmurando va.

La azucena silvestre

RAMÓN DE CAMPOAMOR

(1817–1901)

Cabeza y corazón

(*A Blanca Quiroga y Pardo Bazán*)

Un ángel y el demonio a Eva un día
contemplan con amor.
Y " ¿ qué opináis, decid, de esa obra mía ? "
les preguntó el Señor.

Mirando de Eva la gentil cabeza
dijo el demonio así:
" ¡ La mujer ! A pesar de su belleza
es inferior a mí.
¡ Sentir sin comprender ! ¡ Perpetua ilusa
que goza en delirar,
que tiene, sin razón, la ciencia infusa
del arte de engañar !
Uniendo la inconstancia a la hermosura,"—
el demonio añadió—
" creedme, Señor, vuestra mejor hechura
vale menos que yo."

" La mujer,"—siguió el ángel,—" de tal modo
desafía el dolor,
que, aunque débil su fe, se arriesga a todo
por servir al amor.
De la santa piedad hija querida,
ni piensa ni hace el mal,
y, próvida, transmite con la vida
la sed de lo ideal.
La mujer es tan buena "—enardecido
el ángel concluyó—
" que, aunque soy en el cielo un elegido,
ella es mejor que yo."

Tú, dotada de espíritu sublime
y de gran corazón,
Blanca, entre el ángel y el demonio, dime:
¿ quién tiene más razón ?

El candil del emperador Carlos V

En Yuste, en la pobre cama
de una pobre habitación
alumbrada por la llama
de un candil, medio velón,

soñando está Carlos quinto
que en un duelo personal
ve a sus pies, en sangre tinto,
al rey francés, su rival.
Se incorporó de ira loco;
mas pasó un viento sutil
que movió la luz un poco
del velón, medio candil,
y, tosiendo, con cuidado
se arropó el emperador,
por si aquel aire colado
puede más que su valor;
y "¿Por qué el cielo consiente
—dice el héroe febril—
que mata a todo un valiente
lo que no apaga un candil?"

El pájaro mensajero

Un pájaro solté que, alzando el vuelo,
en busca de mi amor entró en el cielo.
En la carta que el pájaro llevaba,
recordando mis íntimas ternuras,
a mi amor le encargaba
que me hablase del cielo y sus venturas.
El pájaro volvió con la respuesta;
pero llegó borrada,
porque entre el hombre y Dios se halla interpuesta,
la noche sin estrellas de la nada.

CAROLINA CORONADO

(1823–1911)

La luna es una ausencia

Y tú, ¿quién eres de la noche errante
aparición que pasas silenciosa,
cruzando los espacios ondulante
tras los vapores de la nube acuosa?

Negra la tierra, triste el firmamento,
ciegos mis ojos sin tu luz estaban,
y suspirando entre el obscuro viento
tenebrosos espíritus vagaban.

Yo te aguardaba, y cuando vi tus rojos
perfiles asomar con lenta calma,
como tu rayo descendió a mis ojos,
tierna alegría descendió a mi alma.

Y a mis ruegos acudes perezosa
cuando amoroso el corazón te ansía?
Ven a mí, suave luz, nocturna, hermosa
hija del cielo, ven: ¡por qué tardía!

Bardo amante, esa hechicera
fiel y sola compañera
de tu solitaria amiga,
presurosa mensajera
mis pensamientos te diga.

Yo me encontré en unos valles
a esa misteriosa guía
cuando lenta recorría
de olivos desiertas calles
tristes, como el alma mía.

Yo de entre la tierra obscura
la vi brotar, como pura
memoria de tu pasión,
en medio de la desventura
de mi ausente corazón.

Y como el recuerdo amante
me siguió en mi soledad,
callada, tierna, constante,
sin apartarse un instante
esa nocturna beldad.

Porque si yo caminaba
y con pasos fugitivos
árbol tras árbol cruzaba,
ella al par se deslizaba
entre los negros olivos.

Si un instante suspendía
mi carrera silenciosa,
sobre la copa sombría
del árbol se detenía
como una paloma hermosa.

Por eso, el tierno quebranto
sabe de mi ausencia, sola,
porque al escuchar mi canto
vino a sorprender mi llanto
con la luz de su aureola.

Y pues es la verdadera
fiel y sola compañera
de tu solitaria amiga,
presurosa mensajera
mis pensamientos te diga.

GASPAR NÚÑEZ DE ARCE

(1834–1903)

La luz y las tinieblas

La fiera, la tiránica batalla
dura y persiste aún:
es el combate entre la ciega sombra
y la fecunda luz.

¡ Ni un instante de tregua y de reposo !
En la tierra, en el mar,
en el espacio, en la conciencia humana
siempre lidiando están.

Al través de los siglos que se empujan
con sorda confusión,
ruedan mezclados la verdad, el día,
la noche y el error.

¿ Quién vencerá por fin ? ¿ La negra sombra ?
¿ La excelsa claridad ?
¡ Ay, no lo preguntéis ! La horrenda lucha
nunca terminará.

Cuando la creación rota y deshecha
vuelva al caos otra vez ;
cuando desierta impenetrable y muda,
la inmensidad esté ;

en el seno del tiempo, en el espacio
sin mundos y sin sol
seguirá eterno el duelo formidable
entre Satán y Dios.

GUSTAVO ADOLFO BÉCQUER

(1836–70)

Rimas

I

Yo sé un himno gigante y extraño
que anuncia en la noche del alma una aurora,
y estas páginas son de ese himno
cadencias que el aire dilata en las sombras.

Yo quisiera escribirlo, del hombre
domando el rebelde, mezquino idioma,
con palabras que fuesen a un tiempo
suspiros y risas, colores y notas.

Pero en vano es luchar; que no hay cifra
capaz de encerrarlo y apenas, ¡oh hermosa!
si, teniendo en mis manos las tuyas,
pudiera al oído cantártelo a solas.

II

Saeta que voladora
cruza, arrojada al azar,
sin adivinarse dónde
temblando se clavará:

hoja del árbol seca
arrebata el vendaval,
sin que nadie acierte el surco
donde a caer volverá;

gigante ola que el viento
riza y empuja en el mar,
y rueda y pasa, no sabe
qué playa buscando va;

luz que en cercos temblorosos
brilla, próxima a expirar,
ignorándose cuál de ellos
el último brillará.

Eso soy yo, que al acaso
cruzo el mundo, sin pensar
de dónde vengo, ni adónde
mis pasos me llevarán.

V

Espíritu sin nombre
indefinible esencia
yo vivo con la vida
sin formas de la idea.

Yo nado en el vacío,
del sol tiemblo en la hoguera,
palpito entre las sombras
y floto con las nieblas.

Yo soy el fleco de oro
de la lejana estrella;
yo soy de la alta luna
la luz tibia y serena.

Yo soy la ardiente nube
que en el caos ondea;
yo soy del astro errante
la luminosa estela.

Yo soy nieve en las cumbres.
Soy fuego en las arenas,
azul onda en los mares,
y espuma en la ribera.

En el laúd soy nota,
perfume en la violeta,
fugaz llama en las tumbas,
y en las ruinas hiedra.

Yo atrueno en el torrente,
y silbo en la centella,
y ciego en el relámpago,
y rujo en la tormenta.

Yo río en los alcores,
susurro en la alta yerba,
suspiro en la onda pura,
y lloro en la hoja seca.

Yo ondulo con los átomos,
del humo que se eleva,
y al cielo lento sube
en espiral inmensa.

Yo, en los dorados hilos
que los insectos cuelgan,
me mezco entre los árboles.
en la ardorosa siesta.

Yo corro tras las ninfas
que en la corriente fresca
del cristalino arroyo
desnudas juguetean.

Yo, en bosques de corales
que alfombran blancas perlas,
persigo en el Océano
las náyades ligeras.

Yo, en las cavernas cóncavas
do el sol nunca penetra,
mezclándome a los gnomos,
contemplo sus riquezas.

Yo busco de los siglos
las ya borradas huellas,
y sé de esos imperios
de que ni el nombre queda.

Yo sigo en raudo vértigo
los mundos que voltean,
y mi pupila abarca
la creación entera.

Yo sé de esas regiones
a do un rumor no llega,
y donde informes astros,
de vida un soplo esperan.

Yo soy sobre el abismo
el puente que atraviesa;
yo soy la ignota escala
que el cielo une a la tierra.

Yo soy el invisible
anillo que sujeta
el mundo de la forma
al mundo de la idea.

Yo, en fin, soy ese espíritu,
desconocida esencia,
perfume misterioso,
de que es vaso el poeta.

VII

Del salón en el ángulo oscuro,
de su dueño tal vez olvidada,
silenciosa y cubierta de polvo
veíase el arpa.

¡ Cuánta nota dormía en sus cuerdas,
como el pájaro duerme en las ramas,
esperando la mano de nieve
que sabe arrancarlas !

¡ Ay !—pensé, ¡ cuántas veces el genio
así duerme en el fondo del alma ¡,
y una voz, como Lázaro, espera
que le diga : " ¡ Levántate y anda ! "

VIII

Cuando miro el azul horizonte
perderse a lo lejos,
al través de una gasa de polvo
dorado e inquieto,
me parece posible arrancarme
del mísero suelo,
y flotar con la niebla dorada
en átomos leves,
cual ella deshecho.

Cuando miro de noche en el fondo
oscuro del cielo
las estrellas temblar, como ardientes
pupilas de fuego,
me parece posible a do brillan
subir en un vuelo,
y anegarme en su luz, y con ellas
en lumbre encendido
fundirme en un beso.

En el mar de la duda en que bogo
ni aun sé lo que creo;
¡ Sin embargo, estas ansias me dicen
que yo llevo algo
divino aquí dentro !

IX

Besa el aura que gime blandamente
las leves ondas que jugando riza;
el sol besa a la nube en occidente
y de púrpura y oro la matiza;
la llama en derredor del tronco ardiente
por besar a otra llama se desliza,
y hasta el sauce, inclinándose a su peso,
al río que le besa, vuelve un beso.

X

Los invisibles átomos del aire
en derredor palpitan y se inflaman;
el cielo se deshace en rayos de oro;
la tierra se estremece alborozada;
oigo flotando en olas de armonía
rumor de besos y batir de alas;
mis párpados se cierran . . . ¿ Qué sucede ?
— ¡ Es el amor que pasa !

XV

Cendal flotante de leve bruma,
rizada cinta de blanca espuma,
rumor sonoro
de arpa de oro,
beso del aura, onda de luz,
eso eres tú.

Tú, sombra aérea, que cuantas veces
voy a tocarte, te desvaneces
como la llama, como el sonido,
como la niebla, como el gemido
del lago azul.

En mar sin playas onda sonante,
en el vacío cometa errante,
largo lamento
del ronco viento,
ansia perpetua de algo mejor,
eso soy yo.

¡ Yo, que a tus ojos en mi agonía
los ojos vuelvo de noche y día ;
yo, que incansable corro y demente
tras una sombra, tras la hija ardiente
de una visión !

XIX

Cuando sobre el pecho inclinas
la melancólica frente,
una azucena tronchada
me pareces.

Porque al darte la pureza,
de que es símbolo celeste,
como a ella te hizo Dios
de oro y de nieve.

XLI

Tú eres el huracán, y yo la alta
torre que desafía su poder:
¡ tenías que estrellarte o abatirme!
¡ No pudo ser!

Tú eras el océano, y yo la enhiesta
roca que firme aguarda su vaivén:
¡ tenías que romperte o que arrancarme!
¡ No pudo ser!

Hermosa tú, yo altivo; acostumbrados
uno a arrollar, el otro a no ceder;
la senda estrecha, inevitable el choque.
¡ No pudo ser!

LX

Mi vida es un erial:
flor que toco se deshoja;
que en mi camino fatal,
alguien va sembrando el mal
para que yo lo recoja.

ROSALÍA DE CASTRO

(1837–85)

' *As de Cantar . . .*'

As de cantar
que ch' ei de dar zonchos;
as de cantar
que ch' ei de dar moitos.

" As de cantar,
meniña gaitera,
as de cantar,
que me morro de pena. . . .

Co son da gaitiña
co son da pandeira,
che pido que cantes,
rapaza morena.

Co son da gaitiña,
co son do tambor,
che pido que cantes
meniña, por Dios."

'*Cantart' ei, Galicia . . .*'

Cantart' ei, Galicia,
teus doçes cantares,
qu' así mô pediron
na veira do mare.

Cantart' ei, Galicia,
na lengua gallega.
consuelo dos males,
alivio das penas.

Mimosa, soave,
sentida, queixosa;
encanta si ríe,
conmove si chora . . .

Cantares gallegos

Vaguedás

Tal com' as nubes
que leva o vento,
y agora asombran, y agora alegran
os espaços inmensos d'o ceo,
así as ideas
loucas qu'eu teño,

as imaxes de múltiples formas
das extrañas feituras, de cores incertos,
agora asombran,
agora acraran,
o fondo sin fondo d'o meu pensamento.

Follas novas

Negra sombra

Cando penso que te fuches,
negra sombra que m'asombras,
ô pe d' os meus cabezales
tornas facéndome mofa.

Cando maxino qu'es ida
n' o mesmo sol te m'amostras,
y eres a estrela que brila,
y eres o vento que zoa.

Si cantan, ês ti que cantas;
si choran, ês ti que choras,
y ês o marmurio d'o río,
y ês a noite y es a aurora.

En todo estás e ti ês todo,
pra min y en min mesma moras;
nin m'abandonarás nunca,
sombra que sempre m'asombras.

Follas novas

' *Los unos altísimos . . .*'

Los unos altísimos,
los otros menores,
con su eterno verdor y frescura,
que inspira a las almas
agrestes canciones,

mientras gime al chocar con las aguas
la brisa marina, de aromas salobres,
van en ondas subiendo hacia el cielo
los pinos del monte.

De la altura la bruma desciende
y envuelve las copas
perfumadas, sonoras y altivas
de aquellos gigantes
que al " castro " coronan;
brilla en tanto a sus pies el arroyo
que alumbra risueña
la luz de la aurora,
y los cuervos sacuden sus alas,
lanzando graznidos
y huyendo la sombra.

El viajero rendido y cansado
que ve del camino la línea escabrosa
que aun le resta que andar, anhelará,
deteniéndose al pie de la loma,
de repente quedar convertido
en pájaro o fuente,
en árbol o en roca.

En las orillas del Sar

' *Era apacible el día . . .*'

Era apacible el día
y templado el ambiente,
y llovía, llovía,
callada y mansamente;
y mientras silenciosa
lloraba yo y gemía,
mi niño, tierna rosa,
durmiendo se moría.
Al huir de este mundo, ¡ qué sosiego en su frente!
Al verle yo alejarse, ¡ qué borrasca en la mía!

Tierra sobre el cadáver insepulto
antes que empiece a corromperse . . . ¡ tierra !
Ya el hoyo se ha cubierto, sosegaos ;
bien pronto en los terrones removidos
verde y pujante crecerá la hierba.

¿ Qué andáis buscando en torno de las tumbas,
torvo el mirar, nublado el pensamiento ?
¡ No os ocupéis de lo que al polvo vuelve ! . . .
Jamás el que descansa en el sepulcro
ha de tornar a amaros ni a ofenderos.

¡ Jamás ! ¿ Es verdad que todo
para siempre acabó ya ?
No ; no puede acabar lo que es eterno,
ni puede tener fin la inmensidad.

Tú te fuiste por siempre ; mas mi alma
te espera aún con amoroso afán,
y vendrás o iré yo, bien de mi vida,
allí donde nos hemos de encontrar.

Algo ha quedado tuyo en mis entrañas
que no morirá jamás,
y que Dios, porque es justo y porque es bueno,
a desunir ya nunca volverá.
En el cielo, en la tierra, en lo insondable
yo te hallaré y me hallarás.
No, no puede acabar lo que es eterno,
ni puede tener fin la inmensidad. . . .

Del rumor cadencioso de la onda
y el viento que muge ;
del incierto reflejo que alumbra
la selva o la nube ;
del piar de alguna ave de paso ;

del agreste ignorado perfume
que el céfiro roba
al valle o a la cumbre,
mundos hay donde encuentran asilo
las almas que al peso
del mundo sucumben.

En las orillas del Sar

La canción que oyó en sueños el viejo

I

Su ciega y loca fantasía corrió arrastrada por el vértigo,
tal como arrastra las arenas el huracán en el desierto.
Y cual halcón que cae herido en la laguna pestilente,
cayó en el cieno de la vida, rotas las alas para siempre.
Mas aun sin alas cree o sueña que cruza el aire, los espacios,
y aun entre el lodo se ve limpio, cual de la nieve el copo blanco.

II

No maldigáis del que, ya ebrio, corre a beber con nuevo afán ;
su eterna sed es quien le lleva hacia la fuente abrasadora,
cuanto más bebe, a beber más.
No murmuréis del que rendido ya bajo el peso de la vida
quiere vivir y aun quiere amar ;
La sed del beodo es insaciable, y la del alma lo es aun más. . . .

En las orillas del Sar

La eterna belleza

De la vida entre el múltiple conjunto de los seres,
no, no busquéis la imagen de la eterna belleza,
ni en el contento y harto seno de los placeres,
ni del dolor acerbo en la dura aspereza.

Ya es átomo impalpable o inmensidad que asombra,
aspiración celeste, revelación callada;
la comprende el espíritu y el labio no la nombra,
y en sus hondos abismos la mente se anonada.

En las orillas del Sar

La felicidad

I

En los ecos del órgano o en el rumor del viento,
en el fulgor de un astro o en la gota de lluvia,
te adivinaba en todo y en todo te buscaba,
sin encontrarte nunca.

Quizás después te ha hallado, te ha hallado y te ha perdido
otra vez, de la vida en la batalla ruda,
ya que sigue buscándote y te adivina en todo,
sin encontrarte nunca.

Pero sabe que existes y no eres vano sueño,
hermosura sin nombre, pero perfecta y única;
por eso vive triste, porque te busca siempre,
sin encontrarte nunca.

II

Yo no sé lo que busco eternamente
en la tierra, en el aire y en el cielo;
yo no sé lo que busco, pero es algo
que perdí no sé cuándo y que no encuentro,
aun cuando sueñe que invisible habita
en todo cuanto toco y cuanto veo.

Felicidad, no he de volver a hallarte
en la tierra, en el aire ni en el cielo,
¡Aun cuando sé que existes
y no eres vano sueño!

En las orillas del Sar

Pensamientos

¡ Pensamientos de alas negras !, huid, huid azorados,
como bandadas de cuervos por la tormenta acosados,
o como abejas en quien el fuego hizo presa
dejad que amanezca el día de resplandores benditos,
en cuya luz se presienten los placeres infinitos . . .
¡ Y huid con vuestra perenne sombra que en el alma pesa !

¡ Pensamientos de alas blancas !, ni gimamos ni roguemos
como un tiempo, y en los mundos luminosos penetremos,
en donde nunca resuena la débil voz del caído,
en donde el dorado sueño para en realidad segura,
y de la humana flaqueza sobre la inmensa amargura
y sobre el amor que mata sus alas tiende el olvido. . . .

Más rápidos que el rayo,
más aladas que el viento,
inquietos vagamundos que no pueden
refrenar nunca el inconstante vuelo,
así descienden de la mar al fondo
como escalan la altura de los cielos.

Mas si son impalpables e incorpóreos
y múltiples y varios,
¿ Por qué llamarles pensamientos negros
o pensamientos blancos,
si no tienen color, esos del alma
invisibles
eternos e invisibles soberanos ?

En las orillas del Sar

El tiempo pasa

Hora tras hora, día tras día,
entre el cielo y la tierra que quedan
eternos vigías,
como torrente que se despeña
pasa la vida.

Devolvedle a la flor su perfume
después de marchita;
de las ondas que besan la playa
y unas tras otras besándola expiran,
recoged los rumores, las quejas,
y en las planchas de bronce grabar su armonía.

Tiempos que fueron, llantos y risas,
negros tormentos, dulces mentiras,
¡ay! ¿en dónde su rastro dejaron,
en dónde, alma mía?

En las orillas del Sar

JOSÉ ASUNCIÓN SILVA

(1865–96)

Día de difuntos

La luz vaga . . . opaco el día . . .
la llovizna cae y moja
con sus hilos penetrantes la ciudad desierta y fría;
por el aire, tenebrosa, ignorada mano arroja
un obscuro velo opaco, de letal melancolía,
y no hay nadie que en lo íntimo no se aquiete y se recoja
al mirar las nieblas grises en la atmósfera sombría,
y al oír en las alturas
melancólicas y obscuras
los acentos dejativos
y tristísimos e inciertos
con que suenan las campanas,
las campanas plañideras,
que les hablan a los vivos
de los muertos.

Y hay algo angustioso e incierto
que mezcla a ese sonido su sonido,
e inarmónico vibra en el concierto

que alzan los bronces al tocar a muerto
por todos los que han sido.
Es la voz de la campana
que va marcando la hora
hoy lo mismo que mañana,
rítmica, igual y sonora;
una campana se queja
y la otra campana llora,
ésta tiene voz de vieja
y ésa de niña que ora.

Las campanas más grandes que dan un doble recio
suenan con acento de místico desprecio;
mas la campana que da la hora
ríe, no llora;
tiene en su timbre seco sutiles armonías;
su voz parece que habla de fiestas, de alegrías,
de citas, de placeres, de cantos y de bailes,
de las preocupaciones que llenan nuestros días;
es una voz del siglo entre un coro de frailes,
y con sus notas se ríe
escéptica y burladora
de la campana que gime,
de la campana que implora,
y de cuanto aquel coro conmemora;
y es que con su retintín
ella midió el dolor humano
y marcó del dolor el fin.

Por eso se ríe del grave esquilón
que suena allá arriba con fúnebre son;
por eso interrumpe los tristes conciertos
con que el bronce santo llora por los muertos.
No la oigáis, oh bronces, no la oigáis, campanas,
que con la voz grave de ese clamoreo
rogáis por los seres que duermen ahora
lejos de la vida, libres del deseo,
lejos de las rudas batallas humanas;

seguid en el aire vuestro bamboleo,
¡ no la oigáis, campanas! . . .
Contra lo imposible ¿ qué puede el deseo? . . .

Y eso es lo angustioso e incierto
que flota en el sonido;
esa es la nota irónica que vibra en el concierto
que alzan los bronces al tocar a muerto
por todos los que han sido.
Es la voz fina y sutil
de vibraciones de cristal
que con acento juvenil,
indiferente al bien y al mal,
mide lo mismo la hora vil
que la sublime y la fatal,
y resuena en las alturas
melancólicas y obscuras
sin tener en su tañido
claro, rítmico y sonoro,
los acentos dejativos
y tristísimos e inciertos
de aquel misterioso coro
con que suenan las campanas . . .
¡ las campanas plañideras
que les hablan a los vivos
de los muertos! . . .

SALVADOR RUEDA SANTOS

(1861–1933)

Ascua

Vierte la cigarra
su vaso de fuego,
su ánfora armoniosa de trémula lumbre
cual si de una fuente manase cayendo.

Un bordón de guitarra morisca
que nunca ve roto su largo lamento,
un bordón de una llama tejido,
un alambre armónico de sones de incendio,
parece la cuerda de lumbre cantora
del cálido insecto.
Desde el alto púlpito de un chumbo dorado,
lanza la cigarra su sermón violento,
toca la cantora su fibra estallante
y arranca a la cuerda su lírico estruendo.
Es ascua canora,
arpa de dos élitros,
lira de dos alas,
pandero africano, monocordio griego,
crótalo incansable de dos brasas roncas
que tocan el himno del sol y del fuego.
Oídla en el pecho naciente de Cloe
madurar el doble racimo del seno,
cual si en él cantaran los altos capullos
formados de broches rosados de almendro.
La cigarra es la voz de la vida,
una gota del sol hecha verso,
un ascua sonante,
arpa de dos élitros,
lira de dos alas,
pandero morisco, crótalo bohemio. . . .

Los pavos reales

Cuando vuelvo cantando de los trigales
ya al morir entre púrpuras el sol caído,
en medio del paisaje hieren mi oído
con su grito estridente los pavos reales.
Me escondo tras las ramas de los frutales,
y el ave egregia acecho sin hacer ruido,

y miro los colores de su vestido
y su moño de breves flechas triunfales.
   Repitiendo su canto que el aire aleja,
hace el amor en torno de su pareja
y alza la cola augusta de hebras lustrosas;
   y a los ojos abriendo sus galas sumas,
deja brillar cien rosas sobre cien plumas,
y cien iris prendidos a las cien rosas.

MIGUEL DE UNAMUNO

(1864–1936)

Paz en la guerra

¡Ya estás en paz, la de la muerte, amigo!
Tú que a traernos guerra descendiste
a nuestro mundo, guerra creadora,
manantial de deseos desmedidos,
huracán de las almas que levantan
como olas sus ahincos con la tema
de anegar las estrellas en su seno;
guerra con Dios, como Jacob cuando iba
en busca de su hermano, pues padece
fuerza la gloria; guerra que es la base
del que ansia la paz; guerra que es gloria.
Sólo en la guerra espiritual nos cabe
tomar la paz, tu beso de saludo;
sólo luchando por el cielo, Cristo,
vivir la paz podremos los mortales.
Pero tu paz, Hermano, y no el embuste
que como tal da el mundo, hasta aquel día
en que el león con paja se apaciente,
y anide el gavilán con la paloma;
porque guerra de paz fué tu pasión.

El Cristo de Velázquez

Alba

Blanco estás como el cielo en el naciente
blanco está al alba antes que el sol apunte
del limbo de la tierra de la noche:
que albor de aurora diste a nuestra vida
vuelta alborada de la muerte, porche
del día eterno; blanco cual la nube
que en columna guiaba por el yermo
al pueblo del Señor mientras el día
duraba. Cual la nieve de las cumbres
ermitañas, ceñidas por el cielo,
donde el sol reverbera sin estorbo,
de tu cuerpo, que es cumbre de la vida,
resbalan cristalinas aguas puras,
espejo claro de la luz celeste,
para regar cavernas soterrañas
de las tinieblas que el abismo ciñe.
Como la cima altísima, de noche,
cual luna, anuncia el alba a los que viven
perdidos en barrancos y hoces hondas,
¡así tu cuerpo níveo, que es cima
de humanidad y es manantial de Dios,
en nuestra noche anuncia eterno albor!

El Cristo de Velázquez

Castilla

Tú me levantas, tierra de Castilla,
en la rugosa palma de tu mano,
al cielo que te enciende y te refresca,
al cielo, tu amo.

Tierra nervuda, enjuta, despejada,
madre de corazones y de brazos,
toma el presente en ti viejos colores
del noble antaño.

Con la pradera cóncava del cielo
lindan en torno tus desnudos campos,
tiene en ti cuna el sol y en ti sepulcro
y en ti santuario.

Es todo cima tu extensión redonda
y en ti me siento al cielo levantado,
aire de cumbre es el que se respira
aquí en tus páramos.

¡ Ara gigante, tierra castellana,
a ese tu aire soltaré mis cantos,
si te son dignos bajarán al mundo
desde lo alto !

Poesías

Soneto

Es una antorcha al aire esta palmera,
verde llama que busca al sol desnudo
para beberle sangre ; en cada nudo
de su tronco cuajó una primavera.
Sin brotes ni eslabones, altanera
y erguida, pisa el yermo seco y rudo,
para la miel del cielo es un embudo
la copa de sus venas, sin madera.
No se retuerce ni se quiebra al suelo ;
no hay sombra en su follaje, es luz cuajada
que en ofrenda de amor se alarga al cielo
la sangre de un volcán que enamorada
del padre Sol se revistió de anhelo
y se ofrece, columna, a su morada.

De Fuerteventura a París

Sub specie momenti

Verdor nativo ; la niñez que vuelve
y el porvenir disuelve ;
juega el sol con las nubes y sonríe,
la mar me cuna,
y en sus olas la cuita se deslíe,
—con ello mi fortuna—
brotan aquí, en Hendaya,
las aguas lentas de mi fiel Vizcaya.
Leo el Apocalipsis, lo releo,
y en eterna marea me mareo ;
pasa el que es, ha sido y viene,
miro su fuerte voz
pasar sobre la mies de mi alma en hoz
y el alma ¿ qué retiene ?
Todo es momento ;
espacio condensado ; el viento
se lleva el aire de esta leve Francia
y a España lo remonta ; allí se cuela,
¿ formará escuela ?

Romancero del destierro

Arroyuelo

Arroyuelo sin nombre ni historia
que a la sombra del roble murmuras
bañando sus raíces
¿ quién llama a tus aguas ?
Al nacer en la cumbre, en el cielo,
con la mar te sueñas,
con la mar que en el cielo se acuesta,
arroyuelo sin nombre ni historia.

Romancero del destierro

RUBÉN DARÍO

(1867–1916)

Rimas

Yo quisiera cincelarte
una rima
delicada y primorosa
como una áurea margarita
o cubierta de irisada
pedrería,
o como un joyel de Oriente
o una copa florentina.

Yo quisiera poder darte
una rima
como el collar de Zobeída,
el de perlas ormuzinas
que huelan como las rosas
y que brillan
como el rocío en los pétalos
de la flor recién nacida.

Yo quisiera darte
una rima
que llevara la amargura
de las hondas penas mías
entre el oro del engarce
de las frases cristalinas.

Yo quisiera poder darte
una rima
que no produjera en ti
la indiferencia o la risa,
sino que la contemplaras
en su plácida alegría,
y que después de leerla.
te quedaras pensativa.

Responso a Verlaine

Padre y maestro mágico, liróforo celeste,
que al instrumento olímpico y a la siringa agreste
diste tu acento encantador;
¡ Panida ! ¡ Pan tú mismo, que coros condujiste
hacia el propíleo sacro que amaba tu alma triste,
al son del sistro y del tambor !

Que tu sepulcro cubra de flores Primavera,
que se humedezca el áspero hocico de la fiera,
de amor, si pasa por allí;
que el fúnebre recinto visite Pan bicorne;
que de sangrientas rosas el fresco abril te adorne,
y de claveles de rubí.

Que si posarse quiere sobre la tumba el cuervo,
ahuyenten la negrura del pájaro protervo
el dulce canto de cristal
que Filomela vierta sobre tus tristes huesos,
o la harmonía dulce de risas y de besos
de culto oculto y florestal.

Que púberes canéforas te ofrenden el acanto,
que sobre tu sepulcro no se derrame el llanto,
sino rocío, vino, miel:
que el pámpano allí brote, las flores de Citeres,
y que se escuchen vagos suspiros de mujeres
bajo un simbólico laurel.

Que si un pastor su pífano bajo el frescor del haya,
en amorosos días, como en Virgilio, ensaya,
tu nombre ponga en la canción;
y que la virgen náyade, cuando ese nombre escuche,
con ansias y temores entre las linfas luche,
llena de miedo y de pasión.

De noche en la montaña, en la negra montaña
de las Visiones, pase gigante sombra extraña,
sombra de un Sátiro espectral;
que ella al centauro adusto con su grandeza asuste;
de una extra-humana flauta la melodía ajuste
a la harmonía sideral.

Y huya el tropel equino por la montaña vasta;
tu rostro de ultratumba bañe la luna casta
de compasiva y blanca luz;
y el Sátiro contemple sobre un lejano monte
una cruz que se eleve cubriendo el horizonte
y un resplandor sobre la cruz.

Prosas profanas

Sinfonía en gris mayor

El mar como un vasto cristal azogado
refleja la lámina de un cielo de cinc;
lejanas bandadas de pájaros manchan
el fondo bruñido de pálido gris.

El sol como un vidrio redondo y opaco
con paso de enfermo camina al cenit;
el viento marino descansa en la sombra
teniendo de almohada su negro clarín.

Las ondas que mueven su vientre de plomo
debajo del muelle parecen gemir.
Sentado en un cable, fumando su pipa,
está un marinero pensando en las playas
de un vago lejano brumoso país.

Es viejo ese lobo. Tostaron su cara
los rayos de fuego del sol del Brasil;
los recios tifones del mar de la China
le han visto bebiendo su frasco de gin.

La espuma impregnada de yodo y salitre
ha tiempo conoce su roja nariz,
sus crespos cabellos, sus biceps de atleta,
su gorra de lona, su blusa de dril.

En medio del humo que forma el tabaco
ve el viejo el lejano brumoso país,
adonde una tarde caliente y dorada
tendidas las velas partió el bergantín . . .

La siesta del trópico. El lobo se aduerme.
Ya todo lo envuelve la gama del gris.
Parece que un suave y enorme esfumino
del curvo horizonte borrara el confín.

La siesta del trópico. La vieja cigarra
ensaya su ronca guitarra senil,
y el grillo preludia un solo monótono
en la única cuerda que está en su violín.

Prosas profanas

Elogio de la seguidilla

Metro mágico y rico que al alma expresas
llameantes alegrías, penas arcanas,
desde en los suaves labios de las princesas
hasta en las bocas de las gitanas.

Las almas armoniosas buscan tu encanto,
sonora rosa métrica que ardes y brillas,
y España ve en tu ritmo, siente en tu canto
sus hembras, sus claveles, sus manzanillas.

Vibras al aire alegre como una cinta,
el músico te adula, te ama el poeta;
Rueda en ti sus fogosos paisajes pinta
con la audaz policromia de su paleta.

En ti el hábil orfebre cincela el marco
en que la idea-perla su oriente acusa,
o en tu cordaje armónico formas el arco
con que lanza sus flechas la airada musa.

A tu voz en el aire crujen las faldas,
los piececitos hacen brotar las rosas
e hilan hebras de amores las esmeraldas
en ruecas invisibles y misteriosas.

La andaluza hechicera, paloma arisca,
por ti irradia, se agita, vibra y se quiebra,
con el lánguido gesto de la odalisca
o las fascinaciones de la culebra.

Pequeña ánfora lírica de vino llena
compuesto por la dulce musa Alegría
con uvas andaluzas, sal macarena,
flor y canela frescas de Andalucía.

Subes, creces y vistes de pompas fieras
retumbas en el ruido de las metrallas,
ondulas con el ala de las banderas,
suenas con los clarines de las batallas.

Tienes toda la lira; tienes las manos
que acompasan las danzas y las canciones;
tus órganos, tus prosas, tus cantos llanos
y tus llantos que parten los corazones.

Ramillete de dulces trinos verbales,
jabalina de Diana la Cazadora,
ritmo que tiene el filo de cien puñales,
que muerde y acaricia, mata y enflora.

Las Tirsis campesinas de ti están llenas,
y aman, radiosa abeja, tus bordoneos;
así riegan tus chispas las nochebuenas,
como adoras la lira de los Orfeos.

Que bajo el sol dorado de Manzanilla
que esta azulada concha del cielo baña,
polítona y triunfante, la seguidilla
es la flor del sonoro Pindo de España.

Prosas profanas

Marcha triunfal

¡Ya viene el cortejo!
¡Ya viene el cortejo! Ya se oyen los claros clarines.
¡La espada se anuncia con vivo reflejo;
ya viene, oro y hierro, el cortejo de los paladines!
Ya pasa debajo los arcos ornados de blancas Minervas y Martes,
los arcos triunfales en donde las Famas erigen sus largas trompetas,
la gloria solemne de los estandartes
llevados por manos robustas de heroicos atletas.
Se escucha el ruido que forman las armas de los caballeros,
los frenos que mascan los fuertes caballos de guerra,
los cascos que hieren la tierra,
y los timbaleros
que el paso acompasan con ritmos marciales.
¡Tal pasan los fieros guerreros
debajo los arcos triunfales!

Los claros clarines de pronto levantan sus sones,
su canto sonoro,
su cálido coro,
que envuelve en un trueno de oro
la augusta soberbia de los pabellones.
Él dice la lucha, la herida venganza,
las ásperas crines,

los rudos penachos, la pica, la lanza,
la sangre que riega de heroicos carmines
la tierra;
los negros mastines
que azuza la muerte, que rige la guerra.

Los áureos sonidos
anuncian el advenimiento
triunfal de la Gloria;
dejando el picacho que guarda sus nidos,
tendiendo sus alas enormes al viento,
los condores llegan. ¡Llegó la victoria!

Ya pasa el cortejo.
Señala el abuelo los héroes al niño:
"Ved como la barba del viejo
los bucles de oro circundan de armiño."
Las bellas mujeres aprestan coronas de flores,
y bajo los pórticos vense sus rostros de rosa;
y la más hermosa
sonríe al más fiero de los vencedores.
¡Honor al que trae cautiva la extraña bandera!
¡Honor al herido y honor a los fieles
soldados que muerte encontraron por mano extranjera!
¡Clarines! ¡Laureles!

Las nobles espadas de tiempos gloriosos
desde sus panoplias saludan las nuevas coronas y lauros
—las viejas espadas de los granaderos más fuertes que osos,
hermanos de aquellos lanceros que fueron centauros—,
Las trompas guerreras resuenan;
de voces los aires se llenan . . .
—A aquellas antiguas espadas,
a aquellos ilustres aceros,
que encarnan las glorias pasadas.—
¡Y al sol que hoy alumbra las nuevas victorias ganadas,
y al héroe que guía su grupo de jovenes fieros;
al que ama la insignia del suelo materno;

al que ha desafiado, ceñido el acero y el arma en la mano,
los soles del rojo verano,
las nieves y vientos del gélido invierno,
la noche, la escarcha
y el odio y la muerte, por ser por la patria inmortal,
saludan con voces de bronce las trompas de guerra que tocan la
marcha
triunfal! . . .

Cantos de vida y esperanza

A Cervantes

Horas de pesadumbre y de tristeza
paso en mi soledad. Pero Cervantes
es buen amigo. Endulza mis instantes
ásperos, y reposa mi cabeza.
Él es la vida y la naturaleza,
regala un yelmo de oros y diamantes
a mis sueños errantes.
Es para mí: suspira, ríe y reza.
Cristiano y amoroso y caballero
parla como un arroyo cristalino.
Así le admiro y quiero,
viendo cómo el destino
hace que regocije al mundo entero
la tristeza inmortal de ser divino.

Cantos de vida y esperanza

Melancolía

Hermano, tú que tienes la luz, dime la mía.
Soy como un ciego. Voy sin rumbo y ando a tientas.
Voy bajo tempestades y tormentas
ciego de ensueño y loco de armonía.

Ése es mi mal. Soñar. La poesía
es la camisa férrea de mil puntas cruentas
que llevo sobre el alma. Las espinas sangrientas
dejan caer las gotas de mi melancolía.
Y así voy, ciego y loco, por este mundo amargo;
a veces me parece que el camino es muy largo,
y a veces que es muy corto . . .
Y en este titubeo de aliento y agonía,
cargo lleno de penas lo que apenas soporto.
¿No oyes caer las gotas de mi melancolía?

Cantos de vida y esperanza

La dulzura del ángelus

La dulzura del ángelus matinal y divino
que diluyen ingénuas campanas provinciales
en un aire inocente a fuerza de rosales,
de plegaria, de ensueño de virgen y de trino
de ruiseñor, opuesto todo al rudo destino
que no cree en Dios . . . El áureo ovillo vespertino
que la tarde devana tras opacos cristales
por tejer la inconsútil tela de nuestros males,
todos hechos de carne y aromados de vino.
Y esta atroz amargura de no gustar de nada,
de no saber adónde dirigir nuestra prora
mientras la pobre esquife en la noche cerrada
va en las hostiles olas huérfano de la aurora . . .
(¡Oh, suaves campanas entre la madrugada!)

Cantos de vida y esperanza

El soneto de trece versos

De una juvenil inocencia
¡qué conservar sino el sutil
perfume, esencia de su abril,
la más maravillosa esencia!

Por lamentar a mi conciencia
quedó de un sonoro marfil
un cuento que fué de las *Mil*
y una noches de mi existencia . . .
Scherazada se entredurmió . . .
El visir quedó meditando . . .
Dinarzada el día olvidó . . .
Mas el pájaro azul volvió . . .
Pero . . .
No obstante . . .
Siempre . . .
Cuando . . .

Cantos de vida y esperanza

Vesper

Quietud, quietud . . . Ya la ciudad de oro
ha entrado en el misterio de la tarde.
La catedral es un gran relicario.
La bahía unifica sus cristales
en un azul de arcaicas mayúsculas
de los antifonarios y misales.
Las barcas pescadoras estilizan
el blancor de sus velas triangulares
y como un eco que dijera : "Ulises",
junta alientos de flores y de sales.

El canto errante

Hondas

Yo soñé que era un hondero
mallorquín.
Con las piedras que en la costa
recogí,
cazaba águilas al vuelo,
lobos, y
en la guerra iba a la guerra
contra mil.

Un guijarro de oro puro
fué al cenit
una tarde en que en la altura
azul vi
un enorme gerifalte
perseguir
a una extraña ave radiante,
un rubí
que rayara el firmamento
de zafir.

No tornó mi piedra al mundo.
Pero sin
vacilar vino a mí el ave—
querubín.
" Partió herida—dijo—el alma
de Goliat, y vengo a ti.
¡ Soy el alma luminosa
de David ! "

El canto errante

La canción de los pinos

¡ Oh pinos, oh hermanos en tierra y ambiente,
yo os amo ! Sois dulces, sois buenos, sois graves.
Diríase un árbol que piensa y que siente,
mimado de auroras, poetas y aves.

Tocó vuestras frentes la alada sandalia ;
habéis sido mástil, proscenio, curul,
¡ oh pinos solares, oh pinos de Italia !,
bañados de gracia, de gloria, de azul.

Sombríos, sin oro del sol, taciturnos,
en medio de brumas glaciales y en
montañas de ensueños, ¡ oh pinos nocturnos,
oh pinos del Norte, sois bellos también !

Con gestos de estatuas, de mimos, de actores,
tendiendo a la dulce caricia del mar,
¡ oh pinos de Nápoles, rodeados de flores,
oh pinos divinos, no os puedo olvidar!

Cuando en mis errantes pasos peregrinos
la Isla Dorada me ha dado un rincón
do soñar mis sueños, encontré los pinos,
los pinos amados de mi corazón. . . .

El canto errante

RAMÓN MARÍA DEL VALLE-INCLÁN

(1869–1935)

Milagro de la mañana

Tañía una campana
en el azul cristal
de la santa mañana.
Oración campesina
que temblaba en la azul
santidad matutina.

Y en el viejo camino
cantaba un ruiseñor,
y era de luz su trino.
La campana de aldea
le dice con su voz
al pájaro que crea.
La campana aldeana
en la gloria del sol
era alma cristiana.
Al tocar esparcía
aromas del rosal
de la Virgen María.

Esta santa conseja
la recuerda un cantar
en una fabla vieja:

"Campana, campaniña do Pico Sacro
toca porque floreza o rosal do milagro."

Aromas de leyenda

Resol de Verbena

Ingrata la luz de la tarde,
la lejanía en gris de plomo,
los olivos de azul cobarde,
el campo amarillo de cromo.

Se merienda sobre el camino
entre polvo y humo de churros,
y manchan las heces del vino
las chorreras de los baturros.

Agria y dramática la nota
del baile. La sombra morada,
el piano desgrana una jota,
polvo en el viento de tronada . . .

El tíovivo su quimera
infantil, erige en el raso:
en los caballos de madera
bate el reflejo del ocaso. . . .

Corona el columpio su juego
con cantos. La llanura arde:
tornóse el ocaso de fuego;
los nardos ungieron la tarde.

Por aquel rescoldo de fragua
pasa el inciso transparente
de la voz que pregona :—¡ Agua,
azucarillos y aguardiente !

Vuela el columpio con un vuelo
de risas. Cayóse en la falda
de la niña, la rosa del pelo,
y Eros le ofrece una guirnalda.

Se alza el columpio alegremente,
con el ritmo de onda en la arena,
onda azul donde asoma la frente
vespertina de una sirena. . . .

¡ Un real, la cabeza parlante !
¡ A la suerte del pajarito !
¡ La foca y el hombre gigante !
¡ Los gozos del Santo Bendito !

¡ Naranjas ! ¡ Torrados ! ¡ Claveles !
¡ Claveles ! ¡ Claveles ! ¡ Claveles !
Encadenados, los pregones
hacen guirnaldas de babeles.

Se infla el buñuelo. La aceituna
aliñada reclama el vino
y muerde el pueblo la moruna
rosquilla de anís y comino.

La pipa de kif

Bestiario

¡ Romántica casa de fieras
del Buen Retiro, he vuelto a ver
la alegría de tus banderas,
bajo la tarde, como ayer ! . . .

Y me detuve emocionado
ante aquel viejo carcamal
estilizado
en el escudo nacional.

¡ Viejo león que entre las rejas
bostezando agitas la crin,
sobre tus cejas
sus arrugas puso el esplín !

El canguro antediluviano
huyó con saltos de flin-flan :
es australiano
y tiene trazas de alemán. . . .

El tigre se agita ondulante
tras los hierros de su cubil :
belfo tremante :
garra rampante y ojo hostil.

¡ Qué triste el oso se espereza
sobre las pajas de su coy !
¡ Cuando bosteza
recuerda al Conde de Tolstoy !

Sonríe el lobo. Tras la reja,
con un guiño de curial
rasca la oreja
y la estameña del sayal.

Y la romántica jirafa,
solterona que bebe hiel,
las rosas chafa
en la cúpula del laurel.

¡ Arquitectura bizantina,
imposible de razonar,
de la divina
silueta de Sara Bernhardt ! . . .

Ruge encendida la pantera
su ensueño de arenas y sol,
sabe la fiera
un aljamiado de español.

Recuerda el índico elefante
los bosques sagrados de Anam,
sueña el gigante,
como un fakir ebrio de baham,

meditaciones eruditas
que oyó Rubén alguna vez:
letras sanscritas
y problemas del ajedrez. . . .

Encumbrado sobre una rama
el triunfo del pavo-real,
es una llama
del Paraíso Terrenal.

Un ensueño de surtidores,
un cuento de viejo jardín
con los olores
de la albahaca y el jazmín. . . .

El mono acrobático salta
y hace del mundo trampolín.
Mima y esmalta
cada salto con un mohín.

Y la cotorra verdigualda,
retaleando su papel,
luce una falda
que fué de la Infanta Isabel. . . .

Y a Dionisio Aereopagita
en penitencia sobre un pie,
desacredita
la cigüeña falta de fe. . . .

Esponja el flamenco la pluma
y su absurdo monumental
trémula esfuma
sobre dos rayas de coral. . . .

Y el cocodrilo faraónico
las fauces abre en el fangal
al sol que irónico
hace llorar su lacrimal.

¡ Olvidada Casa de Fieras,
con los ojos de la niñez
tus quimeras
vuelvo a gozar en la vejez !

Muere la tarde.—Un rojo grito
sobre la fronda vesperal.—
Y abre el círculo de su mito
el Gran Bestiario Zodiacal.

La pipa de kif

JOSÉ MARÍA GABRIEL Y GALÁN

(1870–1905)

Mi montaraza

I

No hay bajo el cielo divino
del campo salamanquino,
moza como Ana María
ni más alegre alquería
que Carrascal del Camino.

En Carrascal nació ella,
y si antes no fuese bella
su natal tierra bendita,
fuéralo porque la habita
la rosa de monte aquella.

No nace en tierra cristiana
flor silvestre más lozana,
ni hormiga más vividora,
ni moza más castellana,
ni mujer más labradora. . . .

Sencilla para pensar,
prudente para sentir,
recatada para amar,
discreta para callar,
y honesta para decir;

robusta como una encina,
casera como golondrina
que en casa canta la paz,
algo arisca y montesina
como paloma torcaz;

agria como una manzana,
roja como una cereza,
fresca como una fontana,
vierte efluvios de alma sana
y olor de Naturaleza.

¿Qué extraño que los favores
implore yo del destino,
si estoy enfermo de amores
por la reina de las flores
de Carrascal del Camino?

Castellanas

Mi música

Naturales armonías,
populares canturías
cuyo acento musical
no es engendro artificioso,
sino aliento vigoroso
de la vida natural:

vuestras notas, vuestros ruidos,
vuestros ecos repetidos
en ritornello hablador,
son mis goces más risueños,
son el arte de mis sueños,
¡son mi música mejor!...

brava música sincera
de la ronda callejera
de los mozos del lugar,
que con guitarras sonoras
y bandurrias trinadoras
acompañan su cantar;

alegre esquilón de ermita,
voz de amores que recita
la romántica canción;
ruido de aire que adormece,
son de lluvia que entristece,
manso arrullo de pichón; . . .

jugueteos musicales
que modula entre zarzales
el callado manantial
cuyo hililllo intermitente
da la nota transparente
de una lira de cristal; . . .

hálitos del bosque frío,
lejano zumbar de río,
hachazos del leñador,
explosivos en la sierra,
eco incógnito que yerra,
hijo ignoto de un rumor; . . .

tonadilla peregrina
que modula en la colina
la gaitilla del zagal,
la que vierte blancas notas
que de miel parecen gotas
desprendidas del panal. . . .

aire quedo de alameda
que una música remeda
que el alma nunca entendió,
una música increada
que en el seno de la nada
para siempre se quedó. . . .

ya os lo dije; vuestros ruidos,
vuestros ecos repetidos
en ritornello hablador,
son el pan de mi deseo,
son el arte que yo creo,
¡son mi música mejor!

Nuevas castellanas

La jurdana

I

Era un día crudo y turbio de febrero
que las sierras azotaba
con el látigo iracundo
de los vientos y las aguas . . .
Unos vientos que pasaban restallando
las silbantes finas alas . . .
Unos turbios desatados aguaceros,
cuyas gotas aceradas
descendían de los cielos como flechas
y corrían por la tierra como lágrimas.
Como bajan de las sierras tenebrosas
las famélicas hambrientas alimañas,
por la cuesta del serrucho va bajando
la paupérrima jurdana . . .
lleva el frío de las fiebres en los huesos,
lleva el frío de las penas en el alma,
lleva el pecho hacia la tierra,
lleva el hijo a las espaldas . . .
Viene sola, como flaca loba joven
por el látigo del hambre flagelada,
con la fiebre de sus hambres en los ojos
con la angustia de sus hambres en la entraña.
Es la imagen del serrucho solitario
de misérrimos lentiscos y pizarras;
es el símbolo del barro empedernido
de los álveos de las fuentes agotadas. . . .

Ni sus venas tienen fuego,
ni su carne tiene savia,
ni sus pechos tienen leche,
ni sus ojos tienen lágrimas. . . .
Ha dejado la morada nauseabunda
donde encueva sus tristezas y sus sarnas,
donde roe los mendrugos indigestos,
de dureza despiadada,
cuando torna de la vida vagabunda
con el hijo y los mendrugos a la espalda.
Y ahora viene, y ahora viene de sus sierras
a pedirnos a las gentes sin entrañas
el mendrugo que arrojamos a la calle
si a la puerta no lo pide la jurdana. . . .

III

Por la cuesta del serrucho pizarroso
va bajando la paupérrima jurdana
con miserias en el alma y en el cuerpo,
con el hijo medio imbécil a la espalda. . . .

Yo les pido dos limosnas para ellos
a los hijos de mi Patria :
¡ pan de trigo para el hambre de sus cuerpos !
¡ pan de ideas para el hambre de sus almas ! . . .

Campesinas

MANUEL MACHADO

(1874–1947)

Cantares

Vino, sentimiento, guitarra y poesía
hacen los cantares de la patria mía . . .
Cantares . . .
Quien dice cantares, dice Andalucía.

A la sombra fresca de la vieja parra
un mozo moreno rasguea la guitarra . . .
Cantares . . .
Algo que acaricia y algo que desgarra.

La prima que canta y el bordón que llora . . .
Y el tiempo callado se va hora tras hora.
Cantares . . .
Son dejos fatales de la raza mora.

No importa la vida, que ya está perdida;
y después de todo, ¿qué es eso, la vida? . . .
Cantares . . .
Cantando la pena, la pena se olvida.

Madre, pena, suerte, pena, madre, muerte,
ojos negros, negros, y negra la suerte . . .
Cantares . . .
En ellos el alma del alma se vierte.

Cantares. Cantares de la patria mía . . .
Cantares son sólo los de Andalucía.
Cantares . . .
No tiene más cuerdas la guitarra mía.

Castilla

El ciego sol se estrella
en las duras aristas de las armas,
llaga de luz los petos y espaldares
y flamea en las puntas de las lanzas.

El ciego sol, la sed y la fatiga.
Por la terrible estepa castellana,
al destierro, con doce de los suyos
—polvo, sudor y hierro—el Cid cabalga

Cerrado está el mesón a piedra y lodo . . .
Nadie responde. Al pomo de la espada
y al cuento de las picas el postigo
va a ceder . . . ¡ Quema el sol, el aire abrasa !

A los terribles golpes,
de eco ronco, una voz pura, de plata
y de cristal, responde . . . Hay una niña
muy débil y muy blanca
en el umbral. Es toda
ojos azules y en los ojos lágrimas.
Oro pálido nimba
su carita curiosa y asustada.

—Buen Cid, pasad . . . El rey nos dará muerte,
arruinará la casa,
y sembrará de sal el pobre campo
que mi padre trabaja . . .
Idos. El cielo os colme de venturas . . .
¡ En nuestro mal, oh Cid, no ganáis nada !

Calla la niña y llora sin gemido . . .
Un sollozo infantil cruza la escuadra
de feroces guerreros,
y una voz inflexible grita : " ¡ En marcha ! "

El ciego sol, la sed y la fatiga.
Por la terrible estepa castellana,
al destierro, con doce de los suyos
—polvo, sudor y hierro—, el Cid cabalga.

La hija del ventero

La hija callaba, y de cuando en cuando sonreía.
CERVANTES, *Don Quijote*

" La hija callaba
y se sonreía . . ."
Divino silencio,

preciosa sonrisa,
¿ por qué estáis presentes
en la mente mía?

La venta está sola.
Maritornes guiña
los ojos, durmiéndose.
La ventera hila.
Su mercé el ventero,
en la puerta, atisba
si alguien llega . . . El viento
barre la campiña.

. . . Al rincón de fuego,
sentada, la hija
—soñando en los libros
de caballerías—,
con sus ojos garzos
ve morir el día
tras el horizonte . . .

Parda y desabrida,
la Mancha se hunde
en la noche fría.

Domingo

La vida, el huracán, bufa en mi calle. Sobre
la turba polvorienta y vociferadora,
el morado crepúsculo desciende . . . El sol ahora
se va, y el barrio queda enteramente pobre.
¡ Fatiga del domingo, fatiga . . . Extraordinario
bien conocido y bien corriente! . . . No hay remedio.
¡ Señor, tú descansaste; aleja, en fin, el tedio
de este modesto ensueño consuetudinario!
Voces, gritos, canción apenas . . . Bulla. Locas
carcajadas . . . ¿ Será que pasa la alegría?

Y yo aquí, solo, triste y lejos de las fiestas . . .
Dame, Señor, las necias palabras de estas bocas;
dame que suene tanto mi risa cuando ría;
dame un alma sencilla como cualquiera de éstas.

La infanta Margarita

Como una flor clorótica el semblante,
que hábil pincel tiñó de leche y fresa,
emerge del pomposo guardainfante,
entre sus galas cortesanas presa.
La mano,—ámbar de ensueño—entre tules
de la falda desmáyase y sostiene
el pañuelo riquísimo, que viene
de los ojos atónitos y azules.
Italia, Flandes, Portugal . . . Poniente
sol de la gloria el último destello
en sus mejillas infantiles posa . . .
Y corona no más su augusta frente
la dorada ceniza del cabello,
que apenas prende el leve lazo rosa.

ANTONIO MACHADO

(1875–1939)

Orillas del Duero

Se ha asomado una cigüeña a lo alto del campanario.
Girando en torno a la torre y el caserón solitario,
ya las golondrinas chillan. Pasaron del blanco invierno,
de nevascas y ventiscas los crudos soplos de infierno.

Es una tibia mañana.
El sol calienta un poquito la pobre tierra soriana.

Pasados los verdes pinos,
casi azules, primavera
se ve brotar en los finos
chopos de la carretera
y del río. El Duero corre, terso y mudo, mansamente.
El campo parece, más que joven, adolescente.

Entre las hierbas alguna humilde flor ha nacido,
azul o blanca. ¡ Belleza del campo apenas florido,
y mística primavera !

¡ Chopos del camino blanco, álamos de la ribera,
espuma de la montaña
ante la azul lejanía,
sol del día, claro día !
¡ Hermosa tierra de España !

Crepúsculo

Las ascuas de un crepúsculo morado
detrás del negro cipresal humean . . .
En la glorieta en sombra está la fuente
con su alado y desnudo Amor de piedra,
que sueña mudo. En la marmórea taza
reposa el agua muerta.

Cante hondo

Yo meditaba absorto, devanando
los hilos del hastío y la tristeza,
cuando llegó a mi oído,
por la ventana de mi estancia, abierta

a una caliente noche de verano,
el plañir de una copla soñolienta,
quebrada por los trémolos sombríos
de las músicas magas de mi tierra.

. . . Y era el Amor, como una roja llama . . .
—Nerviosa mano en la vibrante cuerda
ponía un largo suspirar de oro
que se trocaba en surtidor de estrellas—

. . . Y era la Muerte, al hombro la cuchilla,
el paso largo, torva y esquelética.
—tal cuando yo era niño la soñaba—

Y en la guitarra, resonante y trémula,
la brusca mano, al golpear, fingía
el reposar de un ataúd en tierra.

Y era un plañido solitario el soplo
que el polvo barre y la ceniza aventa.

'*Era una mañana . . .*'

Era una mañana y abril sonreía.
Frente al horizonte dorado moría
la luna, muy blanca y opaca; tras ella,
cual tenue ligera quimera, corría
la nube que apenas enturbia una estrella.

. . . .

Como sonreía la rosa mañana
al sol del oriente abrí mi ventana;
y en mi triste alcoba penetró el oriente
en canto de alondras, en risa de fuente
y en suave perfume de flora temprana.

Fué una clara tarde de melancolía.
Abril sonreía. Yo abrí las ventanas
de mi casa al viento . . . El viento traía
perfume de rosas, doblar de campanas . . .

Doblar de campanas lejanas, llorosas,
suave de rosas aromado aliento . . .
. . . ¿ Dónde están los huertos floridos de rosas ?
¿ Qué dicen las dulces campanas al viento ?

. . . .

Pregunté a la tarde de abril que moría :
¿ Al fin la alegría se acerca a mi casa ?
La tarde de abril sonrió : La alegría
pasó por tu puerta—y luego, sombría :
Pasó por tu puerta. Dos veces no pasa.

La noria

La tarde caía
triste y polvorienta.

El agua cantaba
su copla plebeya
en los canjilones
de la noria lenta.

Soñaba la mula
¡ pobre mula vieja !
al compás de sombra
que en el agua suena.

La tarde caía
triste y polvorienta.

Yo no sé qué noble,
divino poeta,
unió a la amargura
de la eterna rueda,

la dulce armonía
del agua que suena,
y vendó tus ojos,
¡ pobre mula vieja ! . . .

Mas sé que fué un noble
divino poeta,
corazón maduro
de sombra y de ciencia.

'Anoche, cuando dormía . . .'

Anoche, cuando dormía,
soñé, ¡ bendita ilusión !
que una fontana fluía
dentro de mi corazón.
Dí, ¿ por qué acequia escondida,
agua, vienes hasta mí,
manantial de nueva vida
en donde nunca bebí ?

Anoche, cuando dormía,
soñé, ¡ bendita ilusión !
que una colmena tenía
dentro de mi corazón ;
y las doradas abejas
iban fabricando en él
con las amarguras viejas,
blanca cera y dulce miel.

Anoche, cuando dormía,
soñé, ¡ bendita ilusión,
que un ardiente sol lucía
dentro de mi corazón.
Era ardiente porque daba
calores de rojo hogar,
y era sol porque alumbraba
y porque hacía llorar.

Anoche, cuando dormía,
soñé, ¡ bendita ilusión !,
que era Dios lo que tenía
dentro de mi corazón.

Tres poemas

¡ Oh tarde luminosa !
El aire está encantado.
La blanca cigüeña
dormita volando,
y las golondrinas se cruzan, tendidas
las alas agudas al viento dorado,
y en la tarde risueña se alejan
volando, soñando . . .

Y hay una que torna como la saeta,
las alas agudas tendidas al aire sombrío,
buscando su negro rincón del tejado.

La blanca cigüeña,
como un garabato,
tranquila y disforme ¡ tan disparatada !
sobre el campanario.

. . . .

Señor, ya me arrancaste lo que yo más quería.
Oye otra vez, Dios mío, mi corazón clamar.
Tu voluntad se hizo, Señor, contra la mía.
Señor, ya estamos solos mi corazón y el mar.

. . . .

Dice la esperanza : un día
la verás, si bien esperas.
Dice la desesperanza :
sólo tu amargura es ella.
Late, corazón . . . No todo
se lo ha tragado la tierra.

La saeta

¡ Oh, la saeta, el cantar
al Cristo de los gitanos,
siempre con sangre en las manos,
siempre por desenclavar !
¡ Cantar del pueblo andaluz
que todas las primaveras
anda pidiendo escaleras
para subir a la cruz !
¡ Cantar de la tierra mía,
que echa flores
al Jesús de la agonía,
y es la fe de mis mayores !
¡ Oh, no eres tú mi cantar !
¡ No puedo cantar, ni quiero
a ese Jesús del madero,
sino al que anduvo en el mar !

Mis poetas

El primero es Gonzalo de Berceo llamado,
Gonzalo de Berceo, poeta y peregrino,
que yendo en romería acaeció en un prado,
y a quien los sabios pintan copiando un pergamino.
Trovó a Santo Domingo, trovó a Santa María,
y a San Millán, y a San Lorenzo y Santa Oria.
Y dijo : Mi dictado non es de juglaría ;
escrito lo tenemos ; es verdadera historia.
Su verso es dulce y grave : monótonas hileras
de chopos invernales en donde nada brilla ;
renglones como surcos en pardas sementeras,
y lejos las montañas azules de Castilla. . . .

A don Francisco Giner de los Ríos

Como se fué el maestro,
la luz de esta mañana
me dijo: Van tres días
que mi hermano Francisco no trabaja.
¿Murió? . . . Sólo sabemos
que se nos fué por una senda clara,
diciéndonos: Hacedme
un duelo de labores y esperanzas.
Sed buenos y no más, sed lo que he sido
entre vosotros: alma.
Vivid, la vida sigue,
los muertos mueren y las sombras pasan;
lleva quien deja y vive el que ha vivido.
¡Yunques sonad; enmudecid, campanas!

Y hacia otra luz más pura
partió el hermano de la luz del alba,
del sol de los talleres,
el viejo alegre de la vida santa.
. . . Oh, sí, llevad, amigos;
su cuerpo a la montaña,
a los azules montes
del ancho Guadarrama.
Allí hay barrancos hondos
de pinos verdes donde el viento canta.
Su corazón repose
bajo una encina casta,
en tierra de tomillos, donde juegan
mariposas doradas . . .
Allí el maestro un día
soñaba un nuevo florecer de España.

Los sueños dialogados

I

¡Cómo en el alto llano tu figura
se me aparece!... Mi palabra evoca
el prado verde y la árida llanura,
la zarza en flor, la cenicienta roca.

Y al recuerdo obediente, negra encina
brota en el cerro, baja el chopo al río;
el pastor va subiendo a la colina;
brilla un balcón de la ciudad: el mío,

el nuestro. ¿Ves? Hacia Aragón, lejana,
la sierra de Moncayo, blanca y rosa...
Mira el incendio de ese nube grana,

y aquella estrella en el azul, esposa.
Tras el Duero, la loma de Santana
se amorata en la tarde silenciosa.

II

¿Por qué, decisme, hacia los altos llanos,
huye mi corazón de esta ribera,
y en tierra labradora y marinera
suspiro por los yermos castellanos?

Nadie elige su amor. Llevóme un día
mi destino a los grises calvijares
donde ahuyenta, al caer, la nieve fría
las sombras de los muertos encinares.

De aquel trozo de España, alto y roquero,
hoy traigo a ti, Guadalquivir florido,
una mata del áspero romero.

Mi corazón está donde ha nacido,
no a la vida, al amor, cerca del Duero . . .
¡ El muro blanco y el ciprés erguido !

FRANCISCO VILLAESPESA

(1877–1935)

Sonata de abril

Fresco aroma de rosas . . . Los horizontes rojos
arden en el crepúsculo . . . Por los verdes caminos
florecientes, cantando, pasan los peregrinos . . .
¡ El alma, el alma entera de abril brilla en sus ojos !
¡ Abrid vuestras ventanas, abridlas a los vientos
llenos de ruiseñores, los vientos sosegados
que ahuyentan, con sus besos de rosas perfumados,
sobre las frentes pálidas los tristes pensamientos !
Es la hora en que el alma melancólica espera
la divina palabra que le dé la alegría . . .
Un beso, una caricia de amor, la vida entera
se escapa de los labios, buscando en este día,
bajo el eterno júbilo de la azul primavera,
un alma que no sueñe y un labio que no ría.

Huerto cerrado

¿ Dónde la hermana dirige sus huellas ?
¿ Tan tempranito por qué amaneció,
si los remansos florecen estrellas,
si la alborada sus rosas no abrió ?

—Voy en mi falda a cortar un tesoro
de siemprevivas y rosas de luz,
de margaritas y lirios de oro
para la celda de Juan de la Cruz.

—¿ Dónde florecen tan lindas estrellas?
—En los jardines de Nuestro Señor . . .
—¿ Quién hizo abrirse corolas tan bellas?
—Santa Teresa con llantos de amor.

—¿ Cómo llegar a tan ricos jardines?
—Por los caminos que no tienen fin.
—¿ Y quién custodia sus amplios confines?
—La ígnea espada de algún serafín.

—Dame, hermanita, tus manos piadosas . . .
Quiero ver esos jardines de luz,
y recoger las más fúlgidas rosas
para la celda de Juan de la Cruz.

Romance de las ocho hermanas

Cantares de Andalucía! . . .
¡ Qué bien rima la guitarra
las sonrisas de Sevilla,
los suspiros de Granada
con el silencio de Córdoba
y la alegría de Málaga!
Almería sus amores
sueña al pie de su alcazaba.
Jaén se adormece a la sombra
de un olivo y de una parra . . .
Huelva, la heroica y altiva
Adelantada de España,
sueña con un Nuevo Mundo
en el seno de otras aguas!
Y Cádiz, la danzarina
baila desnuda en la playa,
más blanca en sus desnudeces
que las espumas más blancas!

ENRIQUE DE MESA

(1878–1929)

'*Dime la copla, Jimena . . .*'

Ya se van los ganados
  a Extremadura;
ya se queda la sierra,
  triste y oscura.
Ya se van los pastores,
  ya van marchando.
Más de cuatro zagalas
  quedan llorando.

  Dime la copla, Jimena . . .
aroma la cantilena
su voz armoniosa y pura:
  Ya se van los ganados
a Extremadura.

  En silencio el majadal;
desierto el agreste chozo,
refugio del pastor mozo
a orillas del pastizal.
Tenue ventisca otoñal
presagia invernada dura.
  Ya se queda la sierra
triste y oscura.

  Ya blanquean los borregos
el verdor de la cañada;
los zagales cañariegos
dan al aire su tonada.
  Ya van marchando.
Más de cuatro zagalas
quedan llorando.

  Hacia remoto confín,
a un silbo el rebaño arranca:
armado de su carlanca
le escolta, fiero, el mastín.

Morena moza, fragante
como tomillo salsero,
ve partir el trashumante
rebaño desde el sendero.

¡ Noche alegre de San Juan,
noche de fuego y de amor
en que al ejido, galán,
bajó del hato el pastor !

¿ Será su amor zalamero
flor de almendro tempranero
que mata el cierzo invernizo,
o será tronco roblizo
de la lumbre trashoguero ? . . .

Como el agua del regato,
saltarín y bullidor,
bajaba el zagal del hato
por las veredas en flor.—

En la paz de la mañana,
junto al dulzor del balido,
disuena el agrio ladrido
de la perra trujillana.
El cristal de una fontana
entre las guijas murmura :
Ya se van los ganados
a Extremadura.

Zagala, cierra tu zarzo,
que es duro el viento invernal ;
si viene dulzura en marzo
pronto tornará el zagal.
Hay niebla en el roquedal
y otoño nieva la altura.
Ya se queda la sierra
triste y oscura.

Al tramontar el alcor,
perdidos entre la bruma,
lejano silba el pastor
al rebaño que trashuma.
Tras el mastín ladrador
van los corderos balando.

Ya van marchando.
Más de cuatro zagalas
quedan llorando.

Cancionero castellano

Voz del agua

Era pura nieve,
y soles me hicieron cristal.
Bebe, niña, bebe
la clara pureza de mi manantial.

Canté entre los pinos
al bajar desde el blanco nevero;
crucé los caminos,
di armonía y frescura al sendero.

No temas que, aleve,
finja engaños mi voz de cristal.
Bebe, niña, bebe
la clara pureza de mi manantial.

Allá, cuando el frío,
mi blancura las cumbres entoca;
luego en el estío,
voy cantando a morir en tu boca.

Tan sólo soy nieve,
no me enturbian ponzoña ni mal.
Bebe, niña, bebe
la clara pureza de mi manantial.

Cancionero castellano

La alegre carreta

En la paz virgiliana de la mañana quieta,
se oye la perezosa marcha de la carreta.

Envuelve la frescura de la brisa sutil,
con fragancia de pinos, una risa infantil.

Un reír que ilumina la mañana serena:
ríen Carmen, Dolores, Ana, Jaime, Jimena.

¡Que sea con vosotros la paz de los caminos,
de la vida que empieza, nacientes peregrinos!

Que la ventura os brinde un sendero sin fin,
abierto, cual los ojos del pequeño Monchín.

Llenad vuestros pulmones con aura de pinares,
capullos de la vida, sin riego de pesares.

Y mirad reflejadas las tersas, puras frentes
en los limpios cristales de las aguas corrientes.

¡Oh, qué dulce bullicio, qué alegría tan franca
cuando el carro en las piedras del camino se atranca!

Reíd, temblad de gozo bajo los delantales,
mis pequeños amigos, mis amigos leales.

Vuestros ojos reflejan vuestros ánimos nobles,
claros como las aguas, fuertes como los robles.

No importuna la risa la tristeza de un lloro;
azulada sonríe la mañana de oro.

En quietud amorosa la llanura se baña;
recórtase en el cielo soberbia la montaña.

Fresca risa ilumina la mañana serena.
Ríen Carmen, Dolores, Ana, Moncho, Jimena.

Cancionero castellano

Sin caballero

Un molino,
perezoso a par del viento.
Un son triste de campana.
Un camino,
que se pierde polvoriento,
surco estéril de la tierra castellana.

Ni un rebaño
por las tierras. Ni una fuente
que dé alivio al caminante.
Como antaño,
torna al pueblo, lentamente,
triste y flaco sucesor de Rocinante.

Una venta.
Un villano gordo y sucio,
de miserias galeote . . .
Soñolienta
la andadura de su rucio.
¡No aparece en la llanada Don Quijote!

Terruñero
de la faz noblota y ancha,
descendiente del labriego castellano:

Escudero,
ya no tienes caballero ;
ya no templas con prudencia de villano
las locuras del hidalgo de la Mancha.

Cancionero castellano

RAMÓN PÉREZ DE AYALA

(1880–)

La playa

En el cristal del cielo las agudas gaviotas,
como un diamante en un vidrio, hacen una raya.
Nordeste y sol. La sombra de las aves remotas
se desliza por sobre el oro de la playa.
¡ Oh tristeza de las cosas vagas y errantes,
de todo lo que en el silencio se desliza !
Nuestro paso por el vivir es, caminantes,
como tenue sombra en la arena movediza.

El sendero andante

El niño en la playa

Sobre la arena dorada, el niño juega en la orilla.
El ir y venir del agua el niño en su juego imita.
Aguarda un punto la ola, que de lejos viene henchida,
—el niño tan delicado, la mar tan bronca y arisca . . .
En los bordes del abismo tiembla la flor de la vida.
¡ Ay si el dragón con sus fauces alcanza la florecilla !
Llega rugiendo la ola. El niño, al verla, vacila ;
pero, huye, al cabo, la cara por el terror contraída.
Párase a poco. La ola, derrumbada, casi extinta,
le lame los pies al niño, con lengua hipócrita y fría.

El sendero andante

‘*En el azul de luz increada . . .*’

En el azul de luz increada
flota al viento la hermosa gaviota blanca,
sin mover las alas.
El alma hacia ella se levanta.
La gaviota grazna.
Desarmonía, desilusión.
¿Por qué no canta la hermosa gaviota
como la fea alondra
y el feo ruiseñor?

El sendero innumerable

‘*En un prado, a la vera del mar . . .*’

En un prado, a la vera del mar
bajo un árbol,
estoy tendido,
con los ojos cerrados.
El zumbido del mar eterno
colma la copa del cielo.
Hay sol.
En torno a mi cabeza
revuela un moscardón.
Gira. Gira. Me oprime.
como una obsesión.
Y el zumbido del insecto
es más penetrante e intenso
que el zumbido del mar eterno.

El sendero innumerable

Ocaso

El mar está terso y bruñido.
Una tersura y bruñido mates.
Es de nácar, con tonos púrpura, plata, malva,
azul, gris, violeta, confundidos y suaves.

Están el mar y el cielo
como las valvas interiores de una concha
de nácar; entreabierta. Y está asido en el quicio
el sol, como una perla rosa.
¡ Oh, si esta concha al pronto se cerrase
para siempre, cerrándome en su ámbito,
solo entre el mar y el cielo, frente al sol,
con esta luz y este color seráficos ! . . .

El sendero innumerable

Signos

Nace de cada onda una palabra alada
que vuela hacia el ocaso y se sume en su fuego.
Sobre el agua, una mano, que se hurta a la mirada,
escribe raros signos y se derriten luego.

El sendero innumerable

JUAN RAMÓN JIMÉNEZ
(1881–)

Crepúsculo

El poniente me invade con sus flores
de oro, mientras, largo y lento, canta
el ruiseñor de todos mis amores,
ahogándose casi en mi garganta.
Al ver este oro entre el pinar sombrío,
me he acordado de mí tan dulcemente,
que era más dulce el pensamiento mío
que toda la dulzura del poniente.
¡ Oh dulzura de oro ! ¡ Campo verde,
corazón con esquilas, humo en calma !
No hay en la vida nada que recuerde
estos dulces ocasos de mi alma.

Olvidanzas

Verde verderol

Verde verderol,
¡ endulza la puesta del sol !

Palacio de encanto,
el pinar tardío
arrulla con llanto
la huída del río.
Allí el nido umbrío
tiene el verderol.
Verde verderol,
¡ endulza la puesta del sol !

La última brisa
es suspiradora ;
el sol rojo irisa
al pino que llora.
¡ Vaga y lenta hora
nuestra, verderol !
Verde verderol,
¡ endulza la puesta del sol !

Soledad y calma ;
silencio y grandeza.
La choza del alma
se recoge y reza.
De pronto, ¡ oh belleza !
canta el verderol.
Verde verderol,
¡ endulza la puesta del sol !

Su canto enajena.
—¿ Se ha parado el viento ?—
El campo se llena
de su sentimiento.

Malva es el lamento,
verde el verderol.
Verde verderol,
¡ endulza la puesta del sol !

Baladas de primavera

La fuente seca

Fuente seca y ruinosa, ¡ ya no eres más que piedra !
—¡ Oh antigua voz de plata, oh dulce y clara fuente !—
Un verdón se equivoca con tu fosa, y la yedra
cuelga de ti, lo mismo que una hermana indolente.
¡ Palacio abandonado de un agua, te secaste,
lo mismo que mi vida, para callar tu historia ;
pero el sol de la tarde sueña en lo que dejaste,
como un agua de oro que canta en mi memoria !

La soledad sonora

Marina

El cielo de tormenta, pesado y retumbante,
se raja en el ocaso. Un agudo cuchillo
de luz agria y equívoca, orna el medroso instante,
de un estraño esplendor, delirante y amarillo.
Lo que hiere la luz, como un grito, se inflama ;
carmín de oro es la costa de altas rocas ;
las galeras se encendian, y una lívida llama
va por las olas negras, trájicamente locas ;
Furioso, el viento da, y atormentado y hondo,
contra la irisación del día trastornado ;
y, en una alegoría fantástica, en el fondo
del oriente, persiste el sol falso y dorado . . .

Marinas de ensueño

Hojas nuevas

¡ Mira, por los chopos
de plata, cómo trepan al cielo niños de oro !
Y van mirando al cielo,
y suben, los ojos en el azul, cual puros sueños.

¡ Mira, por los chopos
de plata, cómo trepan al cielo niños de oro !
Y el azul de sus bellos
ojos y el cielo se tocan . . . ¡ Son uno ojos y cielo !
¡ Mira, por los chopos
de plata, cómo trepan al cielo niños de oro !

Poemas agrestes

Abril

A Ramón de Basterra

Riegan nuestro jardín. Huele a violetas
aún. En el renovado laurel, el gorrión inicia
la Marsellesa. ¡ Oh qué delicia,
amigo, ser poetas
y esperar, como a un dios, a abril florido !
¡ Trueque de almas y de cielos !
En los huevos del nido
del corazón, a la serena luz templada,
sentimos un moverse de polluelos,
entre un olor a lirio apetecido
y a rosa deseada.
¡ Corazón perenal, laurel sin nombre, blando
sol del alma : ¡ Viva la hora venidera !
. . . Bajo el arco que, afuera,
nos pone el agua azul de primavera,
la nidada, por dentro, está piando

Pureza

Cielos

Un cielo cada día,
cada noche . . .
Cóncavas manos cazadoras
de la fe de un instante por el mar.

Mas yo, pequeño, escapo, día
tras día, noche
tras noche,
como una mariposa. . . .

Diario de un poeta recién casado

Tarde en ninguna parte

(*Mar de adentro*)

¡ Este instante
de paz—sombra despierta—,
en que el alma se sume
hasta el nadir del cielo de su esfera !

¡ Este instante feliz, sin nueva dicha,
como un lago de oro
rodeado de miserias !
—. . . Todo lo inunda el alma,
y ella se queda
alta, sola,
fuera—

¡ Este instante infinito—cielo bajo—,
entre una larga y lenta
ola del corazón—despierta sangre—
y una antigua, olvidada
y nuevamente vista estrella !

Diario de un poeta recién casado

Oasis

¡ Qué ruido sin voces !
¡ qué sol sin astro !
¡ ay, qué alegría triste !
¡ qué desierto tan lleno y tan sin sombra !

. . . Y el árbol sólo de mi alma crece
raudo, y con sus ramajes ideales
lo va guardando todo;
y su silencio húmedo
tiende sobre el desierto seco
y lleno todo,
un campo, nido eterno
de soledad, de paz y de dulzura.

Diario de un poeta recién casado

Mar despierto

¡Oh, cuán despierto tú, mar rico,
siempre que yo, voluble y trasnochado,
salgo a mirarte; siempre
que yo, los ojos ojerosos,
salgo, a mirarte, cada aurora!

Tu corazón sin carcel,
de todo tu tamaño,
no ha menester reposo;
ni porque desordenes
tu hondo y alto latir sin cuento,
te amedrenta la muerte
por ningún horizonte.

¡Cuál juegas con tu fuerza,
de todos los colores
de las horas! ¡qué alegre y loco,
levantas y recoges, hecho belleza innúmera,
tu ardiente y frío dinamismo,
tu hierro hecho movimiento,
de pie siempre en ti mismo, árbol de olas,
y sosteniendo en tu agua todo el cielo!

¡ Mar fuerte, oh mar sin sueño,
contemplador eterno, y sin cansancio
y sin fin, del espectáculo alto y solo
del sol y las estrellas, mar eterno!

Diario de un poeta recién casado

'*Vino, primero, pura, . . .*'

Vino, primero, pura,
vestida de inocencia;
y la amé como un niño.
Luego se fué vistiendo
de no sé qué ropajes;
y la fuí odiando, sin saberlo.
Llegó a ser una reina
fastuosa de tesoros . . .
¡ Qué iracundia de yel y sin sentido!
. . . Mas se fué desnudando.
Y yo le sonreía.
Se quedó con la túnica
de su inocencia antigua.
Creí de nuevo en ella.
Y se quitó la túnica
y apareció desnuda toda. . . .
¡ Oh pasión de mi vida, poesía
desnuda, mía para siempre!

Eternidades

'*El dormir es como un puente . . .*'

El dormir es como un puente
que va del hoy al mañana.
Por debajo, como un sueño,
pasa el agua.

Eternidades

Cuesta arriba

¡ Inmenso almendro en flor,
blanca la copa en el silencio pleno de la luna,
el tronco negro en la quietud total de la sombra ;
cómo, subiendo por la roca agria a ti,
me pareces que hundes tu troncón
en las entrañas de mi carne,
que estrellas con mi alma todo el cielo !

Piedra y cielo

‘ *Quisiera que mi libro . . .*’

Quisiera que mi libro
fuese como es el cielo por la noche,
todo verdad presente, sin historia.
Que como él, se diera en cada instante,
todo, con todas sus estrellas ; sin
que niñez, juventud, vejez quitaran
ni pusieran encanto a su hermosura inmensa.
¡ Temblor, relumbre, música
presentes y totales !
¡ Temblor, relumbre, música en la frente
—cielo del corazón—del libro !

Piedra y cielo

Mar ideal

El faro,
como la voz de un niño, que quisiera
ser Dios casi se ve, desde nosotros.

—¡ Qué lejos !—

No parece
que está encendido para el mar funesto,
sino para el fatídico infinito.

Belleza

PEDRO SALINAS

(1892–1951)

Suelo

Suelo. Nada más.
Suelo. Nada menos.
Y que te baste con eso.
Porque en el suelo los pies hincados,
y en los pies torso derecho,
en el torso la testa firme,
y allá, al socaire de la frente,
la idea pura y en la idea pura
el mañana, la llave
—mañana—de lo eterno.
Suelo. Ni más ni menos.
Y que te baste con eso.

Presagios

Cigarra

Cigarra que estás cantando
en un rincón ignorado
del árbol que me da sombra,
no tengo ningún deseo
de saber cuál es la rama,
de tantas que me cobijan,
en que apoyas tu cantar.
Y no me importa si existes,
y no me importa si existe
algo más que ese vaivén
de tu lanzadera, esos
hilillos áureos y tensos
con que tejes el cordaje
de ese barco mañanero
de la mañana de agosto
barco de los rumbos dulces
que no lleva a ningún puerto.

Presagios

‘ *Para vivir no quiero . . .*’

Para vivir no quiero
islas, palacios, torres.
¡ Qué alegría más alta :
vivir en los pronombres !

Quítate ya los trajes,
las señas, los retratos ;
yo no te quiero así,
disfrazada de otra,
hija siempre de algo.
Te quiero pura, libre,
irreductible : tú.
Sé que cuando te llame
entre todas las gentes
del mundo,
sólo tú serás tú.
Y cuando me preguntes
quién es el que te llama,
el que te quiere suya,
enterraré los nombres,
los rótulos, la historia.
Iré rompiendo todo
lo que encima me echaron
desde antes de nacer.
Y vuelto ya al anónimo
eterno del desnudo,
de la piedra, del mundo,
te diré :
“ Yo te quiero, soy yo.”

La voz a ti debida

Underwood Girls

Quietas, dormidas están,
las treinta, redondas, blancas.
Entre todas
sostienen el mundo.

Míralas, aquí en su sueño,
como nubes.
redondas, blancas, y dentro
destinos de trueno y rayo,
destinos de lluvia lenta,
de nieve, de viento, signos.
Despiértalas,
con contactos saltarines
de dedos rápidos, leves,
como a músicas antiguas.
Ellas suenan otra música :
fantasías de metal
valses duros, al dictado.
Que se alcen desde siglos
todas iguales, distintas
como las olas del mar
y una gran alma secreta.
Que se crean que es la carta,
la fórmula, como siempre.
Tú alócate
bien los dedos, y las
raptas y las lanzas,
a las treinta, eternas ninfas
contra el gran mundo vacío,
blanco en blanco.
Por fin a la hazaña pura,
sin palabras, sin sentido,
ese, zeda, jota, i. . . .

Fábula y signo

JORGE GUILLÉN

(1893–)

Primavera delgada

Cuando el espacio, sin perfil, resume
con una nube

su vasta indecisión a la deriva . . .
¿Dónde la orilla?,

mientras el río con el rumbo en curva
se perpetúa

buscando sesgo a sesgo, dibujante,
su desenlace,

mientras el agua, duramente verde,
niega sus peces

bajo el profundo equívoco reflejo
de un aire trémulo . . .

Cuando conduce la mañana, lentas,
sus alamedas

gracias a las estelas vibradoras
entre las frondas,

a favor del avance sinuoso
que pone en coro

la ondulación suavísima del cielo
sobre su viento

con el curso ágil de las pompas
que agudas bogan . . .

¡Primavera delgada entre los remos
de los barqueros!

Cántico

Las sombras

Sol. Activa persiana:
Laten sombras.—¿Quién entra?. . . .
Huyen. Soy yo: pisadas.

(¡ Oh, con palpitación
de párpado, persiana
de soledad o amor !)

Quiero lo trasparente.
También las sombras quiero,
trasparentes y alegres.

(¡ Las sombras, tan esquivas,
soñaban con la palma
de la mano en caricia !)

¿ Tal vez mi mano ? . . . Pero
no, no puede. ¡ Las sombras
son intangibles ! : sueños.

Cántico

Esos cerros

¿ Pureza, soledad ? Allí : son grises.
Grises intactos que ni el pie perdido
sorprendió, soberanamente leves.
Grises junto a la Nada melancólica,
bella, que el aire acoge como un alma,
visible de tan fiel a un fin : la espera.
—¡ Ser, ser, y aun más remota, para el humo,
para los ojos de los más absortos,
una Nada amparada : gris intacto
sobre tierna aridez, gris de esos cerros !

Cántico

El ruiseñor

A don Luis de Góngora

El ruiseñor, pavo real
facilísimo del pío,
envía su memorial
sobre la curva del río,

lejos, muy lejos, a un día
parado en su mediodía,
donde un ave carmesí,
cenit de una primavera
redonda, perfecta esfera,
no responde nunca : sí.

Cántico

La rosa

A Juan Ramón Jiménez

Yo vi la rosa : clausura
primera de la armonía,
tranquilamente futura.
Su perfección sin porfía
serenaba al ruiseñor,
cruel en el esplendor
espiral del gorgorito.
Y al aire ciñó el espacio
con plenitud de palacio,
y fué ya imposible el grito.

Cántico

Electra frente al sol

Un resto de crepúsculo resbala,
gris de un azul que fué feliz. ¿ Ceniza
nuestra ? La claridad final, melliza
del filo, hiere al bosque : fronda rala.

Cae talando el sol. ¡ Cruel la tala,
cruel ! No queda tronco. Se encarniza
la lumbre en la hermosura quebradiza,
y ante el cielo el país se descabala.

¿ Todo a la vez ? Ahora van despacio
los juntos por su ruta de regreso.
Ya es íntimo, ya es dulce el día lacio.

Todo a la vez. Se encienden las primeras
luces humanas. ¡ Ah, con qué embeleso
ven al sol las nocturnas mensajeras!

Cántico

GERARDO DIEGO

(1896–)

Romance del Duero

Río Duero, río Duero,
nadie a acompañarte baja;
nadie se detiene a oír
tu eterna estrofa de agua.

Indiferente o cobarde,
la ciudad vuelve la espalda.
No quiere ver en tu espejo
su muralla desdentada.

Tú, viejo Duero, sonríes
entre tus barbas de plata,
moliendo con tus romances
las cosechas mal logradas.

Y entre los santos de piedra
y los álamos de magia
pasas llevando en tus ondas
palabras de amor, palabras.

Quién pudiera como tú,
a la vez quieto y en marcha,
cantar siempre el mismo verso
pero con distinta agua.

Río Duero, río Duero,
nadie a estar contigo baja,
ya nadie quiere atender
tu eterna estrofa olvidada,

sino los enamorados
que preguntan por sus almas
y siembran en tus espumas
palabras de amor, palabras.

Soria

El ciprés de Silos

Enhiesto surtidor de sombra y sueño,
que acongojas el cielo con tu lanza.
Chorro que a las estrellas casi alcanza,
devanando a sí mismo en loco empeño.

Mástil de soledad, prodigio isleño,
flecha de fe, saeta de esperanza.
Hoy llego a ti, riberas del Arlanza,
peregrina al azar, mi alma sin dueño.

Cuando te vi, señero, dulce, firme,
qué ansiedades sentí de diluirme
y ascender como tú, vuelto en cristales,

como tú, negra torre de arduos filos,
ejemplo de delirios verticales,
mudo ciprés en el fervor de Silos.

Versos humanos

Columpio

A caballo en el quicio del mundo
un soñador jugaba al sí y al no
Las lluvias de colores

emigraban al país de los amores
Bandadas de flores
Flores de sí   Flores de no

Cuchillos en el aire
que le rasgan las carnes
forman un puente

Sí   No
Cabalga el soñador
Pájaros arlequines
cantan el sí   cantan el no

Imagen

DÁMASO ALONSO

(1898–)

Soneto

¿ Cómo era, Dios mío, cómo era ?
JUAN RAMÓN JIMÉNEZ

La puerta, franca.
Vino queda y suave.
Ni materia ni espíritu. Traía
una ligera inclinación de nave
y una luz matinal de claro día.
No era de ritmo, no era de armonía
ni de color. El corazón la sabe,
pero decir cómo era no podría
porque no es forma ni en la forma cabe.
Lengua, barro mortal, cincel inepto,
deja la flor intacta del concepto
en esta clara noche de mi boda,
y canta mansamente, humildemente,
la sensación, la sombra, el accidente,
mientras ella me llena el alma toda!

Poemas puros

Calle de arrabal

Se me quedó en lo hondo
una visión tan clara,
que tengo que entornar los ojos cuando
pretendo recordarla.

A un lado hay un calvero de solares;
al otro, están las casas alineadas
porque esperan que de momento a otro
la Primavera pasará.

Las sábanas,
aún goteantes, penden
de todas las ventanas.
El viento juega con el sol en ellas
y ellas ríen del juego y de la gracia.

Y hay las niñas bonitas
que se peinan al aire libre.

Cantan
los chicos de una escuela la lección.
Las once dan.
Por el arroyo pasa
un viejo cojitranco
que empuja su carrito de naranjas.

Poemillas de la ciudad

A una habitación

Prisión de cal y canto,
ataúd de piso y techo,
anclado en la cruz exacta
de los espacios y el tiempo,
en mar de campos, marina
de horas mansas, tierra adentro.

Seis planos pulcros velaban
un corazón volandero
(puerto patente a la vida;
ventana abierta al ensueño),
y una lámpara soñaba,
dormida, en la noche, puerto.

Desarraigado de ti,
por mar, por tierra, me muevo.
Por forma y luz: hondo tajo
de olvido, que cruza el tiempo,
puente, roto hacia mi vida,
de orillas de tu recuerdo.

Que, aguas azules, los días
te irán los muros lamiendo,
y un viento frío, el espacio,
te impele, navío muerto,
a medida que tu carne
rasgo, mi tierra, y me alejo.

Antología 1915–31

Noche

Pozo que entre tus altos calofríos
y el hervir de tus burgas azuladas,
con pulular de estrellas enjambradas
riegas a Dios sus lóbregos baldíos,
aun hay más noche en los veneros míos,
donde las aguas rugen represadas,
más lívidas estrellas derramadas,
más turbias nebulosas, más vacíos.
Acaso tú, al brocal de tu ancho cielo,
entre mis negras aguas de amargura
miras mi torpe rebullir lejano.
Yo interrogo a tu abismo desde el suelo.
¡Oh doble pozo oscuro! ¡Oh doble hondura!
Tú, pozo sideral; yo, pozo humano.

Oscura noticia

'No me digas . . .'

No me digas
que estás llena de arrugas, que estás llena de sueño,
que se te han caído los dientes,
que ya no puedes con tus pobres remos hinchados, deformados por el veneno del reuma.

No importa madre, no importa.
Tú eres siempre joven,
eres una niña,
tienes once años.
Oh, sí, tú eres para mí eso : una candorosa niña.

Y verás que es verdad si te sumerges en esas lentas aguas, en esas aguas poderosas,
que te han traído a esta ribera desolada.
Sumérgete, nada a contracorriente, cierra los ojos,
y cuando llegues, espera allí a tu hijo.
Porque yo también voy a sumergirme en mi niñez antigua,
pero las aguas que tengo que remontar hasta casi la fuente,
son mucho más poderosas, son aguas turbias, como teñidas de sangre.
Óyelas, desde tu sueño, cómo rugen,
cómo quieren llevarse al pobre nadador.
¡ Pobre del nadador que somorguja y bucea en ese mar de la memoria !

. . . Ya ves : ya hemos llegado.
No es una maravilla que los dos hayamos arribado a esta prodigiosa ribera de nuestra infancia ?
Sí, así es como a veces fondean un mismo día en el puerto de Singapoor dos naves,
y la una viene de Nueva Zelanda, la otra de Brest.
Así hemos llegado los dos, ahora, juntos.
Y ésta es la única realidad, la única maravillosa realidad :
que eres tú una niña y que yo soy un niño.

Hijos de la ira

FEDERICO GARCÍA LORCA

(1899–1936)

La balada del agua del mar

El mar
sonríe a lo lejos.
Dientes de espuma,
labios de cielo.

¿ Qué vendes, ¡ oh joven turbia !,
con los senos al aire ?
—Vendo, señor, el agua
de los mares—.

¿ Qué llevas, ¡ oh negro joven !,
mezclado con tu sangre ?
—Llevo, señor, el agua
de los mares—.

Esas lágrimas salobres,
¿ de dónde vienen, madre ?
—Lloro, señor, el agua
de los mares—.

Corazón, y esta amargura
seria, ¿ de dónde nace ?
—Amarga mucho el agua
de los mares !—

El mar
sonríe a lo lejos.
Dientes de espuma,
labios de cielo.

Libro de poemas

La sombra de mi alma

La sombra de mi alma
huye por un ocaso de alfabetas
niebla de libros
y palabras.
La sombra de mi alma.
Un turbio laberinto
de estrellas ahumadas
enreda mi ilusión
casi marchita.
¡ La sombra de mi alma !

Libro de poemas

Cazador

¡ Alto pinar !
Cuatro palomas por el aire van.

Cuatro palomas
vuelan y tornan.
Llevan heridas
sus cuatro sombras.

¡ Bajo pinar !
Cuatro palomas en la tierra están.

Canciones

Canción de jinete

Córdoba.
Lejana y sola.

Jaca negra, luna grande,
y aceitunas en mi alforja.
Aunque sepa los caminos
yo nunca llegaré a Córdoba

Por el llano, por el viento,
jaca negra, luna roja.
La muerte me está mirando
desde las torres de Córdoba.

¡ Ay qué camino tan largo !
¡ Ay mi jaca valerosa !
¡ Ay que la muerte me espera,
antes de llegar a Cordóba !

Córdoba.
Lejana y sola.

Canciones

Paso

Virgen con miriñaque,
Virgen de la Soledad,
abierta como un inmenso
tulipán.
En tu barco de luces
vas
por la alta marea
de la ciudad,
entre saetas turbias
y estrellas de cristal.
Virgen con miriñaque
tú vas
por el río de la calle,
¡ hasta el mar !

Poema del cante jondo

¡ Ay !

El grito deja en el viento
una sombra de ciprés.

(Dejadme en este campo
llorando)

Todo se ha roto en el mundo.
No queda más que el silencio.

(Dejadme en este campo
llorando)

El horizonte sin luz
está mordido de hogueras.

(Ya os he dicho que me dejéis
en este campo
llorando.)

Poema del cante jondo

Pueblo

Sobre el monte pelado
un calvario.
Agua clara
y olivos centenarios.
Por las callejas
hombres embozados,
y en las torres
veletas girando.
Eternamente
girando.
¡ Oh, pueblo perdido,
en la Andalucía del llanto !

Poema del cante jondo

La guitarra

Empieza el llanto
de la guitarra.
Se rompen las copas
de la madrugada.
Empieza el llanto
de la guitarra.
Es inútil
callarla.
Es imposible
callarla.
Llora monótona
como llora el agua,
como llora el viento
sobre la nevada.
Es imposible
callarla.
Llora por cosas
lejanas.
Arena del Sur caliente
que pide camelias blancas.
Llora flecha sin blanco,
la tarde sin mañana,
y el primer pájaro muerto
sobre la rama.
¡ Oh guitarra !
Corazón malherido
por cinco espadas.

Poema del cante jondo

Muerte de Antoñito el Camborio

Voces de muerte sonaron
cerca del Guadalquivir.
Voces antiguas que cercan
voz de clavel varonil.

Les clavó sobre las botas
mordiscos de jabalí.
En la lucha daba saltos
jabonados de delfín.
Bañó con sangre enemiga
su corbata carmesí,
pero eran cuatro puñales
y tuvo que sucumbir.
Cuando las estrellas clavan
rejones al agua gris,
cuando los erales sueñan
verónicas de alhelí,
voces de muerte sonaron
cerca del Guadalquivir.

—Antonio Torres Heredia,
Camborio de dura crin,
moreno de verde luna,
voz de clavel varonil:
¿Quién te ha quitado la vida
cerca del Guadalquivir?
—Mis cuatro primos Heredias,
hijos de Benamejí.
Lo que en otros no envidiaban,
ya lo envidiaban en mí.
Zapatos color corinto,
medallones de marfil,
y este cutis amasado
con aceituna y jazmín.
—¡Ay, Antoñito el Camborio
digno de una Emperatriz!
Acuérdate de la Virgen
porque te vas a morir.
—¡Ay, Federico García,
llama a la Guardia Civil!
Ya mi talle se ha quebrado
como caña de maíz.

Tres golpes de sangre tuvo
y se murió de perfil.
Viva moneda que nunca
se volverá a repetir.
Un ángel marchoso pone
su cabeza en un cojín.
Otros de rubor cansado
encendieron un candil.
Y cuando los cuatro primos
llegan a Benamejí,
voces de muerte cesaron
cerca del Guadalquivir.

Romancero gitano

Romance sonámbulo

Verde que te quiero verde.
Verde viento. Verdes ramas.
El barco sobre la mar
y el caballo en la montaña.
Con la sombra en la cintura
ella sueña en su baranda,
verde carne, pelo verde,
con ojos de fría plata.
Verde que te quiero verde.
Bajo la luna gitana,
las cosas la están mirando
y ella no puede mirarlas.

Verde que te quiero verde.
Grandes estrellas de escarcha
vienen con el pez de sombra
que abre el camino del alba.
La higuera frota su viento
con la lija de sus ramas,
y el monte, gato garduño,

eriza sus pitas agrias.
Pero ¿quién vendrá? ¿Y por dónde?
Ella sigue en su baranda,
verde carne, pelo verde,
soñando en la mar amarga.

—Compadre, quiero cambiar
mi caballo por tu casa,
mi montura por tu espejo,
mi cuchillo por tu manta.
Compadre, vengo sangrando,
desde los puertos de Cabra.
—Si yo pudiera, mocito,
este trato se cerraba.
Pero yo ya no soy yo,
ni mi casa es ya mi casa.
—Compadre, quiero morir
decentemente en mi cama.
De acero, si puede ser,
con las sábanas de holanda.
¿No ves la herida que tengo
desde el pecho a la garganta?
—Trescientas rosas morenas
lleva tu pechera blanca.
Tu sangre rezuma y huele
alrededor de tu faja.
Pero yo ya no soy yo,
ni mi casa es ya mi casa.
—Dejadme subir al menos
hasta las altas barandas;
¡dejadme subir!, dejadme
hasta las verdes barandas.
Barandales de la luna
por donde retumba el agua.

Ya suben los dos compadres
hacia las altas barandas.
Dejando un rastro de sangre.

Dejando un rastro de lágrimas.
Temblaban en los tejados
farolillos de hojalata.
Mil panderos de cristal
herían la madrugada.

Verde que te quiero verde,
verde viento, verdes ramas.
Los dos compadres subieron.
El largo viento dejaba
en la boca un raro gusto
de hiel, de menta y de albahaca.
¡ Compadre! ¿ Dónde está, dime,
dónde está tu niña amarga?
¡ Cuántas veces te esperó!
¡ Cuántas veces te esperara,
cara fresca, negro pelo,
en esta verde baranda!

Sobre el rostro del aljibe
se mecía la gitana.
Verde carne, pelo verde,
con ojos de fría plata.
Un carámbano de luna
la sostiene sobre el agua.
La noche se puso íntima
como una pequeña plaza.
Guardias civiles borrachos
en la puerta golpeaban.

Verde que te quiero verde.
Verde viento. Verdes ramas.
El barco sobre la mar.
Y el caballo en la montaña.

Romancero gitano

Canción de la gota de lluvia

Yo vuelvo por mis alas
dejadme volver.
Quiero morirme siendo
ayer.
Quiero morirme siendo
amanecer.
Yo vuelvo por mis alas,
dejadme tornar.
Quiero morirme siendo
manantial.
Quiero morirme fuera
de la mar.

Así que pasen cinco años, Act I

El llanto

He cerrado mi balcón
porque no quiero oír el llanto,
pero por detrás de los grises muros
no se oye otra cosa que el llanto.

Hay muy pocos ángeles que canten,
hay muy pocos perros que ladren,
mil violines caben en la palma de la mano:
pero el llanto es un ángel inmenso,
el llanto es un violín inmenso,
las lágrimas amordazan el viento,
y no se oye otra cosa que el llanto.

VICENTE ALEIXANDRE

(1900–)

Adolescencia

Vinieras y te fueras dulcemente,
de otro camino
a otro camino. Verte,
y ya otra vez no verte.
Pasar por un puente a otro puente.
—El pie breve,
la luz vencida alegre—.

Muchacho que sería yo mirando
aguas abajo la corriente,
y en el espejo tu pasaje
fluir, desvanecerse.

Ámbito

Soneto. A Fray Luis de León

¿ Qué linfa esbelta, de los altos hielos
hija y sepulcro, sobre el haz silente
rompe sus fríos, vierte su corriente,
luces llevando, derramando cielos?

¿ Qué agua orquestal bajo los mansos celos
del aire, muda, funde su crujiente
espuma en anchas copias y consiente,
terso el diálogo, signo y luz gemelos?

La alta noche su copa sustantiva
—árbol ilustre—yergue a la bonanza,
total su crecimiento y ramas bellas.

Brisa joven de cielo, persuasiva,
su pompa abierta, desplegada, alcanza
largamente, y resuenan las estrellas.

Ámbito

Las águilas

El mundo encierra la verdad de la vida,
aunque la sangre mienta melancólicamente
cuando como mar sereno en la tarde
siente arriba el batir de las águilas libres.

Las plumas de metal,
las garras poderosas,
ese afán del amor o la muerte,
ese deseo de beber en los ojos con un pico de hierro,
de poder al fin besar lo exterior de la tierra,
vuela como el deseo,
como las nubes que a nada se oponen,
como el azul radiante, corazón ya de afuera
en que la libertad se ha abierto para el mundo.

Las águilas serenas
no serán nunca esquifes,
no serán sueño o pájaro,
no serán caja donde olvidar lo triste,
donde tener guardado esmeraldas u ópalos.

El sol que cuaja en las pupilas,
que a las pupilas mira libremente,
es ave inmarcesible, vencedor de los pechos
donde hundir su furor contra un cuerpo amarrado.

Las violentas alas
que azotan rostros como eclipses,
que parten venas de zafiro muerto,
que seccionan la sangre coagulada,
rompen el viento en mil pedazos,
mármol o espacio impenetrable
donde una mano muerta detenida
es el claror que en la noche fulgura.

Águilas como abismos,
como montes altísimos,
derriban majestades, troncos polvorientos,
esa verde hiedra que en los muslos
finge la lengua vegetal casi viva.

Se aproxima el momento en que la dicha consista
en desvestir de piel a los cuerpos humanos,
en que el celeste ojo victorioso
vea sólo a la tierra como sangre que gira.

Águilas de metal sonorísimo,
arpas furiosas con su voz casi humana,
cantan la ira de amar los corazones,
amarlos con las garras estrujando su muerte.

La destrucción o el amor

El árbol

Bajo la tierra el día
oscurece. Ave rara,
ave arriba en el árbol que cantas para un muerto.
Bajo la tierra duermo
como otra raíz de ese árbol que a solas en mí nutro.
No pesas, árbol poderoso y terrible que emerges a los aires
que de mi pecho naces con un verdor urgente
para asomar y abrirte en rientes ramajes
donde un ave ahora canta, vivaz sobre mi pecho.

Hermosa vida clara de un árbol sostenido
sobre la tierra misma que un hombre ha sido un día.
Cuerpo cabal que aun vive, no duerme, nunca duerme.
Hoy vela en árbol lúcido que un sol traspasa ardiendo.

No soy memoria, amigos, ni olvido. Alegre subo,
ligero, rumoroso por un tronco a la vida.
Amigos, olvidadme. Mi copa canta siempre,
ligera en el espacio, bajo un cielo continuo.

Desamor

El mar

¿ Quién dijo acaso que la mar suspira,
labio de amor hacia las playas, triste ?
Dejad que envuelta por la luz campee.
¡ Gloria, gloria en la altura, y en la mar, el oro !
¡ Ah soberana luz que envuelve, canta
la inmarcesible edad del mar gozante !
Allá, reverberando,
sin tiempo, el mar existe.
¡ Un corazón de dios sin muerte, late !

Sombra del Paraíso

RAFAEL ALBERTI

(1902–)

I

El mar. La mar.
El mar. ¡ Sólo la mar !
¿ Por qué me trajiste, padre,
a la ciudad ?
¿ Por qué me desenterraste
del mar ?
En sueños, la marejada
me tira del corazón.
Se lo quisiera llevar.
Padre, ¿ por qué me trajiste
acá ?

II

Gimiendo por ver el mar,
un marinerito en tierra
iza al aire este lamento:
¡Ay mi blusa marinera!
Siempre me la inflaba el viento
al divisar la escollera.

III

... Y ya estarán los esteros
rezumando azul de mar.
¡Dejadme ser, salineros,
granito del salinar!
¡Qué bien a la madrugada,
correr en las vagonetas,
llenas de nieve salada,
hacia las blancas casetas!
¡Dejo de ser marinero,
madre, por ser salinero!

Marinero en tierra

A Federico García Lorca

Sal tú, bebiendo campos y ciudades,
en largo ciervo de agua convertido,
hacia el mar de las albas claridades,
del martín-pescador mecido nido;
que yo saldré a esperarte, amortecido,
hecho junco, a las altas soledades,
herido por el aire y requerido
por tu voz, sola entre las tempestades.
Deja que escriba, débil junco frío,
mi nombre en esas aguas corredoras,
que el viento llama, solitario, río.
Disuelto ya en tu nieve el nombre mío,
vuélvete a tus montañas trepadoras,
ciervo de espuma, rey del monterío.

Marinero en tierra

A Rosa de Alberti, que tocaba, pensativa, el arpa

(*Siglo* XIX)

Rosa de Alberti allá en el rodapié
del mirador del cielo se entreabría,
pulsadora del aire y prima mía,
al cuello un lazo blanco de moaré.
El barandal del arpa, desde el pie
hasta el bucle en la nieve, la cubría.
Enredando sus cuerdas, florecía
—alga en hilos—la mano que se fué.
Llena de suavidades y carmines,
fanal de ensueño, vaga y voladora,
voló hacia los más altos miradores.
Miradla querubín de querubines,
del vergel de los aires pulsadora,
Pensativa de Alberti entre las flores!

Marinero en tierra

Madrigal al billete de tranvía

Adonde el viento, impávido, subleva
torres de luz contra la sangre mía,
tú, billete, flor nueva,
cortada en los balcones del tranvía,

huyes, directa, rectamente liso,
en tu pétalo un nombre y un encuentro
latentes, a ese centro
cerrado y por cortar del compromiso.

Y no arde en ti la rosa, ni en ti priva
el finado clavel, sí la violeta
contemporánea, viva,
del libro que viaja en la chaqueta.

Cal y canto

El ángel de los números

Vírgenes con escuadras
y compases, velando
las celestes pizarras.

Y el ángel de los números,
pensativo, volando,
del 1 al 2, del 2
al 3, del 3 al 4.

Tizas frías y esponjas
rayaban y borraban
la luz de los espacios.

Ni sol, luna ni estrellas,
ni el repentino verde
del rayo y el relámpago,
ni el aire. Sólo nieblas.

Vírgenes sin escuadras,
sin compases, llorando.

Y en las muertas pizarras,
el ángel de los números,
sin vida, amortajado
sobre el 1 y el 2,
sobre el 3, sobre el 4 . . .

Sobre los ángeles

Tres recuerdos del cielo

Homenaje a Gustavo Adolfo Bécquer

Prólogo

No habían cumplido años ni la rosa ni el arcángel.
Todo, anterior al balido y al llanto.
Cuando la luz ignoraba todavía
si el mar nacería niño o niña.

Cuando el viento soñaba melenas que peinar
y claveles el fuego que encender y mejillas
y el agua unos labios parados donde beber.
Todo, anterior al cuerpo, al nombre y al tiempo.
Entonces, yo recuerdo que, una vez, en el cielo . . .

Tercer recuerdo

. . . detrás del abanico de plumas y de oro . . .
G. A. BÉCQUER

Aún los valses del cielo no habían desposado al jazmín y la nieve,
ni los aires pensado en la posible música de tus cabellos,
ni decretado el rey que la violeta se enterrara en un libro.
No.
Era la era en que la golondrina viajaba
sin nuestras iniciales en el pico.
En que las campanillas y las enredaderas
morían sin balcones que escalar y estrellas.
La era
en que al hombro de un ave no había flor que apoyara la cabeza.
Entonces, detrás de tu abanico, nuestra luna primera.

Sobre los ángeles

Los ángeles muertos

Buscad, buscadlos:
en el insomnio de las cañerías olvidadas,
en los cauces interrumpidos por el silencio de las basuras.
No lejos de los charcos incapaces de guardar una nube,
unos ojos perdidos,
o una sortija rota
o una estrella pisoteada.
Porque yo los he visto:
en esos escombros momentáneos que aparecen en lasn eblinas.

Porque yo los he tocado:
en el destierro de un ladrillo difunto,
venido a la nada desde una torre o un carro.
Nunca más allá de las chimeneas que se derrumban
ni de esas hojas tenaces que se estampan en los zapatos.
En todo esto.
Mas en esas astillas vagabundas que se consumen sin fuego,
en esas ausencias hundidas que sufren los muebles desvencijados,
no a mucha distancia de los nombres y signos que se enfrían
en las paredes.

Buscad, buscadlos:
debajo de la gota de cera que sepulta la palabra de un libro
o la firma de uno de esos rincones de cartas
que trae rodando el polvo.
Cerca del casco perdido de una botella,
de una suela extraviada en la nieve,
de una navaja de afeitar abandonada al borde de un precipicio.

Sobre los ángeles

Galope

Las tierras, las tierras, las tierras de España,
las grandes, las solas, desiertas llanuras.
Galopa, caballo cuatralbo,
jinete del pueblo,
al sol y a la luna.
¡A galopar,
a galopar,
hasta enterrarlos en el mar!
A corazón suenan, resuenan, resuenan
las tierras de España en las herraduras.
Galopa, jinete del pueblo,
caballo cuatralbo,
caballo de espuma.
¡A galopar,
a galopar,
hasta enterrarlos en el mar!

Nadie, nadie, nadie, que enfrente no hay nadie;
que es nadie la muerte si va en tu montura.
Galopa, caballo cuatralbo,
jinete del pueblo,
que la tierra es tuya.
¡A galopar,
a galopar,
hasta enterrarlos en el mar!

De un momento a otro

De los álamos y los sauces

(*En recuerdo de Antonio Machado*)

. . . y por oilla,
los sauces se inclinaron a la orilla.
PEDRO DE ESPINOSA

. . . álamos de las márgenes del Duero,
conmigo vais, mi corazón os lleva!
ANTONIO MACHADO

I

Dejadme llorar a mares,
largamente como los sauces.
Largamente y sin consuelo.
Podéis doleros . . .
Pero dejadme.
Los álamos carolinos
podrán, si quieren, consolarme.
Vosotros . . . Como hace el viento . . .
Podéis doleros . . .
Pero dejadme.

II

No puede, como es pequeño,
con tantos árboles grandes.
Sólo con la yerbabuena,
la flor del aire.

Álamo, me pesas mucho;
me doblas los hombros, sauce.
Se sentó. Y aunque era río,
no vino el agua a ayudarle.

III

Veo en los álamos, veo,
temblando, sombras de duelo.
Una a una, hojas de sangre.
Ya no podréis ampararme.
Negros álamos transidos.
¡Qué oscuro caer de amigos!
Vidas que van y no vienen.
¡Ay, álamos de la muerte! . . .

V

Más que olvidados estaban,
por funerales y pena larga.
Les dije: ¡Fuera de casa!
Lejos,
con esos verdes lamentos
y ese redoble de muerto.
No quiero frente inclinada.
Cabeza alta,
mirada alta, bien alta.
Así les iba diciendo,
sin ver que su largo pelo
me amortajaba,
¡Ay sauces, me amortajaba!

VI

Ahora me siento ligero,
como vosotros, ahora
que estoy cargado de muertos.
Voy a crecer, a subir.
Voy a escalaros
ahora que tengo mil años.

¡ Detenedme, que ya subo !
¡ Paradme, que ya os alcanzo !
No me dejéis, ya en el viento,
mirar abajo.

Entre el clavel y la espada

LUIS CERNUDA

(1904–)

Soledad

La soledad. No se siente
el mundo : sus hojas sella.
Ya la luz abre su huella
en la tersura indolente.
Acogida está la frente
al regazo del hastío.
¿ Qué prisa, qué desvarío
a la belleza hizo ajena ?
Porque solo el tiempo llena
el blanco papel vacío.

Perfil del aire

Nevada

En el estado de Nevada
los caminos de hierro tienen nombres de pájaro
son de nieve los campos
y de nieve las horas.

Las noches transparentes
abren luces soñadas
sobre las aguas o tejados puros
constelados de fiesta.

Las lágrimas sonríen
la tristeza es de alas
y las alas sabemos
dan amor inconstante.

Los árboles abrazan árboles
una canción besa otra canción
por los caminos de hierro
pasa el dolor y la alegría.

Siempre hay nieve dormida
sobre la nieve allá en Nevada.

Un río, un amor

Tierra nativa

Es la luz misma, la que abrió mis ojos
toda ligera y tibia como un sueño,
sosegada en colores delicados
sobre las formas puras de las cosas.

El encanto de aquella tierra llana,
extendida, tal una mano abierta,
adonde el limonero, encima de la fuente,
suspendía su fruto entre el ramaje.

El muro viejo en cuya barda abría
a la tarde su flor azul la enredadera,
y al cual la golondrina en el verano
tornaba siempre hacia su nido antiguo.

El susurro del agua alimentando,
con su música insomne en el silencio
los sueños que la vida aún no corrompe,
el futuro que espera como página blanca.

Todo vuelve otra vez vivo a la mente,
irreparable ya con el andar del tiempo,
y su recuerdo ahora me traspasa
el pecho, tal puñal fino y seguro.

Raíz del tronco verde ¿ quién la arranca?
aquel amor primero ¿ quién lo vence?
tu sueño y tu recuerdo ¿ quién lo olvida,
tierra nativa, más mía cuanto más lejana?

Como quien espera el alba

El arpa

Jaula de un ave invisible,
del agua hermana y del aire,
a cuya voz solicita
pausada y blanda la mano.

Como el agua prisionera
del surtidor, tiembla, sube
en una fuga irisada,
las almas adoctrinando.

Como el aire entre las hojas,
habla tan vaga, tan pura,
de memorias y de olvidos
hechos leyendas en el tiempo.

¿ Qué frutas del paraíso,
cuáles aljibes del cielo
nutren tu voz? Dime, canta,
pájaro del arpa, oh lira.

Como quien espera el alba

MANUEL ALTOLAGUIRRE

(1905–)

I

Mírate en el espejo y luego mira
estos retratos tuyos olvidados,
pétalos son de tu belleza antigua
y deja que de nuevo te retrate
deshojándote así de tu presente;
que cuando ya invisible, sólo seas
alto perfume: alma y recuerdo,
junto al tallo sin flor, pondré caídos
estos retratos tuyos, para verte
como aroma subir y como forma
quedar abandonada en este suelo.

II

Ojos de puente los míos
por donde pasan las aguas
que van a dar al olvido.

Sobre mi frente de acero
mirando por las barandas
caminan mis pensamientos.

Mi nuca negra es el mar,
donde se pierden los ríos,
y mis sueños son las nubes
por y para las que vivo.

Ojos de puente los míos
por donde pasan las aguas
que van a dar al olvido.

Soledades juntas

LIST OF REFERENCE BOOKS

ALONSO, DÁMASO: *Antología de poesía española. Edad media* (Signo. Madrid, 1935).

ALONSO, DÁMASO: *Ensayos sobre poesía española* (Madrid, 1944).

ALONSO, DÁMASO: *Poesía española. Ensayo de métodos y límites estilísticos* (Biblioteca Romanica Hispanica, 1950).

ALONSO, DÁMASO: *Poetas españoles contemporáneos* (Biblioteca Romanica Hispánica, 1952)

BLECUA, J. M.: *Historia y textos de la literatura española* (2 vols.).

BRENAN, GERALD: *The Literature of the Spanish People* (Cambridge University Press, 1951).

DÍAZ-PLAJA, GUILLERMO: *Historia de la poesía lírica española* (Col. Labor.).

DIEGO, GERARDO: *Antología española. Autores contemporáneos* (Signo. Madrid, 1935).

GULLON, RICARDO, Y BLECUA, JOSÉ MANUEL, *La Poesía de Jorge Guillén* (Estudios literarios, Zaragoza).

HENRÍQUEZ UREÑA, PEDRO: *La versificación irregular en la poesía española* (Madrid, 1933).

MENÉNDEZ PIDAL, RAMÓN:

Poesía juglaresca y juglares (Madrid, 1924).

Estudios literarios (ensayo sobre la primitiva poesía lírica española) (Col. Austral).

Los romances de América (Col. Austral).

Flor nueva de romances viejos (Espasa-Calpe).

Poesía árabe y poesía europea (Col. Austral).

RÍO, ÁNGEL DEL: *Historia de la literatura española* (Dryden Press, New York, 1949).

RÍQUER, MARTÍN DE: *Resumen de versificación española* (Seix Barral, 1950).

RODRÍGUEZ MARÍN, FRANCISCO: *Cantos populares españoles*.

TORNER, E. M.: *Cancionero musical español* (Harrap, 1948).

INDEX OF AUTHORS
and titles of anonymous works